NEW DIRECTIONS 50

N D

New Directions in Prose and Poetry 50

Edited by J. Laughlin

with Peter Glassgold and Griselda Ohannessian

A New Directions Book

ACKNOWLEDGMENTS
The selections from *New Directions in Prose and Poetry 1936* are reprinted here with the kind permission of the individual authors, their heirs, and/or their present publishers. Elizabeth Bishop's "Casablanca" (Copyright 1936 by Elizabeth Bishop; copyright renewed 1964 by Elizabeth Bishop), reprinted from *The Complete Collected Poems 1927–1979* by permission of Farrar, Straus & Giroux, Inc. E. E. Cummings' "Three Poems" (Copyright 1938 by E. E. Cummings; copyright renewed 1966 by Marion Morehouse Cummings), reprinted from *Complete Poems 1913-1962* by permission of Harcourt Brace Jovanovich, Inc. Henry Miller's "Into the Night Life" (Copyright © 1963 by Grove Press, Inc.), reprinted by permission of Grove Press, Inc. Marianne Moore's "See in the Midst of Fair Leaves," reprinted by permission of Clive E. Driver, literary executor of the estate of Marianne C. Moore. Lorine Niedecker's "The President of the Holding Company" (Copyright © 1985 by the Estate of Lorine Niedecker), used by permission of Cid Corman, literary executor. Wallace Stevens' "Mystic Garden & Middling Beast" (Copyright 1936 by Wallace Stevens; copyright renewed 1964 by Holly Stevens), reprinted from *The Collected Poems of Wallace Stevens* by permission of Alfred A. Knopf, Inc.

Canto XLVI by Ezra Pound (Copyright 1937 by Ezra Pound); "Elegies" by John Wheelwright (Copyright © 1971 by Louise Wheelwright Damon); "How to Write" by William Carlos Williams (Copyright 1936 by the Estate of William Carlos Williams); "Perpetuum Mobile: The City" by William Carlos Williams (Copyright 1938 by New Directions Publishing Corporation)

Acknowledgment is made to the editors and publishers of magazines in which some of the material in this volume first appeared: for Walter Abish, *Parenthèse;* for Denise Levertov, *Religion & Intellectual Life* and *The Rialto;* for Michael Palmer, *Sulfur* (Copyright © 1986 by *Sulfur*); for Jerome Rothenberg, *Sulfur* (Copyright © 1985 by Jerome Rothenberg).

Grateful thanks are given for permission to reprint the following works: John Ashbery, "37 Haiku," from *A Wave* (Copyright © 1981, 1982,

1983, 1984 by John Ashbery), reprinted by permission of Viking Penguin, Inc., and Carcanet Press Ltd.; John Barth, "Night-Sea Journey," from *Lost in the Funhouse* (Copyright © 1966 by John Barth), first published in *Esquire* magazine and reprinted by permission of Doubleday & Company, Inc.; Donald Barthelme, "The School," from *The Amateurs* (Copyright © 1974, 1976 by Donald Barthelme), reprinted by permission of Farrar, Straus & Giroux, Inc.; Charles Bernstein, "Live Acts," from *Controlling Interests* (Copyright © 1980 by Charles Bernstein) and "The Voyage of Life," from *On Equal Terms* (Copyright © 1984 by Symposium Press), reprinted by permission of the author; Raymond Carver, "The Compartment," from *Cathedral* (Copyright © 1983 by Raymond Carver), reprinted by permission of Alfred A. Knopf, Inc. and Collins Harvill; Allen Ginsberg, "Plutonian Ode," from *Collected Poems: 1947-1980* (Copyright © 1978, 1984 by Allen Ginsberg), reprinted by permission of Harper & Row, Publishers, Inc., and Penguin Books Ltd.; James Merrill, "From the Cutting-Room Floor," from *Late Settings* (Copyright © 1985 by James Merrill), reprinted by permission of Atheneum Publishers, Inc.; W. S. Merwin, "Exercise," from *Writings to an Unfinished Accompaniment* (Copyright © 1973 by W. S. Merwin), reprinted by permission of Atheneum Publishers, Inc.; Jonathan Williams, "O for a Muse of Fire," from *The Empire Finals at Verona* (Copyright © 1960 by Jonathan Williams) and "My Quaker-Atheist Friend . . . ," from *Elite/Elate Poems* (Copyright © 1979 by Jonathan Williams), first published by The Jargon Society and reprinted by permission of the author; "Bea Hensley Hammers from Chinquapin Leaf . . . ," from *Blues and Roots/Rue and Bluets* (Copyright © 1985 by Jonathan Williams), reprinted by permission of Duke University Press; Jonathan Williams, "A Few Clerihews," from *The Fifty-two Clerihews of Clara Hughes* (Copyright © 1983 by Jonathan Williams), reprinted by permission of Pynyon Press. Acknowledgments are continued on page 274.

Manufactured in the United States of America
First published clothbound (ISBN: 0-8112-0993-8) and as New Directions Paperbook 623 (ISBN: 0-8112-0994-6) in 1986
Published simultaneously in Canada by Penguin Books Canada Limited

New Directions Books are published for James Laughlin
by New Directions Publishing Corporation,
80 Eighth Avenue, New York 10011

CONTENTS

I   NEW DIRECTIONS 1936

Mary Barnard
  Playroom   74

Elizabeth Bishop
  Casablanca   51

Kay Boyle
  January the Twenty-Fourth, New York   48

Jean Cocteau
  from The Laïc Mystery   26

E. E. Cummings
  Three Poems   45

Dudley Fitts
  This Country Road, with the Engine Running   60

Eugene Jolas
  Heinrich Heine and the Grain Dance   92

James Laughlin
  Preface: New Directions   3
  The Glacier and Love's Ignorant Tongue   80

Henry Miller
  Into the Night Life   64

Marianne Moore
See in the Midst of Fair Leaves   32

Gorham Munson
New Directions in Economics   17

Lorine Niedecker
The President of the Holding Company   71

Montagu O'Reilly
The Romantic Museum   53

Ezra Pound
Canto XLVI   21

Tasilo Ribischka
The Transcarnation of Acumen and Decible   77

Gertrude Stein
A Water-Fall and a Piano   10

Wallace Stevens
Mystic Garden & Middling Beast   9

John Wheelwright
Elegies   13

William Carlos Williams
How to Write   34
Perpetuum Mobile: The City   39

Louis Zukofsky
"Mantis"   82

II NEW DIRECTIONS—
THE YEARS THAT FOLLOW

Walter Abish
    Happiness   101

David Antin
    from The Structuralist   194

John Ashbery
    37 Haiku   128

John Barth
    Night-Sea Journey   181

Donald Barthelme
    The School   201

Charles Bernstein
    Two Poems   142

Frederick Busch
    Comrades   227

Hayden Carruth
    Lana   205

Raymond Carver
    The Compartment   117

Cid Corman
    Three Poems   225

Gregory Corso
    Was Papa Haydn Born April 1st?   236

Robert Creeley
    Five Poems   222

Guy Davenport
    Wild Clover   253

Coleman Dowell
    The Surgeon   211

Robert Duncan
    Two Poems   190

Lawrence Ferlinghetti
    He with the Beating Wings   151

Allen Ginsberg
    Plutonian Ode   172

Allen Grossman
    The Life and Death of Kisses   209

John Hawkes
    A Little Bit of the Old Slap and Tickle   155

Denise Levertov
    The Showings: Lady Julian of Norwich, 1342–1416   108

James Merrill
    From the Cutting-Room Floor   160

W. S. Merwin
    Exercise   153

Michael McClure
    Two Poems   114

Joyce Carol Oates
    Quartet   144

Toby Olson
    The Scourging at the Pillar   166

George Oppen
Two Poems   126

Michael Palmer
(Baudelaire Series)   140

Kenneth Patchen
When We Were Here Together   165

James Purdy
Rapture   237

Kenneth Rexroth
The Signature of All Things   246

Jerome Rothenberg
Visions of Jesus   249

Gary Snyder
Night Song of the Los Angeles Basin   233

Jonathan Williams
Four Poems   176

Tennessee Williams
Mother Yaws   131

INTRODUCTION

1986 marks the 50th anniversary of New Directions. And this booklet will be included later this year in #50 in the series of *New Directions in Prose and Poetry* anthologies. Much has changed in the field of avant-garde writing in five decades. We reprint here a large part of the contents of *ND 1936*, the first volume, and will append to it a sampling of what some of the most interesting avant-garde writers have been doing in recent years. From Gertrude Stein and Eugene Jolas's "Revolution of the Word" in *transition* to the "Language poets" is perhaps not such a long step (and one can hear the voice of Stein in the Language poets and in David Antin's "talk poems"), but let each reader make his own comparisons and draw his own conclusion. Perhaps the term "avant-garde" is outmoded. We hear more now about semiotics and postmodernism.

In 1986, is there an identifiable avant-garde? But in 1936, when the first "Annual" was assembled, there was a recognizable avant-garde. It was not a cohesive group such as the Dadaists or the Surrealists, or the Russian or Italian Futurists. But revolt against convention, against accepted traditions, was in the air, and the writers searching for new directions published in such magazines as *transition, The Little Review, Broom, Secession, The Dial, Others, Contact,* and a dozen more. Most of the contributors to *ND 1936* represented here were to be found in these ground-breaking periodicals.

It is perhaps relevant to tell how Pound persuaded me to become a publisher, because so many of his friends, at his suggestion, were included in *ND 1936*. In 1934, I took a leave of absence from Harvard and, through a recommendation from Dudley Fitts (my English master at Choate), was accepted as one of the itinerant students who frequented the "Ezuversity" in Rapallo. When it was time for me to go home I asked Pound for "career advice." He had been seeing my poems for months and ruled them hopeless. There could be no future for me in fiction because, he explained, Flaubert, Stendhal, James, and Joyce had "done" the novel. He urged me to finish Harvard and then do "something useful" and promised that he would help me find authors from among his friends. So it was— except that I didn't wait to finish Harvard before starting to print books. I put it that way—"printing"—because I then knew nothing about publishing or distribution. However, I was an editor of the *Harvard Advocate,* the college literary magazine, and could arrange with Wilder Foote, who printed the *Advocate* at his newspaper in Brandon, Vermont, to produce a few hundred copies of *ND 1936.* The ugly cover was of my design, but I forgot to suggest to Wilder that he number the pages.

Each of the early numbers of the anthologies began with my vehement and quite preposterous introductions—remarkable combinations of arrogance, ignorance, and Poundian propaganda—but without Pound's wit and color. I cringe when I reread these introductions now, but they are, I suppose, of some historical interest, if only to compare them with what the alienated young of the '60s were saying. Not only was I certain that I knew how to arrest the decay of literature, I also knew how to save the world with Social Credit. (In fairness to Pound let me say that I still believe that a healthy economy should not be based on the pyramiding of debt, public and private.) Reviewing one of the early anthologies, Randall Jarrell referred to me as "Goody Two-shoes." In Aristotle (*Rhetoric,* 2.12.1389) there is an exact description, to the life, of myself when, at twenty-two, I launched New Directions. The Stagirite is writing about the "characteristics of youth."

> "Young men have strong desires, and whatever they desire they are prone to do. Of the bodily desires the one they let govern them most is the sexual; here they lack self-control. They are shifting and unsteady in their desires, which are vehement for a time, but soon relinquished; for the longings of youth are keen rather than deep—are like sick people's fits of hunger and thirst. The young are passionate, quick to anger, and apt to give way to it. And their angry passions get the better of them; for, since they wish to be honored, young men cannot put up with a slight; they are resentful if they

only imagine that they are unfairly treated. Fond of honor, they are even fonder of victory, for youth likes to be superior, and winning evinces superiority. They love both honor and victory more than they love money. Indeed, they care next to nothing about money, for they have not yet learned what the want of it means. . . ."

J. Laughlin

New Directions

in

Prose &

Poetry

barnard-bishop-boyle-carnevali-cocteau-cummings-dejong-deming-fitts-jolas-laughlin-miller-moore

DREAM
WRITING

AMERICAN
SURREALISM

INDIRECT
CRITICISM

munson-niedecker-o'reilly-pound-ribischka-rudge-stein-stevens-swan-vail-wheelwright-williams-zukofsky

Edited by
James Laughlin IV

I
NEW DIRECTIONS 1936

TO
THE EDITORS
THE CONTRIBUTORS
& THE READERS
of
transition
who have begun successfully
THE REVOLUTION OF THE WORD

PREFACE: NEW DIRECTIONS

A considerable part of the material included in this volume was first printed in the literary section of the Social Credit magazine, *New Democracy*. When, in October, 1935, I chose for the title of that section the name "New Directions" I composed in explanation an editorial in which I proposed that the department would attempt to collect in its pages all the most technically-advanced prose and poetry of American writers, all the work which exhibited a desire on the part of its author to set out in a new philological direction, collect it *because* it, and the fact that it existed at all, reflected the change in the state of the world mind whose spearhead was the New Economics of Major Douglas.

The emphasis of leadership was then upon the economist rather than the poet.

But since that time, nearly a year of hard experience in the propagation of Social Credit has led me to feel that the emphasis should be reversed: it is the poet—the word-worker—who must lead.

The economist (at least *one* economist!) has the right answer to the paradox of poverty amid plenty, but he is confronted by such a solid wall of static thinking that he cannot force his ideas across.

Society has a highly trained incapacity to think along other than familiar lines.

Because poverty has always existed your average educated citizen cannot believe that a system which would do away with it could function. We are faced, finally, by a mass lack of imagination. And the key to that deficiency is language. Only the writer is in a position to fit the key in the lock and turn it.

We think with words. We are entirely dependent upon them for communal action. The amount of thinking that even an isolated individual could do without words to conceptualize his perceptions

3

would be almost negligible—limited in fact to what a horse or a dog can do. Pavlov's dogs could handle two feeling-concepts at once: the hunger-feeling concept and the bell-hearing concept; man, with his system of signs, can work with half a dozen and have any number more on his shelves. No wonder that the words for soul and breath-speech are cognate in almost all languages.

We think with words. And the clarity of our thought (and consequently our actions) depends on the clarity of our language. If we have only a hazy notion of what our words mean we will not be persons of luminous character. If the community allows one word to mean two things mistakes will be made by its members in their social actions. And if we allow many words to mean, in effect, nothing at all we shall be eligible for the presidency of a large university, a national trust, or a legislative body. That sentence is not meant to be funny: it is too tragically true.

Only the word Babel can render the state of the common knowledge in the social sciences today. Only the Pillar of Salt can signify the adaptability of our "intellectual leaders" for tearing down the Tower. Apparently they love the mess they work in like Mexicans their filth.

A few days ago at the Harvard Tercentenary Gilson, the great Medievalist, appealed for a hierarchy of universally accepted logical values to save the "civilized" world from chaos. How right he was! But will his plan be feasible? Not unless there is a housecleaning in every European language. Not unless there is a hacking away of dead wood . . . a polishing of terms . . . a scraping off of barnacles and associational verdigris.

It is the word-worker who must show the way.

The world is in crisis, and language is at once the cause and the cure. New social concepts could stop the waste and the destruction. But they can only be introduced into minds ready to receive them, minds *able* to think along new lines, minds capable of imagination.

Language controls thought. It is not the other way around, as most people think, flattering their human vanity. There is at first, of course, in the development of any culture a vernal period in which thought does dominate. But it doesn't last long in a non-ideographic language. Almost at once, as soon as the culture has advanced to a fairly general literacy, the process of ossification sets in and language, becoming, in its state of sclerosis, a force in itself, impeding by its sclerosis the free flow of ideas, having an obstinate life of its own, begins to condition and then to control the modes of thought.

Language controls thought—as the Church Fathers knew when they insisted on continual care of terminology—as Ogden and Richards knew when they wrote *The Meaning of Meaning*—and the fluidity and flexibility of thought depends upon the fluidity and flexibility of language.

Without the unsubtle lubrication of fresh blood it is hard to conceive of a new social order except by revision of verbal orientation. And it is the writer alone who can accomplish that reorientation. But it will not be the slick paper writers who cater to inferiority complexes, or the editor who will print nothing "unfamiliar to his readers" or the commercial publishers' hair-oil boys. It will be men like Cummings or Carlos Williams who know their business well enough to realize the pass to which language has come and are willing to endure obscurity and poverty to carry on their experiments.

Always, in every age the best writers have understood and resisted ossification. The fertile periods of literature are those of philological innovation. And, as Fenollosa has pointed out, "all nations have written their strongest and most vivid literature before they invented a grammar." Shakspere did not hesitate to invent words. Neither did Rabelais.

Language I conceive as the kinetic sum of two opposing forces— the will of the individual to express his ego in his own way & the will of the community to get things done efficiently by standardizing the system of communication as much as possible. As long as the two opposites are in proper balance a healthy social body can be expected—a reasonable rate of evolution.

But when standardization goes too far, because the resistance of individualism lags, when habits of language are formed which prevent the individual from thinking (and acting) as an indivdual, then the socal cancer begins to proliferate. And nothing but a purification of language can check its spread. Bentham knew this but he couldn't break through the hedge.

The problem, the danger, is the subtlety of the disease. You cannot put your finger on any single word or type of word and say, "Here, look at this chancre!" For ossification operates through groupings, through usage-fixed associations, which are ultimately, in the back of the brain, controlled, I think, by sound. You can picture the whole process of educative assimilation as the building up of sound tracks in the under mind. We can derail ourselves by attention. It is the general inattention through innocence which is responsible for the condition.

Bentham's remedy was simply redefinition. "Phraseoplerosis," he called it. Trace every fictional entity to its material basis, he said, and abuse becomes impossible. But Bentham didn't have to deal with the universal diffusion of print. The groupings were not then indelibly engraved in every mentality by constant repetition. To-day the situation is worse and the physic must be proportionately more drastic.

If every grade school teacher could suddenly, like Saul on the road to Damascus, be struck with the light . . . . If at the same time each could be implemented with enough intelligence and invention to teach language as it has never been taught before, to teach the children every subject from a linguistic axis . . . . If every horse wore gold shoes which were cast before every door-step . . . .

But in the realm of possibility—what we can do now is to support Basic English and experimental writing and practise as much personal verbal chastity as possible (in which I am afraid I set a very bad example!).

Basic English has a distinct national as well as an international value, of which I am sure its backers are aware. Its method of word selection stems from Bentham, and although it cannot turn English into an ideographic language where the material-metaphorical origin of every sign is *visible* in its structure, it can, by its limitation of the vocabulary and simplified syntax, shatter the old sound tracks to pieces. As Ezra Pound has already said, you can be reasonably sure that a "philosopher" is really a philosopher and not another unwitting logodaedalist if he can make his ideas substantial in Basic.

Experimental writing—supposing some circulation for it—is of even greater value in that it attacks more radically the visual and conceptual fronts of the congealed associations as well as the oral one. In this light, it becomes a patriotic duty to read a little Stein now and again, much as it may bore you, simply to physic your sluggish mental intestine. I have made some interesting experiments with Stein texts as verbal cathartics on disinterested subjects. Ten average individuals were asked to write a short paragraph on some such non-material subject as "Religion and the State"; they were then asked to read Stein for ten minutes; then asked to write on the same subject again without consulting their previous effort. The results were all alike—a marked decrease in the use of stereotyped and stock phrases, a greater directness of style.

I believe then, that experimental writing has a real social value, apart from any other. And it is with this in mind that this collection is published at this time. For however my contributors may see themselves I see them as agents of social reform as well as artists. Their propaganda is implicit in their style and in probably every case (originally, at least) unconscious. For their protection I must make it very clear that in this preface I am speaking for myself alone. I hope that they will find themselves in sympathy with my views, but it was not on this basis that the selection of material was made. If I have *used* them I hope it has not been to a degree which transcends the critic's accepted privilege. Their points of departure and immediate objectives are various, but all have a similar ultimate aim—the perfection of a clearer, richer, more meaningful verbal expression.

❅   ❅   ❅

The Cocteau "Mystère Laïc" (in the brilliant translation by the violinist Olga Rudge) is republished because it did not attract at the time of first American publication in *Pagany* the attention which it deserved and because nothing has since appeared from any other hand to supersede its method as the most significant new direction in the technique of criticism of our time. Cocteau's Indirect Criticism is the gravestone of the Polite Paragraph of the preceding century. Pound has adjusted the technique to the requirements of criticism in the social sciences. The impact is that of a short jab to the chin.

Montagu O'Reilly is in close touch with "orthodox" Parisian Surrealism, but Lorine Niedecker is not. She lives in Wisconsin and her ideas are all her own. Among her most interesting experiments were the poems written on three levels of consciousness which appeared about a year ago in the Wilson-Drummond "Westminster" Anthology. Henry Miller, who is extremely versatile, uses Surrealism as part of his repertoire. He is the author of the book which a number of competent judges think the best and an equal number the worst of the past few years: *Tropic of Cancer* is published by the Obelisk Press in Paris and cannot be imported into the United States. In my estimation Miller is the most vivid of living American writers.

Miss Stein is probably more alive to sclerosis of language than any other writer in this collection. Language decay, and not Cubist painting, was the catalyst to her lonely and valourous career. It is to her, through my analyses of her work, that I owe the inception of the train of thought which culminates in this preface, which is, in turn, a partial sketch of the chapter on language in my book *Understanding Gertrude Stein* which is now in progress. "A Waterfall And A Piano" represents a new "period" in Miss Stein's anabasis.

The prototype of Kay Boyle's short-short form is, of course, that of Hemingway's interludes in *In Our Time*, which were published alone under that title by the Three Mountains Press. I have it on second hand that Dr. Hemingstein had great profit of its exercise, and on first hand that Miss Boyle found it very unsatisfactory to write in any other once it was mastered. It is by the kindness of Mr. Charles Pearce that the stories from *365 Days* are reprinted.

It remains only to be said that I consider the metric of my own verse tentative, and that it is always a delight to quote to embattled Georgians who protest the novelty of Mr. Cummings' typography the line of Father Ennius written *ca.* 200 B.C.:

"saxo cere comminuit brum."

I expect that *all* of my contributors would like to do the same to me! J. L. IV

Hancock Point   10 : ix : 36

WALLACE STEVENS

I never got close to Stevens, though Hartford is only an hour's drive from Norfolk, where I live. I had only one brief visit with him in his impressive office at the Hartford Fire Insurance Company. I had loved the poems of Harmonium, *and had come over to ask him for something for ND 1936. He responded most graciously. The question of payment was never raised. In fact, so far as I can remember, no one in ND 1936 got paid. In those days payment was never expected in the avant-garde publications. It was enough to get published. Stevens was cordial that day but in a restrained, almost courtly way. I was just part of the literary landscape and a very unimportant part. He was not easy to talk to, not much bubble, a grave counselor. From Peter Brazleau's "oral biography,"* Parts of a World, *we know that he did not greatly relish casual literary contact though, earlier in his life, he did make visits to New York. He was absorbed in his work at the office and in his poetry and reading. It is said that he composed poems while walking to and from his house and his office. And it is reported that his wife, the lady so beautiful that her head was modeled on the old Liberty dime, did not encourage literary visitors at lunch. He had to take them to the Hartford Canoe Club. Did they actually paddle if the weather was fine—on the broad Connecticut River, or perhaps on the little parallel canal that used to run through the city? It's probably not there anymore; downtown Hartford is now a maze of huge glass boxes.*

MYSTIC GARDEN & MIDDLING BEAST

WALLACE STEVENS

The Poet striding among the cigar stores,
Ryan's lunch, hatters, insurance and medicines,
Denies that abstraction is a vice except

To the fatuous. These are his infernal walls,
A space of stone, of inexplicable base
And peaks outsoaring possible adjectives.
One man, the idea of man, that is the space,
The true abstract in which he promenades.
The era of the idea of man, the cloak
And speech of Virgil dropped, that's where he walks,
That's where his hymns come crowding, hero-hymns,
Chorals for mountain voices and the moral chant,
Happy rather than holy but happy-high,
Day hymns instead of constellated rhymes,
Hymns of the struggle of the idea of God
And the idea of man, the mystic garden and
The middling beast, the garden of Paradise
And he that created the garden and peopled it.

GERTRUDE STEIN

Quite by serendipity, I visited Gertrude Stein and Alice B. Toklas at their beautiful little chateau-ferme near the Lac d'Annecy in the summer of 1934. At the Salzburg Festival I had encountered her great friend Bernard Faÿ, the Sorbonne historian of American culture. He knew that Gertrude liked to instruct young Americans. Bernard wrote to ask if I might visit. "Will he work?" Yes he would.

My work at Bilignin was of two kinds: changing tires on Gertrude's Ford (the rough roads of the region could deflate three tires in an afternoon) on the daily rides through the countryside; and preparing press releases for the lectures (collected in Narrations) of her American lecture tour later in the year. That was as hard work as I ever tackled. The lectures deal with grammar, linguistics, and narrative, but the approaches are epistemological and ontological, all written in vintage Steinese. Trying to reduce them to a page each of what an American reporter would understand was a challenge. It took many drafts and several weeks.

All went well—a sympathetic landscape, two fascinating eccentrics, and good cooking supervised by Alice—until I made a gaffe. Gertrude caught me reading Proust. What a blowup! "J! Don't you know that Proust and Joyce copied their book from my Making of Americans?" *I fell from grace, but we kept up a slight correspondence for some years, and Gertrude sent me "A Water-fall And A Piano" for ND 1936. At one point, I tried to write about her work—* Explaining Gertrude Stein *it was to be called—but I broke down when I came to her period of automatic writing. I know it was automatic writing because I saw her doing it on the terrace at Bilignin. How to explain that? She had nothing to do with the Surrealists.*

A WATER-FALL AND A PIANO

GERTRUDE STEIN

There are so many ways in which there is no crime. A goat comes into this story too. There is always coincidence in crime.

Helen was an orphan that is to say her mother was put away and her father the major was killed in the war.

He went to the war to be killed in the war because his wife was crazy. She behaved strangely when she went to church. She even behaved strangely when she did not. She played the piano and at the same time put cement between the keys so that they would not sound. You see how easy it is to have cement around.

I have often noticed how easy it is to have cement around. Everywhere there are rocks and so everywhere if you have the necessary building and equipment you have cement.

So the mother was put away and the father was dead and the girl was an orphan.

She went to stay where there was a water-fall. Somewhere there some one had two beautiful dogs that were big. One of them was a male and the other was a female, they were to have puppies, their owner a woman wealthy and careful too always wore carpenter's trousers and carpenter's shirts and loved to work. She said when the puppies came there would be nine and they would need more milk than their mother had. She said this was always so. So she said she would buy a goat.

It is difficult to buy a goat not that goats are really rare, but they are not here and there.

A veterinary who could save lives dogs' lives, cows' lives, sheep's lives and even goats' lives he was not so good about horses, because his father and his grandfather had been veterinaries, even his sister always knew what to do, was asked to find a goat a healthy goat. He found one, the goat had been bought and payed for and then no one would let the goat go. This often happens.

Do you see how the whole place was ready now for anybody to be dead.

With them lived an Englishwoman, this was all in France, and the rest were French.

The more you see how the country is the more you do not wonder why they shut the door. They women do in a way and yet if they did not it would be best.

There are many places where every one is married even in the country, some of them are not. Think of it even in the country some of them are not.

The Englishwoman was not. She was not married. The French women either had been or were going to be, but the Englishwoman never had been nor was going to be.

She took care of the gardens and chickens and the nine puppies when they came and she did without the goat, and then she went away for a month's holiday and then she came back.

In the meantime well not in the meantime because they had always known each other the orphan stayed with the lady who had the nine puppies.

Nobody refuses fear. Not only for themselves but for their

dreams because water as if it were a precipice in the moon-light can not disturb because of there being no origin in their dreams.

The Englishwoman came back. She was very cheerful and had seen all her friends and had plans for the nine puppies and the rest of the garden.

Then the dogs found her. She had put her cap beside her and there were two bullets in her head and she was dead.

The police disturbed her they had no business to, the protestant pastor buried her he had no business to, because nobody has been told what had happened to her.

The doctor said nobody could shoot themselves twice. All the doctors said that. An officer said that this was not so. During the war when an officer wanted to be dead he often put a bullet into his head. But it was very often true, that he did not succeed in doing more than putting a bullet into his scalp and then he sent a second one after.

Anyway she was dead, and her family she had a family in England were not satisfied they were satisfied that she was dead oh yes they were satisfied as to that. And the character of the lady who had the nine puppies she kept them all changed and remained changed ever after. And the orphan married an officer.

And every one still talks about it all but not so much now as they did. An American comes to visit in place of the Englishwoman but she has not come to be dead.

JOHN WHEELWRIGHT

Jack Wheelwright was one of the floating group that met for dinner now and then at the Ararat Café in Boston—John Cheever, Robert Fitzgerald, Sherry Mangan (who published the magazine larus *from his Great Eastern Steam Printing Company), R. P. Blackmur, occasionally the painter Maurice Grosser, Howard Blake, S. Foster Damon, Lincoln Kirstein, Hyatt Mayor, Dudley Fitts, and a few aspiring Harvard undergraduates, such as myself.*

Jack was a self-ordained "character." Wheelwrights were Brahmins long before there were any Cabots or Lowells. Six generations in the Bay Colony and one of the early ones scalped by the Indians. Impoverished, but never dependent. Fired out of Harvard, Jack wanted first to be an architect like his father, who designed the Romanesque bridge across the Charles. Took to writing. An Anglican steeped in theology, but also a devout Socialist. So many memories of mad, lovable Jack, my favorite among them when I would pick him up at a fashionable dinner party on Beacon Hill, he in tails, white tie, and top hat, plus a milk crate and his old racoon coat. I would drive him out to Roxbury, a tough quarter of Boston full of Irish. Jack would mount his box, giving me his hat to hold and harangue the crowd about the rights of the workers, often ending up with the story of Sacco and Vanzetti.

*Jack was killed one night in 1940 as he was walking home from a party, hit by a drunken driver at the corner of Marlborough and Mass. Avenue. His funeral was standing room only. Everyone loved Jack—the Anglicans, the Socialists, the Brahmins from Beacon Hill, the writers, the Harvard students and their professors. He pub-*lished several books of poetry, Mirror of Venus, Rock and Shell, Political Self-Portrait. *New Directions did a* Collected Poems *in* 1972.

There is a book about him and Sherry Mangan, The Revolutionary Imagination *by Alan M. Wald. And Matthew Josephson published a wonderfully anecdotal essay about the "improper Bostonian" in* The Southern Review (*Spring 1972*).

ELEGIES

JOHN WHEELWRIGHT

SPRING

Dark (blank dark) incised with intricate, surcharged
you, first dead friend. Day break gun. Birds leave
leaning night towers for fields unbudded, stone-fenced
numb. In this, the voided womb of cult (splayed vines sag
looped between bathed mulberries and behind poplars
the carven hills hang taut) I jump squatting and I would cry out
    loud:
If Dawn follow the far Dark, can Spring far follow Winter?
Budding tear-foetuses tear my throat; I weep, therefore I grieve.
        You (blank indelible
        image of Death on cypress-measured air)
        say with a voice without sound:
        Un-think these things.
        O! Penetrable shade
        how calmly you look out.

SUMMER

The stars we meshed in coral trees of Spring
jumped like fish while we reaped hay moon-
rise past ecstasy, felt then as tears,
or plucked dream berries with noon
eyes through whole days interlocked with spheres.
           The net was torn.

You knew I did not dare be young,
yet did not know your sight was prayer
to give such wing'd cries as belong
beneath a tiger lily's tongue.
                The net was emptied soon.
          Your eyes taught my eyes clarity
          and both were vessels filled with song
          whose words unravelled the unemptied web.
          Now in these dappled twilight clouds I see
          an aspen crescent; but hear no horn call
          while the sarcastic dawn turns gray.

AUTUMN

Upon the Doric plinth of Death
(swag-wreathed, cracked, skull-paved)
hovers a basilika: within, Corinthian-fronded;
projected from the brain-shell; mind-inhabited;
Ionic housed; with outward capitals to spiral
diagramed geometry where rims pierce hubs:
Moth to Lava; Worm to Chrysalis; the Seasons' Wheel;
wheeled Day to Sundown, Night to Dawn; Ice, Water Cloud and
    Rain.
          Since you crushed chrysales of netted stars
          these proofs of ended death prove that their proofs
          draw no diameters to the unending circle.
          Painted as marble, the temple is rubble stone
          drilled by the frost whose wiry eyes
          travel the convolution of a shell.

WINTER

Rock's inner form turned dust reveals
cleft shells to be as stone; and cricket skulls

in powdered light give your quick, analytic mandate:
Un-think these things. Gun-roused at dusk
a cock 'll bugle "Kyrie." Get the geometry of event.
When your lungs failed at war
my mother pulse of dividends revived.
Other theorems of Truth; of Beauty, other corollary!

> As over water when a mill-sluice shuts
> film ice twitches between inverted
> tendril and frond, frond and tendril;
> your rushing brain lay still.
> Our bold-voluted immortality, fallen
> is only rock
> —though proud in ruin, piteous in pride—
> Ned.   Ned.
> Snow on a dome, blown by night wind.

GORHAM MUNSON

Gorham Munson was an editor and man of letters, an important
figure in The Awakening Twenties, *the title of the book in which*
he set down his recollections of that extraordinary period. He had
associations with such arts magazines as Secession, Seven Arts,
Broom, The Little Review, S4N, *and* The Dial, *and he wrote for*
The Nation, The New Republic, *and* The Freeman. *Among his*
close friends were Waldo Frank, Kenneth Burke, Frost, Williams,
many painters, and particularly Hart Crane, whose "untold story"
he gives in his book.

Munson became interested in Social Credit through A. R. Orage,
the editor of The New Age, *who made several visits to New York*
to promote the teachings of Gurdjieff. When I got to know him,
through Pound, in 1935, his enthusiasm for Gurdjieff had waned,

but he had become an impassioned advocate of monetary reform. His book Aladdin's Lamp is the best and most comprehensive I know on that subject. He became, in effect, the leader of the American Social Credit party. (I was a member of the Boston branch. I handed out leaflets on the Boston subway—with no results whatsoever.)

Backed by a Buffalo industrialist, J. Crate Larkin—as I recall he manufactured soap—Munson started New Democracy, a semimonthly "Review of National Economy and the Arts." He hoped that his paper would come to rival The New Republic's and The Nation's influence. But, of course, it never did. The American public is little interested, then or now, in finding out how banks manipulate credit or in abolishing poverty.

But the magazine was of great benefit to me. It was the incubator for New Directions. Munson had the happy idea of giving me two or three pages (it was a large format) for a literary section in each issue, beginning in November 1935 and running to August 1936, when Mr. Larkin lost interest. We christened the section "New Directions."

With the help of Pound and his friends some fine material was collected, and I was able to review books which interested me (Eliot, Orage). Eliot gave me two lovely little poems, "Rannoch, by Glencoe" and "Cape Ann." Williams reviewed the novel Summer Time Ends by John Hargrave, head of the British Social Credit party. Pound sent "Who Gets It?," a diatribe on financial skullduggery, and Canto XLVI. There were choruses from their translation of the Alcestis by Fitts and Fitzgerald; sketches by Kay Boyle, Miller's "Into the Nightlife," and poems by Pound's protégé, Mary Barnard, Elizabeth Bishop, Moore, Cummings, Williams (his great "Perpetuum Mobile"), Wheelwright, and Lorine Niedecker.

NEW DIRECTIONS IN ECONOMICS

GORHAM MUNSON

The world economic crisis; a clash between tradition and the *necessity* for innovation, between old directions and the *necessity* of totally new ones.

    ❀   ❀   ❀   ❀   ❀   ❀

Financial bitchery is the corruption that makes society powerless to cross the threshold of the New Age of Abundance, Leisure and Liberty.

    ❀   ❀   ❀   ❀   ❀   ❀

Death to the Old Economics! We have too long put up with its stupidities, its cruelties, its Black Magic of Numbers, its imperialistic wars and its Red, Black and Brown Fascisms.

    ❀   ❀   ❀   ❀   ❀   ❀

The rebel student wraps a wet towel around his head for many nights. He reads all the masters of orthodox economics from Adam Smith to the revisers of Marx. No light on the anomaly of poverty amidst plenty! At last he turns to the heretics. Here he finds unveiled the guarded secret of the great financiers. A concealed error in loan accountancy, a faking of the books, a swindling of the mind, by which it appears that an increment of physical wealth invariably breeds an increment of debt. The student's brain is dazed by the madness of real wealth turned into financial poverty. He cannot believe that so vast a maleficence can result from a little lie in bookkeeping. He is overwhelmed by the romance of a humdrum bookkeeper falsifying an entire civilization.

    ❀   ❀   ❀   ❀   ❀   ❀

Signposts for the new directions of Douglas:

Attack the problem of distributing the "good things of life," for the production problem has been solved.

Abandon absolutes in economics; the fruitful principle is relativity.

The socialization of credit is the first step.

Justice in the price relation is the key to economic democracy.

The unearned increment of association awaits monetization.

The present generation are tenants-for-life of a common cultural heritage, now unrecognized as a principal factor of wealth-production.

Not the abolition of the dividend system but its extension to all members of society is the direction of the future.

    ❅   ❅   ❅   ❅   ❅   ❅

Social Credit is a mechanism. It re-times the devices of the Private Credit mechanism, slowing down the rate of cancellation of credit to the rate of consumption. Its governor is the Retail Price Discount instead of the rediscount rate of the present banking system. Its National Dividend device modernizes the "open market" policy. Social Credit is the existing financial mechanism remodelled to adjust it to the fact of physical plenty.

    ❅   ❅   ❅   ❅   ❅   ❅

What is it all governments neglect? To keep the books of national production and consumption. A Jeffersonian truth: the best government is the one that by keeping the nation's books needs to govern least.

    ❅   ❅   ❅   ❅   ❅   ❅

Up with the New Economics of Social Credit! Through consumption to prosperity—through material welfare to creation—through creation to the new social order. The Revolution Absolute!

EZRA POUND

The key lines in Canto XLVI are the ones underscored:

"Said Paterson:
        Hath benefit of interest on all
the moneys which it, the bank, creates out of
                                    nothing."

Paterson (1658–1719) *was the chief founder of the Bank of England.*

This indictment is at the core of Pound's economic teaching. Few people understand that banks have for centuries, and still do, legally create money (as credit). If a bank has $1,000 of real deposits, your money or mine, it may lend to borrowers up to seven times that amount. (Ironically, loans are carried on the bank's books as "deposits." Thus banks can charge interest on bookkeeping money.) This system works well when the economy is expanding— and it helps the economy grow. But when depression and panic come along, and bank loans are not repaid, there is Big Trouble.

This, for Pound, was at the root of usury. In his great Canto XLV he tells us how usury affects the arts:

"hath no man a painted paradise on his church wall."

In Canto XLVI, the "fuzzy bloke" is Pound himself, talking to Major C. H. Douglas, the father of Social Credit. The "case" is the economic causes of war and poverty. "Max" is Max Beerbohm, who had a house in Rapallo. A. R. Orage was the social theoretician of Social Credit. "Marmaduke" was the novelist Pickthall, who converted to Mohammedanism. Canto XLVI gives Pound's evidence against the system—which still prevails—but "will any jury convict'um?"

Is it necessary for us to know who all the people in The Cantos *were? The poem has a cast of thousands. A few key characters perhaps. But let the others float. The significance is in the ideas and the excitement of the language.*

CANTO XLVI

EZRA POUND

If you will say that this tale teaches . . .
a lesson, or that the Reverend Eliot
has found a more natural language . . . you who think you will
get through hell in a hurry . . .
                    That day there was cloud over Zoagli
And for three days snow-cloud over the sea
Banked like a line of mountains.
Snow fell. Or rain fell stolid, a wall of lines,
So that you could see where the air stopped open
and where the rain fell beside it
Or the snow fell beside it. Seventeen
Years on this case, nineteen years, ninety years
                    on this case (Inspector!)
Of the centuries. Office/
An' the fuzzy bloke sez (legs no pants ever wd. fit) "IF
that is so, any government worth a damn can
pay dividends?"
The Major chewed it a bit and sez: "Y-es, eh . . .
"You mean instead of collectin' taxes?"
"Instead of collecting taxes." That office?
Didja see the Decennio?
?
Decennio exposition, reconstructed office of Il Popolo,
Waal, ours waz like that, minus the Mills bomb an' the teapot,
Seventeen years, heavy lipped chap at the desk,
One half green eye and one brown one, nineteen
Years on this case, CRIME
Ov two CENturies, 5 millions bein' killed off
to 1919, and before that

Debts of the South to New York, that is to the
banks of the city, two hundred million,
war, I don't think, or have it your own way . . .
about slavery?
Five million being killed off . . . couple of Max's drawings,
one of Balfour and a camel, an'
one w'ich fer *oBviOus* reasons haz
never been published, ole Johnny Bull with a 'ankerchief.
It has never been published . . .
          "He ain't got an opinion."
Sez Orage about G.B.S. sez Orage about Mr. Xtertn.
Sez Orage about Mr. Wells, "He won't HAVE an opinion
trouble is that you mean it, you never will be a journalist."
19 years on this case, suburban garden,
"Greeks!" sez John Marmaduke "a couple of art tricks!
"What else? never could set up a NATION!"
"Wouldn't convert me, wdn't HAVE me converted,
"Said 'I know I didn't *ask* you, your father sent you here
'to be trained. I know what I'd feel.
'send my son to England and have him come back a christian!
'what wd. I feel?' " Suburban garden,
Said Abdul Baha: "I said 'let us speak of religion!'
"Camel driver said: 'I must milk my camel.'
"So when he had milked his camel I said 'let us speak of religion.'
"And the camel driver said: 'It is time to drink milk.
'Will you have some?' For politeness I tried to join him.
"Have you ever tasted milk from a camel?
"I was unable to drink camel's milk. I have *never* been able.
"So he drank all of the milk, and I said: 'let us speak of religion,'
'I have drunk my milk. I must dance.' said the driver.
"We did not speak of religion." Thus Abdul Baha
Third vice-gerent of the First Abdul or whatever Baha,
the Sage, the Uniter, the founder of a religion,
in a garden at Uberton, Guberton or mebbe it was some
other damned suburb, but at any rate a suburban suburb,
amid a flutter of teacups, said Mr. Marmaduke:
"Never will understand us. They lie. I mean personally
"They are mendacious, but if the tribe gets together
"the tribal word will be kept, hence perpetual misunderstanding.

"Englishman goes there, lives honest, word is reliable,
"ten years, they believe him, then he signs terms for the
     government.
"and, naturally, the treaty is broken. Mohammedans,
"Nomads, will never understand how we do this."
17 years on this case, and we not the first lot!
Said Paterson:
     Hath benefit of interest on all
the moneys which it, the bank, creates out of nothing.

     Semi-private inducement
Said Mr. RotSchild, hell knows which Rot schild,
1861, '64 or there sometime, "Very few people
"will understand this. Those who do will be occupied
"getting profits. The general public will probably not
"see it's against their interest."
     Seventeen years on the case; here
Gents, is/are the confession
     "Can we take this into court?
     "Will any jury convict on this evidence?"
1694 anno domini, on through the ages of usury
On right on into hair-cloth, right on into rotten building,
Right on into London houses, ground rents, foetid brick work,
Will any jury convict 'um? The Foundation of Regius
     Professors
Was made to spread lies and teach Whiggery, will any
     JURY convict 'um?
The Macmillan Commission about two hundred and forty years
     LATE
with great difficulty got back to Paterson's
"The bank makes it *ex nihil*"
Denied by five thousand professors, will any
Jury convict 'um? This case, and with it
the first part, draws to a conclusion,
of the first phase of this opus, Mr. Marx, Karl, did not
foresee this conclusion, you have seen a good deal of
the evidence, not knowing it evidence, si monumentum
look about you, look, if you can, at St. Peter's,
Look at the Manchester slums, look at Brazilian coffee

or Chilean nitrates. This case is the first case
Si requieres monumentum?
This case is not the last case or the whole case, we ask a
REVISION, we ask for enlightenment in a case
moving concurrent, but this case is the first case:
Bank creates it *ex nihil*. Creates it to meet a need,
Hic est hyper-usura. Mr. Jefferson met it:
No man hath natural right to exercise profession
of lender, save him who hath it to lend.
Replevin, estopple, what wangle which wangle, Van Buren
        met it.
Before that was tea dumped into harbour, before that was a
great deal still in the school books, placed there
NOT as evidence. Placed there to distract idle minds,
Murder, starvation and bloodshed, seventy four red revolutions
Ten empires fell on this grease spot.
"I rule the Earth" said Antoninus "but LAW rules the sea."
Meaning, we take it, lex Rhodi, the Law Maritime,
        of sea lawyers,
usura and sea insurance
wherefrom no State was erected greater than Athens.
Wanting TAXES to build St. Peter's thought Luther beneath
        civil notice,
1527. Thereafter art thickened. Thereafter design went to hell.
Thereafter barocco, thereafter stone-cutting desisted.
Hic nefas, (narrator) commune sepulchrum.

19 years on this case / first case. I have set down part of
The Evidence. Part! commune sepulchrum
Aurum est commune sepulchrum. Usura, commune sepulchrum.
helandros   kai heleptolis   kai helarxe.
Hic Geryon est. Hic hyper-usura.

FIVE million youths without jobs
FOUR million adult illiterates
15 million "vocational misfits," that is with small chance for jobs
NINE million persons annual, injured in preventable industrial
        accidents

One hundred thousand violent crimes. The Eunited States ov
    America
3rd year of the reign of F. Roosevelt, signed F. Delano, his uncle
CASE for the prosecution. That is one case, minor case
in the series / Eunited States of America, a. d. 1935
England a worse case, France under a foetor of regents.
"Mr. Cummings wants Farley's job" headline in current paper.

30 Jan XIV

JEAN COCTEAU

Pound met Jean Cocteau when he was living in Paris in the Twen-
ties. They became lifelong friends. Pound considered Cocteau the
best French poet among his contemporaries, though as early as
1913 he had met and admired some of the "Effort libre" group—
Vildrac, Duhamel, Romains, Jouve. Remy de Gourmont, who died
in 1915, was his hero in France. Gourmont's Problème du style
influenced the Imagists. Pound translated Gourmont's Physique de
l'amour, *appending to it, in a postscript, his own bizarre sexual*
theories. He knew some of the Dadaists and thought that Picabia,
whose writings he promoted in The Little Review, *had an extraor-*
dinary mind. Valéry did not interest him. Claudel was slop. He
never mentioned the Surrealists or Apollinaire or Reverdy to me,
though he must have read them. Cocteau was the man.
    Modern drama was not an interest for Pound, but he praised
Cocteau's use of figures from Greek mythology in his plays and
liked the novels. His favorite Cocteau poem was "Leoun." It was the
"Mystère laïc" which excited him—as an example of how to write
criticism in a new way. The painter Chirico, the subject of the
piece, meant nothing to him. What attracted him was Cocteau's
indirect criticism, the collage of diary fragments, mini-essays,

aphorisms (here is the famous "Victor Hugo was a madman who thought he was Victor Hugo"), prose poems, aesthetic pronouncements, and verbal acrobatics.

Why did Pound set such store by a work which Francis Steegmuller, Cocteau's best biographer, dispatches in a few sentences as "banal" and "artistic stumbling"? I think it is a case of Pound's affinity for Cocteau's method. Cocteau's little paragraphs jump from one seemingly unrelated topic to another the way Pound would later structure The Cantos.

The English translation was made by Olga Rudge, Pound's longtime companion—they met when he was living in Paris—no doubt with a good deal of help from E.P. The "Mystère laïc" runs to twenty-five pages of which we have chosen five to represent it here.

THE LAÏC MYSTERY

from an essay in indirect criticism: the painter chirico

JEAN COCTEAU

Translated by Olga Rudge

I have been driven from home by the dust, by souvenirs, photographs, letters, and fetishes of all sorts, and from now on I shall doubtless never live anywhere. On the mantle-piece of that nowhere I should like to set up these notes, and my study of Picasso.

I reserve the right to live and to make friendship (more difficult to make than love) in the presence of these portraits, to which I owe recognition, and respect.

*

Chirico's paternal family: a mad uncle and aunt.

One uncle pushed a chair in front of himself to keep from falling over a precipice. His Aunt Olympia used to unwind her magnificent hair, kneel in front of a sofa and rub her head against it until she went bald. Such anecdotes help to eliminate all picturesqueness from Chirico's work.

✻

Chirico's brother, Savinio, was a musician and poet. A naive amateur would ask himself which of the two brothers inspired the other, and why they influence each other. It happens that they authentify themselves. Savinio proves that family spirit and memories of childhood orient Chirico. Two brothers brought up in Greece, Italian in origin, their Mother watching them from an Acropolis, sitting on an ormolu chair holding a bouquet of roses.

✻

The new English process for cleaning pictures requires the use of chloroform. They operate on a painting that has been put to sleep. Specialists in white blouses chloroformed Ucello's battle. On waking it had lost that blear eyed expression without which the public will hardly stand masterworks. Since then I can't look at Chirico's pictures without telling myself that they are asleep.

✻

Seen from above a man falling is a man diminishing, this diminishing stops abruptly, leaving him there like a doll. A man walking away is a man falling gently, instead of being crushed he dissolves like a cloud. All Chirico's perspectives are precipitous drops.

✻

An automobile accident, a railway wreck are masterpieces in the unexpected. One would like to watch them in slow motion, to see speed and immobility twisting iron in their milliners' fingers.

✻

A photographed house is different from a cinematographed house. Even when nothing moves, the cinema registers time passing. Nothing is more disconcerting than photography in the middle of a film.

❧

Characters gripped by fear should be 'statuefied' by this syncope, for a second. Hung near other pictures, Chirico's seem thus changed into statues, the air of ancient calm, of accidents that have just taken place, displays the postures, the grimaces of speed overtaken by immobility without having had time to get ready.

❧

The horror of a street accident comes from immobile swiftness, a cry *changed* to silence (not the silence after a cry). One recognizes the corpses at once by their attitudes that are grotesque but not funny. Distance in Chirico is of death. A picture by Chirico is the brutal passage from one state to another. The peculiar arrangement of the heteroclite objects does not make us laugh; it is this group of dusty puppets about whose nature, though our eyes deceives us, the human soul never errs.

❧

One night returning from Villefranche I came slap on a fresh accident. My headlights lit up the debris, the corpses. I *wanted* to see luggage there in front of me and the people who had fainted. But I *knew*. The remnant of animal in us recognizes death.

❧

Isadora Duncan died yesterday. This tragedy shows more than one relation to the order of things that here concerns us. It demands too strict a complicity between a crapulous little racing car and a fringed shawl not to awaken our suspicions. This shawl detested the victim. I have often seen it catch in the doors of bars, and of lifts, and tangle itself in branches. I perceive quite clearly what the shawl wanted, i.e. to strangle Isadora and give her that Jocasta's death predicted by Duse. But the car's? The latest news is that an American collector has bought it.

P.S.—On top of this they say the shawl has also been bought. Perhaps the two criminal objects have found a means of being reunited.

✤

In the coulisses of the Renaissance, orthopedy, anatomy were merely awaiting a signal from Chirico to "go on."

✤

A pure man's life should contain no action which can be effortlessly legitimized in the courts, and the courts are never worth the pure man's while. A pure man ceases to be such the minute he accepts a favorable position, or profits by a party.

I can see no single detail in Chirico's work that could appear innocent in the judge's eyes; plead not guilty, or save his neck. No one was on the scene of the crime. The smallest possible dry biscuit would come and bear witness against him.

✤

Poetry is exactitude, number.

But people think that inexactitude is poetic, romantic. The crowd adores an inexactitude that looks real. I wonder whether blackmailing newspapers report things incorrectly because they learn them at fourth hand, or whether they distort the truth because of their profound knowledge of the public taste. The public senses a reality behind the apparent unreality of a Chirico painting. It is not going to be fooled.

Picasso. Chirico, Futurists. Expressionists. The newer generation combines them, refines them—but can no more get away from them than from Ducasse or Rimbaud. I can take much more interest in a young painter groping and hunting for the latch to get out. There are too many legitimate children of the bourgeois marriage between Picasso and Chirico. I want an "enfant terrible."

✤

To judge "Le Rappel à l'Ordre" from an æsthetic point of view, is to confuse tools with "objects of art."

✤

I am not interested in determining whether Chirico paints better or worse, if he repeats himself or invents. That would be taking the æsthetic point of view, and Chirico interests me from the ethical.

He proves to me the existence of a soul's truth, never picturesque, though possessing all the elements that evoke picturesqueness.

❋

A great artist is inhuman, vegetable, bestial. If he tries to speak his attempts upset us. Stravinsky in the 'Sacre' is a growing tree. The Stravinsky of 'Histoire du Soldat,' the 'Serenade,' 'Oedipus Rex' is the tree that tries to speak and that does speak. Chirico always speaks. He often speaks by means of ventriloquism. Sometimes he speaks alone. Then he relapses. Nothing is more touching than an animal trying to regain the secret of human speech which it has discovered and then lost.

❋

Chirico takes off his orthopedical corset and no longer hides behind the Italian illusionist (trompe l'oeil) method.

❋

Daring sprouts in brave men's backs. You call a man brave when he prolongs an old audacity. Everyone thought themselves intelligent from 1920 to 1927 because we were watching the rococo of obscurity.

❋

Picasso sucked daggers. It leaves a bitter taste in his mouth. Miro sucks sticks of barley sugar, sucks them to a point. The point gets sharper and sharper but the barley sugar gets shorter.

❋

What saves Miro—his line is alive. If he makes a cross it crucifies.

❋

I consider that art reflects ethics and that one cannot renew oneself without living dangerously and laying oneself open to calumny. This is the only wall between Maritain and myself. At bottom he thinks art a dangerous game, a caricature of creation, a "dawsey" (dar'st ée).

❋

That is true when he looks back over that long reign of æstheticism and cruelty during which heart seemed ridiculous, but this ice is beginning to melt. Everything changes. The plastic code is giving way to a moral plastic not to be judged by the intelligence. The new criticism will require the use of the heart, that is to say it will be more difficult to manipulate and will finally disappear. One of Chirico's merits is that in a completely plastic period he relied more on moral than on visual problems, which latter lead fatally to preciosity.

God's æsthetic escapes judgment.

The utility of a crime, of an accident in his work. Man is in God's image. When I can't follow an artist whom I admire, I have to make an act of faith.

＊

MARIANNE MOORE

Miss Moore—I always called her that, though we went to baseball games (she remembered the records of Connie Mack's teams and knew everything about the Dodgers) and had long talks, rather too long talks, on the telephone—was another of the blessings Pound sent me. Pound knew of her work as early as 1915. That year, writing to Harriet Monroe about an issue of Poetry, *he says that "her titles are nice." By 1918 he is writing her five-page discussions of poems she submitted for* The Little Review. *In 1919 she is "Chère Marianne." They were close friends to the end. When Pound came to the States in 1969—he was silent then, but totally silent* (tempus tacendi)—I *watched him talk like his old self for twenty minutes with M.M. in a little side room of the New York Public Library, away from the crowd that wanted to honor him.*

I find nothing in the correspondence which indicates that M.M. tinkered with Pound's poems when she was at The Dial, *as she did with some of Hart Crane's, to his extreme annoyance. They say she was an incorrigible editorial fixer—always the perfectionist— and I can vouch for her ability. At one point I had sent her a copy of a poem I had written about an airplane crashing into the top of the Empire State Building, an event I witnessed from my office window. Some months later Miss Moore was on the phone. "Mr. Laughlin, I do hope you won't be* too *angry with me. The other evening I was doing a reading, and I wanted to read one of your poems. But I felt that 'Above the City' could be slightly improved in small ways. I hope I was not presumptuous." No, I was not angry, not in the least. I didn't actually see the revision till many years later, when Pat Willis showed it to me in the Moore collection at the Rosenbach Museum in Philadelphia. Miss Moore had remade* the poem—and it's now certainly one of my best.

SEE IN THE MIDST OF FAIR LEAVES

MARIANNE MOORE

and much fruit, the swan—
    one line of the mathematician's
sign greater-than, drawn
    to an apex where the lake is
met by the weight on it; or an angel
standing in the sun, how well
    armed, how manly;

and promenading
    in sloughs of despond, a monster—

man when human nothing
   more, grown to immaturity,
punishing debtors, seeking his due—as
an arrow turned inward has
   no chance of peace.

WILLIAM CARLOS WILLIAMS

It's hard to believe he is so famous now, but in 1936, when I came along, sent by Pound, Bill Williams had no publisher. From the first, he had had a scramble to get published at all. He had the Poems *of 1909 printed himself and nondistributed at Garroway's drugstore in Rutherford. Pound arranged for* The Tempers (1913) *with his publisher, Elkin Mathews, in London. Al Que Quiere (1917), Kora in Hell (1920), and Sour Grapes (1921) were done with Four Seas, a vanity press in Boston. Pound persuaded his friend Bill Bird to do* The Great American Novel (1923) *in the "inquest series" at Three Mountains Press in Paris.* Spring and All (1923), *one of his most important books, could only be done by Robert McAlmon's Contact Editions in Paris. And so it went. When Williams finally did get New York publishers, Boni for* In the American Grain *and Macaulay for* Voyage to Pagany (1928), *they both went out of business.*

Which explains why, when an ardent young man turned up on his doorstep, Williams was willing to take a chance on total inexperience. There were many rewards for me in that wonderful relationship with a great poet who became a generous and understanding friend.

"How to Write" was typical of Williams's informal but invaluable pedagogy. He encouraged and helped young writers all his life. Any tyro could come to him with the most dismal of manuscripts and find sustenance. He started me writing verse again

*after Pound told me I was hopeless, and he helped me work out
my eccentric typewriter metric.*

"Perpetuum Mobile: The City" has been one of my favorite
Williams poems since I first saw it. So much of him is there. The
short, syncopated lines with the superb breaks. WCW had the
finest ear for breaking lines. And eye, too, for the breaks make a
lovely visual pattern, floating the lines on the page. Such rhythm.
Then the use of the collage method which reached its perfection
in Paterson and the "Asphodel." (This to be compared with the
disjuncts of Pound's ideogrammatic method, though each was quite
different and successful in its own way. What is the "connection"
in this poem between the bank holdup and tying the wisps of
kinky hair? Logically, there is none. But in the way that a poem
makes discoveries there is every connection.)

And there is so much here of Williams's own life: the values,
the aspirations, the losses, the abiding presence of love. Once,
toward evening, he walked me up to the knoll above his house in
Rutherford from where we looked across the Jersey meadows to
the distant skyscrapers of New York. In the setting sun they were
indeed like trees in flower. New York was the world he had once
hoped for: a prosperous medical practice, the ready society of
writers and artists. But that was not to be. In the middle section
of the poem he rejects the great but frightening city. Not really
for him. The coda is the farewell to New York, the acceptance of
life in Rutherford. It was a happy choice for us. Would we have
had the great Doctor Stories or the poems where we first hear the
true sounds of American speech, and from that the American idiom,
if Dr. Williams had practiced from a posh office on Park Avenue?

HOW TO WRITE

WILLIAM CARLOS WILLIAMS

One takes a piece of paper, anything, the flat of a shingle, slate, cardboard and with anything handy to the purpose begins to put down the words after the desired expression in mind. This is the anarchical phase of writing. The blankness of the writing surface may cause the mind to shy, it may be impossible to release the faculties. Write, write anything: it is all in all probability worthless anyhow, it is never hard to destroy written characters. But it is absolutely essential to the writing of anything worth while that the mind be fluid and release itself to the task.

Forget all rules, forget all restrictions, as to taste, as to what ought to be said, write for the pleasure of it—whether slowly or fast—every form of resistance to a complete release should be abandoned.

For today we know the meaning of depth, it is a primitive profoundity of the personality that must be touched if what we do is to have it. The faculties, untied, proceed backward through the night of our unconscious past. It goes down to the ritualistic, amoral past of the race, to fetish, to dream, to wherever the "genius" of the particular writer finds itself able to go.

At such a time the artist (the writer) may well be thought of as a dangerous person. Anything may turn up. He has no connection with ordered society. He may perform an imbecility or he may by a freak of mind penetrate with tremendous value to society into some avenue long closed or never yet opened. But he is disconnected with any orderly advance or purpose.

It is now that artists stoutly defend themselves against any usefulness in their art. And it makes no difference whether it is a treatise on mathematics or a poem that is being written. *While* it is being written, as far as possible, the writer be he mathematician or poet, must with a stored mind no doubt, must nevertheless thoroughly abandon himself to the writing in greater or less degree if he wishes to clinch his expression with any depth of significance.

The demonic power of the mind is its racial and individual past, it is the rhythmic ebb and flow of the mysterious life process and unless this is tapped by the writer nothing of moment can result. It is the reason for the value of poetry whose unacknowledged rhythmic symbolism is its greatest strength and which makes all prose in comparison with it little more than the patter of the intelligence.

So poets have been considered unbalanced creatures (as they often are), madmen very often. But the intrinsic reason for this is seldom understood. They are in touch with "voices," but this is the very essence of their power, the voices are the past, the depths of our very beings. It is the deeper, not "lower" (in the usually silly sense) portions of the personality speaking, the middle brain, the nerves, the glands, the very muscles and bones of the body itself speaking.

But once the writing is on the paper it becomes an object. It is no longer a fluid speaking through a symbolism of ritualistic forms but definite words on a piece of paper. It has now left the region of the formative past and come up to the present. It has entered now a new field, that of intelligence. I do not say that the two fields do not somewhat overlap at times but the chief characteristic of the writing now is that it is an object for the liveliest attention that the full mind can give it and that there has been a change in the whole situation.

It is this part of writing that is dealt with in the colleges and in all forms of teaching but nowhere does it seem to be realized that without its spring from the deeper strata of the personality all the teaching and learning in the world can make nothing of the result. Not to have realized this is the greatest fault of those who think they know something of the art.

All that the first phase of writing has accomplished is to place its record on the paper. Is this valuable, is it worthless? These questions it cannot answer and it is of no use for the poet to say:

This is what *I* have done, therefore it is excellent. He may say that and what he has done may be excellent but the reasons should be made clear and they involve the conscious intelligence.

The written object comes under the laws of all created things involving a choice and once the choice has been made there must be an exercise of the will to back it. One goes forward carefully. But the first step must not be to make what has been written under a quasi-hallucinatory state conform to rules. What rules? Rather the writing should be carefully examined for the new and the extraordinary and nothing rejected without clear reason. For in this way the intelligence itself is corrected.

Thus, we know that in language is anchored most or all of the wisdom and follies of our lives. Besides which language may grow stale, meanings may and will be lost, phrases may block our arrival at conclusion. And in the writings of genius, in the poems (if any) the released personality of the artist the very break with stupidity which we are seeking may have occurred. And this will always be in the *form* which that first writing has taken.

But lest a mistake occur I am not speaking of two persons, a poet and a critic, I am speaking of the same person, the writer. He has written with his deepest mind, now the object is there and he is attacking it with his most recent mind, the fore-brain, the seat of memory and ratiocination, the so-called intelligence.

This cannot do more in reviewing that which is before it than reject that which has been said better elsewhere. Whereas in the first phase a man need not seriously have written at all, now it is necessary that he know the work of other men, in other times, as much as possible and from every available angle. This is the student's moment.

And for an American there is one great decision to be made. What language is being written?

A few years ago some American in England wrote an attack upon American writers living in America saying in effect: How can they write English not hearing it spoken every day?—His comment was meant to be ironical but it turned out to be naive. The answer to his question is, naturally: Why bother with English when we have a language of our own?

It is the intelligence which gives us the history of writing and its point of arrival today, the place of Poe, the value of Whitman, the purpose of free verse, why it occurred at just that time, the significance of Gertrude Stein's work, that of the writings of James Joyce and the rationale of modern verse structure.

Briefly all this is the birth of a new language. It is a new allotment of significance. It is the cracking up of phrases which have stopped the mind.

All these things could be gone into in detail, a book could be written and must be written of them, but that is not my purpose here. What I have undertaken is to show the two great phases of writing without either of which the work accomplished can hardly be called mastery. And that, in the phrase of James Joyce, is the he and the she of it.

PERPETUUM MOBILE: THE CITY

WILLIAM CARLOS WILLIAMS

        —a dream
we dreamed
            each
separately
            we two
of love
            and of
desire—

that fused
in the night

in the distance
     over
the meadows—

          by day
impossible—

          The city
disappeared
          when
we arrived—
          A dream
a little false
toward which
          now
we stand
          and stare
transfixed—

All at once
          in the east
rising!

          All white!

          small
as a flower—

a locust cluster
a shad bush
          blossoming

Over the swamps
          a wild
magnolia bud—
          greenish
white
a northern
          flower—

And so
       we live
       looking—

At night
     it wakes
On the black
       sky—
a dream
      toward which
we love—

at night
      more
than a little
      false—

We have bred
we have dug
we have figured up
our costs
we have bought
an old rug—

We batter at our
unsatisfactory
      brilliance—

There is no end
      to desire—

Let us break
     through
and go there—
in
         vain!

—delectable
     amusement:

Milling about—

Money! in
armoured trucks—
Two men
           walking
at two paces from
           each other
their right hands
           at the hip—

on the butt of
an automatic—

till they themselves
hold up the bank
and themselves
           drive off
for themselves
           the money
in an armoured car—

           For love!

Carefully
     carefully tying
carefully

           selected
wisps of long
dark hair
       wisp
by wisp
upon the stubbs
of his kinky wool—

For two hours
three hours
           they worked—

until
he coiled
      the thick
knot upon
that whorish head—
Dragged
      insensible
upon his face
by the lines—
—a running horse

     For love!

Their eyes
     blown out—

—for love, for love!

Neither the rain
nor the storm—

can keep them

     for love!

from the daily
accomplishment
     of their
appointed rounds—

Guzzling
the cream foods
     while
out of sight
     in
the sub-cellar—
the waste fat
the old vegetables
     chucked down

a chute
        the foulest
sink in the world—
And go

on the out-tide
ten thousand
            cots
floating to sea
        like weed
that held back
the pristine ships—

And fattened there
            an eel
in the water pipe—

            No end—
There!
        There!
There!

        —a dream
of lights
        hiding
the iron reason
            and stone
a settled
        cloud—

City
        whose stars
of matchless
        splendor—

            and
in bright-edged
            clouds
            the moon—

            bring
silence
            breathlessly—

Tearful city
          on a summer's day
the hard grey
            dwindling
in a wall of
          rain—

          farewell!

E. E. CUMMINGS

*I was reading Cummings again the other night. What delights!
What sheer pleasure, his and mine, in what the language can do
when conventional patterns are ingeniously disrupted. His writing
and that of Gertrude Stein were quite different. But they had a
similar goal—to "make it new" in the way words are hitched
together. Clean them up, shake them loose, make them fresh and
alive again.*

*The poems which Cummings sent me for ND 1936 were rather
slight. But read some of the big ones and you'll see why he electrified my youth. (I give the page numbers in the Harcourt Collected Poems.) "O Distinct Lady" (37), "somewhere i have never
travelled" (263), "kumrads die because they're told" (296), "this
mind made war" (the poem about Pound) (315), and "my father
moved through dooms of love" (373). Or some of the comic-
satiric poems: "The Cambridge ladies" (58), "Beauty Hurts Mr.
Vinal" (167), "remarked Robinson Jefferson" (232), "May I feel
said he" (288), and "let's start a magazine" (293).*

For me, Cummings is the heir in our time of the Elegiac Poets, crossed with Martial, and of Herrick and Rochester. Like Dylan Thomas, he was the master of the great first line. Pound urged everyone to read Eimi, the prose book about Russia. I found it tedious and much prefer The Enormous Room. Pound probably liked Eimi because it is anti-Communist. Strange that he should have approved word-play prose when he so hated Finnegans Wake.

It was a fine reward for a day's work at the office, which was then in the old triangular building at the corner of Sixth Avenue and 4th Street, when the Cummingses would ask me to drop by for tea in Patchin Place. They were in Number 4 on the ground floor, with Djuna Barnes, whom they mothered with chicken broth when she was poorly, upstairs. The Cummingses lived a rather self-contained life. I seldom saw them around the Village. Marion, who was a fine photographer, was tall and very beautiful. She had once been a fashion model. She was serene but with her special sparkle. Estlin was on the small side, wirey, but even though he seldom left his armchair I felt the energy coming out of him. He talked with a Yankee twang; his eyes seemed to talk as well as his mouth. He wasn't a raconteur, but what he said was always pithy and witty. His laugh had a little cackle in it, not unlike Bill Williams's Jersey cackle. They had been friends for years.

Cummings's relaxation was painting. There were always a number of his oils in the apartment, often changing. I was never greatly taken with his work, but it meant ever so much to him. And I don't forget that when Pound was brought to Washington from Italy for trial Cummings sent the thousand dollars for which he had sold a painting to the defense fund. (Hemingway did the same.)

THREE POEMS

E. E. CUMMINGS

1
lucky means finding
Holes where
pockets aren't lucky
's to spend

laughter
not money lucky are
Breathe
grow dream

die love not
Fear eat sleep kill
and have you am luck
-y is we lucky luck-

ier
luck
-I-
est

2
my specialty is living said
a man (who could not earn his bread
because he would not sell his head)

squads right impatiently replied
two billion public lice inside
one pair of trousers (which had died)

3
economic secu
rity" is a cu
rious excu

se
(in

use among pu
rposive pu
nks) for pu

tting the arse
before the torse

KAY BOYLE

*Kay Boyle was one of the great beauties and figures in expatriate
literary Paris in the Twenties and Thirties. The notation in my
copy of her novel* Year Before Last *shows that I read it at Choate
in 1932. (And "purchased from the* Atlantic Fund" *means that I
bought it from the prize money of* The Atlantic Monthly *contest
for stories by schoolboys.) Dudley Fitts would have told me how
good she was.*

   I think I have all her novels, and they are all exceptional. A superb style that creates its own world of sensibility and color. But robust in a feminine way. No sentimentality, simply a keen perception of what makes people do as they do and feel what they feel. New Directions reprinted Monday Night in our New Classics Series (it is a classic) in 1947 and did a collection of Thirty Stories in 1957.

As often happens when a writer is famous for one genre, few people know that Kay is a remarkable poet. One of ND's earliest books was her A Glad Day in 1931. She wrote long lines that build without much pause into stanzas, often with interpolations of prose; subdued imagery but rich in verbal texture, mentation, and allusion.

In the mid-Thirties Kay became interested in the short-short story—stories which could be printed on one page. She conceived of a collection of 365 Days, a story for each day of the year. She wrote many herself then recruited friends to do the others. I was pleased when she accepted two of mine, one of them a reduction of a rather scabrous piece I had done for the Advocate, for the book which appeared in 1936. She sent me three of these shorts for ND 1936, one of which is reprinted here.

Memories of a week when I was skiing in Megève in France. Kay and her then husband, the writer Lawrence Vail, invited me often for meals at their beautiful chalet. It was called "Les Cinque Enfants"—there was a covey of bright and handsome children with names like Sinbad, Apple, and Pegeen, some his, some hers. A happy household.

Kay wouldn't want me to tell this story—she is a proud and private person—but I will. She was always on the right side of every cause. During the Vietnam War, after she had moved to San Francisco, she picketed the embarkation docks in Oakland where the GIs were shipped off to that glorious conflict. She was arrested, put in prison and, despite her age, set to scrubbing floors on her hands and knees. She was released only when she was found to be seriously ill and sent to the hospital for an operation.

JANUARY THE TWENTY-FOURTH, NEW YORK

KAY BOYLE

I

In one corner of the dormitory, near the roof, was a pigeon-cote in which more than fifty birds were cooing. The chief prisoner was a pigeon-fancier, the warden said with an apologetic smile. The detectives shifted their cigars in their mouths and looked wearily around the room. "Why, he's so soft-hearted he has to leave the building when the cook's killing one of the birds for his supper," the warden went on. "You know what he's in for?" snapped the commissioner. "Burglary, felonious assault, and homicide."

II

The detectives went through the first tier of cells in the west wing, throwing out everything they found. The prisoners were driven out and they huddled at the end of the flats, some of them rouged, their eyebrows painted, two holding blankets around their naked shoulders. Out from the cells sailed corsets, compacts, perfume bottles, a blonde wig, nightgowns, high-heeled slippers and ladies' underwear. The detectives went up to the second tier and herded the prisoners out. "I wouldn't work here for a thousand berries a week," a detective said. "I'm just not that kind of a girl."

III

The commissioner remarked that such characteristics were common in prison, but that it was disgusting to see them flaunted in this way. He didn't think he'd ever get over the shame of what he'd seen. The kingpin had a great weakness for lemonade, said the warden with an indulgent smile. The detectives pried open the locker in his cell: it was filled with tinned peaches, olives, pickled herrings, malted milk, copies of "The New Yorker," and a deck of heroin. "If you lay a finger on my rosary," said the kingpin in a high falsetto, "I warn you I'll scream."

ELIZABETH BISHOP

Marianne Moore told me about a gifted young poet named Eliza-beth Bishop. (The best portrait I know of Miss Moore is the one by E.B. in her Collected Prose. *Especially the account of their meeting. Cautious about being pestered by young admirers, Miss Moore suggested to Miss Bishop that they meet on the steps of the Public Library, near the northern lion. She wanted to look over this Vassar girl before inviting her to Cumberland Street in Brook-lyn. E.B. passed the test, and they became close friends.)*

"Cool and limpid" is a cliché usually applied to streams or lakes. But that is how I always saw Bishop's work. No waste motion of rhetoric, nothing showy. A technique so sure that it didn't show. Under the words a clear intelligence. She set very high standards for herself. In 1938, when she must have been writing for five years, and I asked for a book, she said she had only twenty pub-lishable poems.

Later I could probably have become her publisher if I had not been so stubborn. In 1939 I dreamed up the idea of the "Five Young American Poets" anthologies. Since it is always difficult to sell first books of poetry I reasoned that five poets in the same volume—about fifty pages of each—would be an enticing bargain. I wanted ever so much to have Elizabeth be one of the first five, but she was reluctant. I think she worried she would be grouped with others she didn't care for, just wanted to be by herself, which was natural enough. The first five were George Marion O'Donnell, Randall Jarrell, John Berryman, Mary Barnard, and W. R. Moses. Not bad company.

*I didn't see too much of Elizabeth over the years, especially after
she moved to Brazil, but there were some good encounters when
I was visiting Tennessee Williams in Key West and she was down
there with her friend Louise Crane. She had somehow made the
acquaintance of the motherly (black) madame of Key West's
house of pleasure, The Square Roof. She arranged that we all be
invited to have tea—purely social, of course. Such lovely manners
those young ladies had. Such elevated, if somewhat faltering conversation. All dressed in their go-to-church dresses—they had actually been to Mass that morning—their chaste eyes lowered, their
smiles only polite. Before we left, we were invited by one of the
young ladies to see her room upstairs. It was neat as a pin. Calendar chromos of rural and mountain scenes on the walls. Silver-
framed photographs of family members on the bureau. A little vase
of carnations on the bed table. A large old-fashioned brass bedstead
with coverlet of pink satin, and leaning against the lace-covered
pillows her little family of five dolls—all white.*

CASABLANCA

ELIZABETH BISHOP

Love's the boy stood on the burning deck
Trying to recite "The boy stood on
The burning deck." Love's the son
    Stood stammering elocution
    While the poor ship in flames went down.

Love's the obstinate boy, the ship,
Even the swimming sailors, who

Would like a schoolroom platform, too,
 Or an excuse to stay
 On deck. And love's the burning boy.

MONTAGU O'REILLY

"Montagu O'Reilly," whose real name is Wayne Andrews, was one of my classmates at Harvard—he lived in Dunster House—and has been a close friend ever since. His passions are languages, history, and architecture. By the time he reached Harvard he was already completely at home in French. He had spent a lot of time in Paris, where he became friends with some of the Surrealists. In prep school at Lawrenceville, he published his own magazine, entirely in French.

"The Romantic Museum" shows some influence of the Surrealists but more of the decadent French writers who preceded them, with a whiff of the snobisme of Proust. Another of Wayne's contes fantastiques was Pianos of Sympathy. *It is the intricate story of the beautiful Giulia Davanzati who looses her gentle tresses into the piano strings of the instrument of Baron Giacomo delle Fontane, whose servitor has thoughtfully placed ice under one end of the keyboard and a candle under the other. When warmed music is played the long hair floats aloft; when cold, it subsides. Wayne's sympathetic piano created a small sensation around Harvard Yard when it was published in the* Advocate. *I picked up the type from the magazine for a pamphlet—the first book published by New Directions (1936). It was so successful that it went into two printings of one hundred copies each.*

Later, in 1948, we did a collection of Wayne's délices, Who Has Been Tampering with These Pianos? *After graduation, Wayne's ambition called him to the world of banking. But money was not enough. He turned to historical studies, ending up as professor of art and architecture at Wayne State University in Detroit. He has written many books. My favorites are his biography of Madame de Staël, Architecture, Ambition, and Americans (a study of great or bizarre houses, with his own photographs), Siegfried's Curse (on the role of Jews and anti-Semites in German culture), and a luminous little book on Voltaire. He is now completing an account of the Surrealists for New Directions. Wayne is, I imagine, the only American who has read every novel by Theodor Fontane.*

THE ROMANTIC MUSEUM

MONTAGU O'REILLY

" . . If you could come to visit me in my home, a veritable romantic museum . . ."

The friends of Paul Duval were deeply moved. When they had known him at the Lycée Condorcet, he had been the most charming student of Paris. And now, after fourteen years of seclusion, he was inviting them to dine at his château near Maisons-Lafitte. In their delight at the prospect of seeing him once again, they quite forgot any misgivings which the phrase "romantic museum" might once have aroused in their minds.

In the disorganised early post-war years, elegant young Paul Duval had always been a settling influence in any select student gathering. His ready wit, delightful personality, and reticent cravates had seemed to fit him for the Ecole des Sciences Politiques and a high post in the French Embassy in Rome. And yet, strangely enough, Paul Duval had preferred to retire from the world in complete seclusion. His friends, amazed, could only attribute this oddity to his penchant for the experimental sciences. Sadly they acquiesced when Paul Duval announced his intention of withdrawing from society in order to devote himself to a thorough study of scientific problems. And naturally enough, although all the acquaintances of Paul Duval wished him well, they all secretly regretted the witty comrade of the days of the bachot.

They were then delighted to receive from their old school friend, couched in the polite idiom which of old made him a favorite with the Faubourg St. Germain, an invitation to dine at Maisons-Laffitte. To their wives they expressed their delight at the prospect of renewing that acquaintance. The wives, in their turn, confessed that they were anticipating an entertainment at once congenial and mysterious.

And so, on the appointed day, many of the most pleasant motor cars of France departed for the confines of Maisons-Laffitte. As her motor was passing through Clichy-Levallois, Elaine de Hautecoeur, the youthful bride of a partner of Hasard Frères, determined, to the infinite annoyance of her husband, to relax her hair. First she observed that the automobile was travelling at that moment at a speed of 89 kilometers an hour. She then took the control-cord which ran from her side to the motor, and adjusted the contact at 89. Thereupon, she connected the cord to the mechanical brooch which held her tresses in position. Immediately, her hair collapsed in a cascade at the precise rate of 88.93 kilometers an hour, granting that the non-conductibility of brooch-metal was seven hundredths of one per cent less than unity.

For a moment, the tresses, gasping for breath, clouded the windows of the motor.

"I believe," interrupted Georges-Gaëtan de Hautecoeur, as his bride's hair swept over the editorial of *Le Temps*, "that, as usual, you are inclined to be over-generous. Your attitude toward the crime of Asnières is willful. Please do not allow it to influence your behavior on this day when we go to see a friend, traditional like myself, like myself well-versed in Italian history."

"I believe hair can confuse history," replied Eliane de Hautecoeur. "And I believe that autonomous hands of Asnières can bewilder history too."

Once more, after sudden falls, Eliane's hair breathed normally again. Once more, she thought of Asnières.

This is the story of Asnières.

Young girls, upon leaving the Prisunic of that city, were accosted by an elderly gentleman in correct attire. Spinning from his waist was a black circle upon which a right triangle was revolving, unemployed. In a courteous tone he inquired if they wished their fortunes told. In case the girls acquiesced, they were led into an undistinguished apartment in a nearby street. They were there requested to pose before a boxed mirror. The gentleman then attached the circle with the spinning triangle to one side of the apparatus. As soon as the young ladies were seated on a divan, the stranger began to manipulate three controls on the instrument.

Of a sudden, the young girls felt that they were no longer looking at the mirror, but that the mirror was looking at them.

What was looking at them was the triangle spinning in the circle. It was sighted directly at their hands.

One of the victims later told the police that the velocity control gauge on the motor never mounted higher than 232 revolutions a minute. But, added the victim, as soon as the 232 was reached, our hands were no longer our own. Indeed, free from all control of their personality they were autonomous hands.

Bashfully, the impresario having vanished in a motor, the helpless frails wandered out into the streets of Asnières. Within six minutes, the young girls began making the most unseasonal advances, the most gratifying caresses that that city had yet seen. Wanderers that evening were grateful. And, until the constabulary intervened, Asnières was demoralized. An active prefect of police denounced with indignation such libertine graces. He only began to believe when other customers of the Prisunic that afternoon testified that the interesting impresario had actually led the delinquents away.

When, on other nights, other girls were confined with the same complaint, Asnières realized it faced a malefactor of genius.

Meanwhile, the 87 girls thus far imprisoned in the city, finding that their hands could no longer venture on the streets, now ran their fingers, unemployed, through their own tresses. Already, the capable staff-photographers of *Paris-Soir* had published countless photographs of the free hands in that pose.

And now, once more, as three or four mischievous strands obscured the communiqué from the Palazzo Venezia, did Georges-

Gaëtan de Hautecoeur venture to reprove his wife. "We can only hope that Justice will discover the unfortunate degenerate who has ill advised in that manner 87 young girls of the Third Republic."

"I am sorry, Gaëtan," responded Eliane, "but my generosity does not permit me to agree with your statement. Who knows what the hands have found, up to now undiscovered?"

"We are nearing Schifanoia, Eliane," insisted Georges-Gaëtan de Hautecoeur. "It is time to put up your hair."

Again Eliane observed the speed of the motor car: 42 kilometers. Again she set the dial, this time at 42. In a bound her hair recoiled at a speed of 41.93 kilometers an hour.

Eliane's tresses were still breathing deeply when the old servant of the Duval family opened the carriage door.

"Well, Paul, what bizarre novelties has London been concocting for us these days!" remarked Georges-Gaëtan de Hautecoeur. "We are perhaps already far enough from reality with the Pagan manoeuvres of the Front Populaire."

"It is true, Gaëtan, that sometimes we may consider that in Anthony Eden England is disappointing."

Georges-Gaëtan de Hautecoeur was pleased to see that Paul Duval preserved the moderate outlook which had made him sage in student days.

Presently, in company with myriad other guests, Georges-Gaëtan and Eliane de Hautecoeur began their promenade down the allée leading to the Duval manor. It was a pleasant drive, ending as it did before a pair of massive gates upon which was written the name of the estate: S c h i f a n o i a . Reticently, perhaps, the letters were blurred. Not without interest did Eliane de Hautecoeur observe that the dew which clung to the letters was the identical dew which clung to the eyelashes of dancers in unused poems. Not without passion did Eliane de Hautecoeur observe that the letters themselves were forgotten eyelashes.

Paul Duval desired to interrupt such meditation. "That," he said, "is the entrance to my romantic museum."

"It is a source of pleasure to me," remarked de Hautecoeur to his wife, "that even if Paul Duval has forsaken Paris for Maisons-Laffitte, he has, at least, not abandoned tradition. 'Schifanoia,' as you will recall, my dear Eliane, was the summer palace of Lodovico il Moro at Milan."

Soon all the guests were assembled in the great Dining Hall of the Duval estate. Slowly the guests took their seats. But as the company leaned back in their Louis XV chairs, they noticed that the very touch of their backs on the chairs produced an intense, operatic whistle. When the whistle had run its course, all recognized the tune as the famous Haunting Theme from Schubert's well-known Unfinished Symphony. Bewildered, the ladies and gentlemen arose and stared at the chair backs. To their surprise, they discovered that on the back of each chair was projected a pair of full-size lips. It was, then, the pressure of their backs on the lips of the chair backs which had released the banquet rendering of the Haunting Theme.

"By the way, Georges-Gaëtan," commented Duval, "this might interest you. Those lips are a scientific replica of those of Clarice Orsini, the Roman bride of Lorenzo de' Medici."

Although irritated that Paul Duval had condescended to phenomena while dining, Georges-Gaëtan de Hautecoeur was favorably impressed by the historical accuracy of the tableau vivant.

The dinner was at an end. Tongues were tasting liqueurs when, suddenly, the great majority of guests sensed a chill breathing. Eliane de Hautecoeur was at first embarrassed. Could her own tresses still be tense? A glance at her closed brooch showed her however that her own hair was now completely relaxed.

Paul Duval was at once polite. He summoned a butler. "Open the bay window out into the garden. Let the guests see for themselves."

And outside, in the garden, an immense eyebrow was worrying one quarter acre of authentic winter snow. Emotionally aroused, the titanic accumulation of thoughtful hair was mercilessly assailing the masses of congealed rain. The hoarse breathing of the eyebrow, acutely pained by the occasional counter-attacks of the snow, was what had captured the attention of the guests of Paul Duval.

"Here's something for you, Gaëtan," remarked the host. "The mechanically controlled eyebrow is precisely that of Isotta degli Atti, enlarged exactly 1,200 times. The snow I obtained from a contemporary skating Timini. I am of the opinion that the whole picture is in perfect scale."

Once more, Paul Duval had calmed the fears of Georges-Gaëtan de Hautecoeur. Happy, Georges-Gaëtan de Hautecoeur was eloquent.

"In the name of all those in whom the sentiment of antiquity is still strong, allow me to congratulate you, Duval, on the precision of your researches. Doubtless, as you say, you do live in a romantic museum. But we, your friends of yesterday, will always think more of the latter word than the former. We shall always wish you well, although not without profoundly regretting the old comrade of the days at the Lycée Condorcet. A toast!"

At once the 39 guests of Paul Duval raised their glasses in honor of the most promising student of the school. Immediately 38 guests of Paul Duval drained the liquids. The 39th guest refused. The 39th guest was Eliane de Hautecoeur. A few odd tresses fluttered in nervousness, and she began to speak:

"These eyelashes, lips, and eyebrows have been exclusively historical. They have done splendidly, but really, they are far from being as quick as my hair. Accompany me to the garage, and you will see how the insane speed of my tresses annihilates all history."

Paul Duval was deeply moved. In a slow, moderate voice he counseled his guests not to disturb his mechanics in their work. Already, however, Eliane de Hautecoeur had drawn all the guests along the drive down to the garage. Her chauffeur was, of course, in readiness.

"Victor!" she advised, "Run the Delage up on the greasing rack immediately. Race the motor at a presumed speed of at least 180 kilometers an hour."

The chauffeur obediently ran the machine up on the oiling-terrace. Upon being advised that the engine was nearing 180 kilometers an hour, Eliane took the control cord and adjusted the contact at 180. She then connected the cord to the mechanical brooch which held her tresses in position. Immediately, her hair collapsed, demented, in a cascade at the precise rate of 179.93 kilometers an hour, granting that the non-conductibility of brooch-metal was seven hundredths of one per cent less than unity.

Sublime in the spurious sun of the garage lanterns, the tresses of Eliane de Hautecoeur had descended liquid in speed. And as the onlookers gazed with pleasure at the conquering imitation of light, it was acknowledged by all that hair had indeed vanquished history.

So intent were the spectators upon this first-rate exhibition that no one save Eliane de Hautecoeur noticed that as the tresses breathed deeply, passionately, they clouded a mirror half-hidden behind a sackcloth curtain.

Not without interest did Elaine de Hautecoeur observe that near the clouded portion of the mirror hung an interesting disc with an unemployed triangle.

Later that evening Georges-Gaëtan de Hautecoeur, after having reproved his wife for her misconduct, dared regret the romantic interests of Paul Duval. As the Delage traversed the last of the suburbs, Georges-Gaëtan de Hautecoeur recited knowingly the celebrated verse of Voltaire:

"Un esprit corrompu ne fut jamais sublime."

Eliane de Hautecoeur, in peace, fondled her sublime hair.

DUDLEY FITTS

Were it not for Dudley Fitts, my English master as Choate, I would never have become a scribbler, nor for that matter a publisher. For it was Fitts, in correspondence with Pound, who arranged for me to study at the "Ezuversity" in Rapallo. And Pound, descrying no talent for poetry, ordained that I become a publisher.

Anyone who ever worked with Fitts, either at Choate or later at Andover, would attest that he was the greatest of their teachers. He began his Sixth Form Honors course with Aristotle's Poetics, *went on to the* Oresteia, *then jumped to Chaucer, which we had to recite in the fourteenth-century mode. For the College Board exams we had, of course, to cover the standard English poets, but he ended up with Eliot, Pound, and Williams. And a theme each week which he corrected with devastating humor. On one of my pointilliste masterpieces he wrote "Beaucoup de bruit pour rien." He was a taskmaster, and a caustic disciplinarian, but he treated us as adults and we adored him. He had a great collection of the* right *texts in his study, where he would let some of us come to read if we didn't chatter, interfering with his writing.*

Fitts wrote poems (*ND* brought out a selection in 1937), a few imaginative stories, and many reviews. But his forte was translation. He could sight-read Greek, Latin, French, Spanish, and Italian. Posterity will know him best for the translations of Greek drama, Oedipus Rex *and* Alcestis, *which he did with Robert Fitzgerald, a student at Choate a few years before me. There was much more: witty versions of poems from* The Greek Anthology (*which, it being Fitts, he called* The Palatine Anthology, *since the manuscript had been found in a monastery in the German Palatinate), and a selection from Martial. In the mid-'40s he undertook a vast labor: the compiling and editing of* An Anthology of Contemporary Latin American Poetry. *It was the first broad survey of the field, funded by Nelson Rockefeller when he was Coordinator of Inter-American Affairs in Washington. ND published it in 1942, beautifully printed by Peter Beilenson, who did many of our finest books from his Walpole Printing Office.*

Let me not overlook Fitts's extraordinary letters. No one of us favored with them ever threw a Fitts letter in the wastebasket. Hard to describe. Comical. Sardonic. Double-talk. Triple-talk. Many "types of ambiguities." Macaronics. Joycean puns. Malapropisms. Anecdotal. Erudite. Interlingual. Self-deprecating. Sometimes angry. Always exhilarating. Fortunately John Frederick Nims is now making a selection of them. Fitts was a magical typist; he played his Corona like an organ with many stops. (Actually, he did play the organ in the Choate chapel, and I caroled for him before my voice changed.) He used expressive indentations with rubrics or inserts in red. He had taken over some of Cummings's visual tricks. Fitts's Latin in Cummings's typography was a puzzling pleasure. Dudley's handwriting (he never signed himself "Dudley"—I don't think he liked his name—it was always "D. Fitts") was beautiful. One day it dawned on me, when he had written something for me in Greek, that he had modeled his script on the way he wrote the Greek letters.

Fitts was a handsome but slightly odd-looking man. He couldn't see much without his horn-rimmed glasses, but that wasn't it. Finally, as I observed him in class, it came to me. His forehead.

*His brow was higher by three eighths of an inch than that of any-
one else in the room. He was indeed a highbrow.*

*My first brief conversation with him is forever etched, as they
say, on the plate of memory. As an underformer I had seen him
around, but had never been assigned—we were rotated every two
weeks—to his table in the dining hall. One day when I was rushing up the stairs from the mail room and he was coming down
wearing the black Dracula cape which he affected, I bumped into
him and knocked him half down. The irate gaze of Hermes was
fixed upon me and he uttered: "You young puppies who haven't
even read Thucydides!" And the God continued on his errand.*

THIS COUNTRY ROAD, WITH
THE ENGINE RUNNING

DUDLEY FITTS

(. . . *tendebantque manus*)

. . . and whatever it is I am content to sit here beside you
Holding my tongue because ineptitudes are so easy and
Nothing is better than anything at all.

'You make it all so clear.'

Thank you. The reason I did not just now mention Fear
Is that here we are, you here and I there, say,
Suddenly in a state of mind (at least I am in a state of mind)
Whose *Alone* is as furry and as dense as a dream-beast:
You may touch it, stroke it, feed it your heart (if you like), or
Ignore it. I can do nothing but fear it.

'You make it all so clear.'

Thank you. Believe me, I would not so desperately twist
Your fingers, I would not hurt you so, if I thought you would
        leave me.
This timidity I speak of is suddenly six-year-old,
Bug-in-a-rug, Tamoshanter Cat, cold plaintive piping
Frog, if you recall your *St Nicholas.* It is

('But I don't.')

                    the sort of recession that psychiatrists
Cry sweetly for: "You are sensual (oh I don't mean it in the
        vulgar sense) and
Afraid of it. Come now: Cat?"—*Tail.*
                            "Rain?"—*Vial.*
                                    "Light?"—*Can*

Hear now.
        "Dream?"—*Oh skurcely skurcely in these days.*
                                        "Flame?"—

Twisting twisting.

'Twisting?'

Yes, unfortunately. I wish you would kiss me. This
Fingering interflexion of *Maybes,* of *What ifs,* of *Why nots*—
Cathexis. I said, "I fell downstairs.
And sprained my cathexis." Several laughs, but good God
What are they paid for? I might as well have said,
"Wrap me up a psychosis, sell it to Officer Muldoon,
Tell it by moonlight—"

'You make it all so clear.'

Thank you. Meanwhile you and I sit here
Parked on a country road with the engine running,
Tasting huge silence. The way's dark going tonight,
Neither of us can rightly say we shall not stumble,

Somehow, and the humbler our speech the more sure our right
To reach for—

'For what?'

Pax. I have been saying it all this time,
Prithee peace, I have choked on language, broken
God knows how into a very great wilderness of dreaming,
All silent-seeming . . .

And this is what I told you of furry loves with triangular
small faces
In cold ascension.
All the places,
The stinking jammed wards, the clinical couch, the long wait
at noon,
And here, the dark road now, tense, instant, suddenly the
Nearness of touching the suddensweet nearness of you, dearest
Real—
You : be nearer.

'But it is late, and very still.
You have not spoken a word for an hour or more.
Come: we must go back . . .

(*ripae ulterioris amore* . . .)

HENRY MILLER

*It was Pound who put me in touch with Henry Miller. One day
in 1935 when we were having lunch in the "Albuggero" Rapallo,
he tossed a book across the table with the comment: "Waal, Jas,*

here's a dirty book that's really purty good." Needless to say, I was enthralled. I'd never read anything like that. I didn't even know such things could be written about, or, if they were, written so well. It was the original Obelisk Press edition of Tropic of Cancer which Henry had sent to Ezra.

I wrote to Henry at the address in the book, and a correspondence began which went on for many years. What letters! Though never anything racy. The natural flow of Henry releasing his thoughts. I was never able to do the Tropic books for fear my family would cut off the funds for New Directions, but we did do some twenty Miller books in all.

First was The Cosmological Eye in 1939, a collection of his short pieces, including "Glittering Pie," with which John Slocum and I got the Harvard Advocate banned when we printed it there earlier. (Prosecution was dropped when we provided the Cambridge district attorney with 50-yard-line tickets for the Harvard-Yale game.)

The big eye on the jacket of the first edition of The Cosmological Eye was mine, the left one, superimposed on a picture of clouds by a photographer classmate in Adams House. Some years later I was watching an Ingmar Bergman film. A man and a woman are quarreling in a railway carriage. On the seat between them is Henry's book and my eye. No doubt about it. The camera zooms in and rests on the eye several times. My letter to Mr. Bergman went unanswered. I'll never know what he saw in my eye, or what it had to do with a lovers' quarrel on a train. Such is genius.

Dear Henry. He didn't look like Errol Flynn but like the postmaster in a small rural town. A gentle man of great kindness. He was fascinated by Buddhism and often told me that when he was old he wanted to make his way to Tibet and die there.

He gave me two fragments from Black Spring for ND 1936, "Jabberwhorl Cronstadt," a burlesque on the American Communist poet Walter Lowenfels, and "Into the Night Life," part of which is printed here.

INTO THE NIGHT LIFE

HENRY MILLER

Over the foot of the bed is the shadow of the cross. There are chains binding me to the bed. The chains are clanking loudly, the anchor is being lowered. Suddenly I feel a hand on my shoulder. Some one is shaking me vigorously. I look up and it is an old hag in a dirty wrapper. She goes to the dresser and opening a drawer she puts a revolver away.

There are three rooms, one after the other, like a railroad flat. I am lying in the middle room in which there is a walnut book-case and a dressing table. The old hag removes her wrapper and stands before the mirror in her chemise. She has a little powder puff in her hand and with this little puff she swabs her arm-pits, her bosom, her thighs. All the while she weeps like an idiot. Finally she comes over to me with an atomizer and she squirts a fine spray over me. I notice that her hair is full of rats.

I watch the old hag moving about. She seems to be in a trance. Standing at the dresser she opens and closes the drawers, one after the other, mechanically. She seems to have forgotten what she remembered to go there for. Again she picks up the powder puff and with the puff she daubs a little powder under her arm-pits. On the dressing table is a little silver watch attached to a long piece of black tape. Pulling off her chemise she slings the watch around her neck; it reaches just to the pubic triangle. There comes a faint tick and then the silver turns black.

In the next room, which is the parlor, all the relatives are as-sembled. They sit in a semi-circle, waiting for me to enter. They sit stiff and rigid, upholstered like the chairs. Instead of warts and wens there is horse-hair sprouting from their chins.

I spring out of bed in my night shirt and I commence to dance the dance of King Kotschei. In my night shirt I dance, with a

parasol over my head. They watch me without a smile, without
so much as a crease in their jowls. I walk on my hands for them,
I turn somersaults, I put my fingers between my teeth and whistle
like a blackbird. Not the faintest murmur of approval or disap-
proval. They sit there solemn and imperturbable. Finally I begin
to snort like a bull, then I prance like a fairy, then I strut like a
peacock, and finally I realize that I have no tail and I quit. The
only thing left to do is to read the Koran through at lightning
speed, after which the weather reports, the Rime of the Ancient
Mariner and the Book of Numbers.

Suddenly the old hag comes dancing in stark naked, her hand
aflame. Immediately she knocks the umbrella stand over the place
is in an uproar. From the upturned umbrella stand there issues a
steady stream of writhing cobras travelling at lightning speed.
They knot themselves around the legs of the tables, they carry
away the soup tureens, they scramble into the dresser and jam
the drawers, they wriggle through the pictures on the wall,
through the curtain rings, through the mattresses, they coil up
inside the women's hats, all the while hissing like steam boilers.

Winding a pair of cobras about my arms I go for the old hag
with murder in my eyes. From her mouth, her eyes, her hair, from
her vagina even the cobras are steaming forth, always with that
frightful steaming hiss as if they had been ejected fresh from a
boiling crater. In the middle of the room where we are locked an
immense forest opens up. We stand in a nest of cobras and our
bodies come undone.

I am in a strange, narrow little room, lying on a high bed. There
is an enormous hole in my side, a clean hole without a drop of
blood showing. I can't tell any more who I am or where I came
from or how I got here. The room is very small and my bed is
close to the door. I have a feeling that some one is standing on
the door-sill watching me. I am petrified with fright.

When I raise my eyes I see a man standing at the door-sill.
He wears a gray derby cocked on the side of his head; he has a
flowing moustache and is dressed in a checkerboard suit. He asks
my name, my address, my profession, what I am doing and where
I am going and so on and so forth. He asks endless prying questions to which I am unable to respond, first because I have lost
my tongue, and second because I cannot remember any longer

what language I speak. "Why don't you speak?" he says, bending over me jeeringly, and taking his light rattan stick he jabs a hole in my side. My anguish is so great that it seems I must speak even if I have no tongue, even if I know not who I am or where I came from. With my two hands I try to wrench my jaws apart, but the teeth are locked. My chin crumbles away like dry clay, leaving the jaw-bone exposed. "Speak!" he says, with that cruel, jeering smile, and taking his stick once again he jabs another hole through my side.

I lie awake in the cold dark room. The bed almost touches the ceiling now. I hear the rumbling of trains, the regular, rhythmic bouncing of the trains over the frozen ties, the short, throttled puffs of the locomotive, as if the air were splintered with frost. In my hand are the pieces of dry clay which crumbled from my chin. My teeth are locked tighter than ever; I breathe through the holes in my side. From the window of the little room in which I lie I can see the Montreal bridge. Through the girders of the bridge, driven downward by the blinding blizzard, the sparks are flying. The trains are racing over the frozen river in wreaths of fire. I can see the shops along the bridgeway gleaming with pies and hamburger sandwiches. Suddenly I do remember something. I remember that just as I was about to cross the border they asked me what I had to declare and, like an idiot, I answered: "I want to declare that I am a traitor to the human race." I remember distinctly now that this occurred just as I was walking up a tread-mill behind a woman with balloon skirts. There were mirrors all around us and above the mirrors a balustrade of slats, series after series of slats, one on top of another, tilted toppling, crazy as a nightmare. In the distance I could see the Montreal bridge and beneath the bridge the ice-floes over which the trains raced. I remember now that when the woman looked round at me she had a skull on her shoulders, and written into the fleshless brow was the word sex stony as a lizard. I saw the lids drop down over her eyes and then the sightless cavern without bottom. As I fled from her I tried to read what was written on the body of a car racing beside me, but I could catch only the tail end and it made no sense.

At the Brooklyn Bridge I stand as usual waiting for the trolley to swing round. In the heat of the late afternoon the city rises up like a huge polar bear shaking off its rhododendrons. The forms waver, the gas chokes the girders, the smoke and the dust wave like amulets. Out of the welter of buildings there pours a jellywash of hot bodies glued together with pants and skirts. The tide washes up in front of the curved tracks and splits like glass combs. Under the wet headlines are the diaphanous legs of the amoebas scrambling on to the running boards, the fine, sturdy tennis legs wrapped in cellophane, their white veins showing through the golden calves and muscles of ivory. The city is panting with a five o'clock sweat. From the tops of the skyscrapers plumes of smoke soft as Cleopatra's feathers. The air beats thick, the bats are flapping, the cement softens, the iron rails flatten under the broad flanges of the trolley wheels. Life is written down in headlines twelve feet high with periods, commas and semicolons. The bridge sways over the gasoline lakes below. Melons rolling in from Imperial Valley, garbage going down past Hell Gate, the docks clear, the stanchions gleaming, the hawsers tight, the moss splitting and spelching in the ferry slips. A warm sultry haze lying over the city like a cup of fat, the sweat trickling down between the bare legs, around the slim ankles. A mucous mass of arms and legs, of half-moons and weather-vanes, of cock-robins and round-robins, of shuttle-cocks and bright bananas with the light lemon pulp lying in the bell of the peel. Five o'clock strikes through the grime and sweat of the afternoon, a strip of bright shadow left by the iron girders. The trollies wheel round with iron mandibles, crunching the papier-maché of the crowd, spooling it down like punched transfers.

As I take my seat I see a man I know standing on the rear platform with a newspaper in his hand. His straw hat is tilted on the back of his head, his arm rests on the motorman's brass brake. Back of his ears the cable web spreads out like the guts of a piano. His straw hat is just on a level with Chambers Street; it rests like a sliced egg on the green spinach of the bay. I hear the cogs slipping against the thick stub of the motorman's toe. The wires are humming, the bridge is groaning with joy. Two little rubber knobs on the seat in front of me, like two black keys on a piano. About the size of an eraser, not round like the end of a cane. Two gummy thingamajigs to deaden the shock. The dull thud of a rubber hammer falling on a rubber skull.

The countryside is desolate. No warmth, no snugness, no closeness, no density, no opacity, no numerator, no denominator. It's like the evening newspaper read to a deaf mute standing on a hat rack with a palmetto leaf in his hand. In all this parched land no sign of human hand, of human eye, of human voice. Only headlines written in chalk which the rain washes away. Only a short ride on the trolley and I am in a desert filled with thorns and cactus.

In the middle of the desert is a bath-house and in the bath-house is a wooden horse with a log-saw lying athwart it. By the zinc-covered table looking out through the cob-webbed window, stands a woman I used to know. She stands in the middle of the desert like a rock made of camphor. Her body has the strong white aroma of sorrow. She stands like a statue saying good-bye. Head and shoulders above me she stands, her buttocks swoopingly grand and out of all proportion. Everything is out of proportion—hands, feet, thighs, ankles. She's an equestrian statue without the horse, a fountain of flesh worn away to a mammoth egg. Out of the ball-room of flesh her body sings like iron. Girl of my dreams, what a splendid cage you make! Only where is the little perch for your three-pointed toes? The little perch that swung backward and forward between the brass bars. You stand by the window, dead as a canary, your toes stiff, your beak blue. You have the profile of a line drawing done with a meat-axe. Your mouth is a crater stuffed with lettuce leaves. Did I ever dream that you could be so enormously warm and lop-sided? Let me look at your lovely jackal paws, let me hear the croaking, dingy chortle of your dry breath.

Through the cob-webs I watch the nimble crickets, the long, leafy spines of the cactus oozing milk and chalk, the riders with their empty saddle-bags, the pommels humped like camels. The dry desert of my native land, her men gray and gaunt, their spines twisted, their feet shod with rowel and spur. Above the cactus bloom the city hangs upside down, her gaunt, gray men scratching the skies with their spurred boots. I clasp her bulging contours, her rocky angles, the strong dolmen breasts, the iron nipples with their champing bits, the cloven hoofs, the plumed tail. I hold her close in the choked spume of the canyons under the locked watersheds twisted with golden sands while the hour runs out. In the blinding surge of grief the sand slowly fills my bones.

A pair of blunt, rusty scissors lies on the zinc-covered table beside us. The arm which she raises is webbed to her side. The hoary inflexible movement of her arm is like the dull raucous screech of day closing and the cord which binds us is wired with grit. The sweat stands out on my temples, clots there and ticks like a clock. The clock is running down with nervous wiry sweat. The scissors move between on slow rusty hinges. My nerves race along the teeth of the comb, my spurs bristle, the veins glow. Is all pain dull and bearable like this? Along the scissors' dull edge I feel the rusty blunt anguish of day closing, the slow webbed movement of hunger satisfied, of clean space and starry sky in the arms of an automaton.

I stand in the midst of the desert waiting for the train. In my heart there is a little glass bell and under the bell there is an edelweiss. All my cares have dropped away. Even under the ice I sense the bloom which the earth prepares in the night.

LORINE NIEDECKER

I'm sorry that I never actually met Lorine Niedecker. From her many letters over the years I think of her as an old friend. She was an original in the best sense, hoeing her own row in poetry with complete disregard for literary fashion. She seldom left her hometown of Fort Atkinson, Wisconsin, where, I'm told, few people knew that she was a poet.

At the time of her death in 1970 I wrote of her: "She was the genuine U.S. article, a person who knew what she wanted to do and did it. Had she wished, or troubled, to play the game of poetry politics, she could probably have ended up as well known as the ladies who are now wearing the establishment's 'laurels,' but that just wasn't her way, so it will be up to time to prove her merit. I have no doubt what the judgment will be." Jonathan Williams last year brought out in his Jargon Society series her complete writings under the title From This Condensery. *A must book for students of modern poetry.*

Some of the old letters are missing from the archive, but it would have been through Louis Zukofsky that I learned of Lorine. She sent in two little plays for ND 1936 which remind me a bit of Russell Edson. Here is one of them. Because the tone is different from her more characteristic poems, I would like to quote from one of those to give the echt Niedecker flavor.

"My life is hung up
in the flood
    a wave-blurred
        portrait

Don't fall in love
with this face—
    it no longer exists
        in water
            we cannot fish"

THE PRESIDENT OF THE HOLDING COMPANY

LORINE NIEDECKER

PRESIDENT
I will enforce it that after supper you speak about dusk.

SECRETARY
I have this concrete immolence

VOICE OUTSIDE
this messenger from the dead.

PRESIDENT

Have you looked up Sumatra's defence of cat-tails?

SECRETARY

Pardon sir, who gives you fanatic worry when the rest of us boop
on the stairs?

PRESIDENT

I consume it my dignity

VOICE OUTSIDE

to go straight to the devil

PRESIDENT

Stuff and retain him . . . I'll have him by the stem of his hat.

SECRETARY

O Matchbox, save him, he's the best timidity we have.

PRESIDENT

O why am I tired why haven't I
a circumlocus of design
someone to come in and say
the pears smell ripe here . .

But I'm bound to the fears of my weathers.
Are you ready to release the evening?

SECRETARY

Maygo is waving his voice by the well.

PRESIDENT

Success like raisins comes first in the mouth.
But who wants a mouthful of raisins.

VOICES OUTSIDE

Sylva Wergles was a worty witchwoo
She lived by the side of a tree.
She combed the worldside for pennies and peas
And wood a few sallies to sea.

O my, said the counterfeit judge, By the boo
You cost me a tendril and then a long shoot.
Get thee from me and relate
How frogs come out of a gate.

SECRETARY

? It can't be commercial poetry.

PRESIDENT

I doubt its prowess. It lacks compulsion.

VOICES OUTSIDE

O sweet little Tilda's an open sale
She comes from a baudy and lands in a gale.
She tunes up the strings of her gay rig-a-roo
And plays a high banner to how so come who.

PRESIDENT

The traffic is ended. The last star is a bonded issue. Sighing is
extinct. I've gone to the morning entry.

MARY BARNARD

In her autobiography Assault on Mount Helicon, *which is both
engaging and valuable as literary history, Mary Barnard tells how
she first sent some of her poems to Pound in 1933—expecting no
answer. But he replied at once:*

> *"Age? intentions? . . . how much intention?
> I mean how hard and how long are
> you willing to work at it?"*

Some thirty further letters from EP to MB quoted in her book evidence both Pound's concern for the young and that she was "willing to work at it."

Pound told her to continue her study of Greek and set her to doing Sapphics in English, but "NOT persistently using a spondee like that blighter Horrace [sic], for the second foot."

MB pursued Pound's suggestion with long persistence, and some twenty-five years later, in 1958, her superb translation of the complete Sappho came out with California University Press. I say "persistence" because that's what it takes—I know—to find the right tone in English for rendering a classical language. She says that one influence which helped her find her "spare but musical" tone was the Italian of Quasimodo's Lirici Greci. Whatever, she fulfilled Pound's precept:

> "The job of the writer of verse is to get the LIVE language AND the prosody simultaneously. Prosody: articulation of the total sound of a poem (not bits of certain shapes gummed together.)"

MB came into my life in 1936 with eleven poems in New Democracy, then with the group in ND 1936, then through her friendship with William Carlos Williams—there are so many fine letters from Bill to MB in Assault on Mount Helicon (and from Marianne Moore)—and finally in 1940 when she was one of the elect in the Five Young American Poets anthology, the same year as Jarrell and Berryman.

Our first visual inspection of each other was at lunch in New York with Robert Fitzgerald and Florence Codman, the enterprising publisher of Arrow Editions. MB wrote that I was then between recuperations from skiing accidents. She found me "much less serious [than Fitzgerald]. In fact my first impression seems to have been that he didn't have very good sense." She remembers my saying that I loved painting but never went to museums. From which she deduced that there were "Rembrandts and Picassos in his own home." Hardly correct.

The part I like best in Assault on Mount Helicon is MB's account of a few weeks she spent at Norfolk in 1937 doing odd jobs for

Jimmy Higgins, who was there running the New Directions office in the stable which my aunt had converted for that purpose. She has caught with gentle wit the character of that bizarre situation— the literary slaves huddled in a caretaker's cottage (Mary was paid thirty-five cents an hour, but she did get free board) while my aunt and her consort exemplified what he liked to call "gracious living" in the great house up the road. I was in Norfolk for only a few days of MB's visit, being enrolled again that year at Harvard. MB reports that Higgins "was bombarded by dozens of instructions that arrived daily from Cambridge."

My aunt, whom Higgins called "the great arranger," took a liking to MB. She thought her most suitable and tried to persuade her to succeed him permanently in the Norfolk post. But MB decided that Norfolk was too isolated and that she didn't have the physical strength to tote heavy book packages to the village post office.

We have remained good friends over the years, seeing each other as my travels permitted. MB relates at one point that "JL skied down off a mountain [Mount Hood] and took me to dinner at the old Portland Hotel, and afterwards to see Greta Garbo in Camille." We had a fine reunion four years ago when I was lecturing at Centrum in Port Townsend, Washington. MB dropped in from Vancouver to size up my last incarnation as Professor Turbojet.

PLAYROOM

MARY BARNARD

Wheel of sorrow, centerless.
Voices, sad without cause,
Slope upward, expiring on grave summits.

Mournfulness of muddy playgrounds,
Raw smell of rubbers and wrapped lunches
When little girls stand in a circle singing
Of windows and of lovers.

Hearing them, no one could tell
Why they sing sadly, but there is in their voices
The pathos of all handed-down garments
Hanging loosely on small bodies.

TASILO RIBISCHKA

Tasilo Ribischka (the last name is that of a famous Austrian skier)
was the first of my pseudonymous Doppelgängers. I used him when
I wrote something silly, such as "Acumen and Decible." When he
resurfaced in ND 1937 *he was described in the contributors' notes*
as "night watchman in an industrial plant in Saugus, Mass., which
gives him a lot of time to think."

Next there was William Candlewood, named for Candlewood
Lake near New Milford. He was used to write rejection letters to
authors. He was also the whipping boy. If something was fouled
up at New Directions it was always blamed on Candlewood. The
apology letters said he would be fired immediately.

Finally there is Hiram Handspring, who is very much alive. Too
alive. His luminous parodies get published in The Iowa Review,
while I can only make it into Oink! *and* Exquisite Corpse.

Doubles can be dangerous. Read James Hogg's classic Confessions of a Justified Sinner. *Or look what happened to Romain Gary.*
His Émile Ajar became so much more famous that he blew his
brains out. (That is an oversimplification of a complicated story
which I have dealt with more fully in the afterword to the New
Directions reprint of Gary-as-Ajar's The Life Before Us.)

THE TRANSCARNATION OF
ACUMEN AND DECIBLE

TASILO RIBISCHKA

Acumen cam ernst. Wars springing, rearalay! Wars spring end sing end wing end ring, wars springing rearalay! Sone Acumen wars straight as string end lutifule to whit to woo, oh lutifule vas slith and moon of lutes.

Acumen wars a Quinceline, so quinceley ser nourich crept she wars flay oor gholyfolly end bahbahed to her. Sud Acumen's marley niever niggled her for she wars soo prifogulated with ser crins and duples, ser melins and ser oneaks. This crulpet Quince ser beard and Cune fat baldered in a dun basky wor he murreled moor end plered. Ipoo the Cune, Ipoo!

Sone Acumen wan ser sussle nourich did storp waywendered wanly end wantly in the welds. How flare the tay, how flay the weld, how troomerish our wendeling Quinceline! The picky priddies twilled sud Acumen nit ceard. The acquelly runners ruled sud Acumen nenly plered end ploored. Plure old Phun phizzelated plure she woonwent. Loo roo, how soor a tay for Acumen! Ser sussle nourich wars storp, ser marley wars eccliebable, end ser folward the Cune log soully bebaldered end murrelent in the basky. Plerendlessly waywendeled wan Acumen, so lutifule in the springing welds.

So thor in the weld sunter a gronant woad did Decible Decible troune her, trine Acumen drafening by a pule of plers sunter a gronant woad. How moorly lutifule wars she! How edible! How corzamining ser murrel!

Decible wars ippity subsorcellated. Sen corz eplert marmoorly to vene her thor so lutifule end dravening all amurreled. Sutty he trent end bassied her tifity, tifity bassied Acumen on ser twick.

Acumen surled, she slippered, she riddled, she wagout. Decible she vent end surled daboo. Wars blue. Acumen surled end Decible whirled.

"Woo too?" fleg Acumen.

"Decible" fleg Decible.

"Wa foo?" fleg Acumen.

"Sam Agnavel" fleg Decible.

"Vel bassy me?"

"Moor marrily!"

Nadderdadder Acumen end Decible urred andander ippity. Nadderdadder, vas rex en aller blue.

"Urr me moor?" fleg Acumen.

"Moor! moor! moor!" fleg Decible.

"Edible Decible!"

"Vel cingo, Acumen parabel?" fleg Decible.

"Bassy me ernst daboo!"

Ippity appixit from nixwo a wondershining flay, all shizzeling end ruisselent with brinkles.

"Peccadour, Acumen!" fleg this flay, "Hacoo too cingo end bassy wan ter folward the Cune lieg murreling in the basky?"

Acumen mert.

"Bi, pin this zabbermagger end gal!" Sone ippity quip pippity exspixit the wondershining flay.

Decible end Acumen pun the zabbermagger, a lutifule gelsilber zabbermagger, end gan vor the kloss paddy en paddy.

Wan se cam to the kloss Decible waggered the zabbermagger end ippity ovvered the rams. "Zabber!" fleg Acumen ve wars moor cerlibrate, end se gan en.

Se troune the Quince en ser crippy foguling with ser oneaks.

"Blithers!" fleg the Quince, "Wa vel, flancey?"

"Crulpet marley," fleg Acumen, "Ter dool is dondered!"

End Acumen waggered the zabbermagger end ser marley the crulpet Quince wars mogged en a pinxkitchen end sutty all ser crins end duples, ser melins end ser oneaks biggered to pinx her.

"Loooooo" plered the pinxkitchen sud Acumen end Decible nit ceard. Se wars gun en the basky.

End wan the blue Cune vent Acumen end Decible en the balder basky he plered namoor sud fleg sussely:

"Benidoo mer kimbi!"

End se all gan gammer en gep.

"Cingi me!" fleg Acumen.

"Moor marrily!" fleg Decible.

Gippered the gep end the loor blue Cune, benider, wummered the zabbermagger.

JAMES LAUGHLIN

Needless to say, the poem which follows has never been reprinted. But it does speak for my obsession with skiing, and particularly ski mountaineering, part of my life which has annoyed many New Directions authors when I was not in the office to attend personally to their books.

Most American skiers think that skiing is riding up a ski lift and skiing down a slope packed by a Thiokol snow-groomer. How many thousand feet can you do in a day? For me, that is not skiing. Skiing is going off into the high peaks of our West or the European Alps with a pack on your back and seal skins attached to the bottom of the skis to make them grip. You spend the nights in little huts and climb to peaks where the views seem limitless. When you ski down it's in fresh, untracked snow. With each turn you send up a cloud of snow-spray. It feels like a sensual rhythmic dance.

I never was able to persuade Pound that there should be a few lines of skiing in the Cantos. *God knows everything else is there, including troutfly-tying. The only reply I ever got related to my pleas was this in a letter of 1947:*

> *"Are you doing ANYTHING? Of course if you spend ¾s of your time slidin' down ice cream cones on a tin tea tray . . ."*

Actually, skiing on glaciers is not very exciting because they are almost all very flat. Only high up, under the ice-falls below a peak, is it interesting. Up there are the crevasses, where the surface of the glacier has been fractured by pressure. To ski such slopes you must go roped to a guide who will haul you out if you break a snowbridge. That never happened to me.

The most famous glacier skiing is the Haute Route between Zermatt in Switzerland and Chamonix in France. Five days of it down several connecting glaciers, spending the night in huts. Wonderful vistas of peaks and unbroken snow. And there is the Fox Glacier on the South Island of New Zealand. It runs from the west flank of Mount Cook down to the Tasman Sea. As you descend, the landscape around the glacier changes from arctic to flowering spring. But it's a long climb back up.

THE GLACIER AND LOVE'S IGNORANT TONGUE

JAMES LAUGHLIN

The sloth of the glacier
surpasseth understanding
"like I could fly" he said

"just like I could fly
in the air like an angel
like a bird fly all over

hell and see everything
everywhere all at once"
the life of the glacier

its whole life turning
slow flanks of snow from
generation to generation

would be too short except
that a breath one breath
is far too long & "it's

just like somebody" he said
"kept hitting you and you
said go ahead mister please

hit me again only harder"
dear ice dear ageless ice
tell me the word you know

it won't burn my tongue
because her kiss "time?"
asked the glacier "what's

that?—look at these tiny
flowers blooming in clumps!
isn't rain wonderful?" Oh

tongue ignorant tongue
find me the word I don't
care if you cut yourself

to pieces on my teeth just
find me this word that
glaciers know to tell her.

LOUIS ZUKOFSKY

*The number of students in the "Ezuversity" was irregular. Rapallo
is on the main line between Paris and Rome, so there were many
transients. Some stayed for several months, as I did, but others
were only stopovers for a few weeks or even days. While I was*

there with Pound, Basil Bunting turned up and the young poet Pound called "Tangle-on Angleton." I was impressed by Louis Zukofsky, who stayed for three weeks. What an intense mind! But he was not at all impressed with me. We had little conversation. I simply listened to him talking with Pound. I think he thought I was a parasite. My only point of superiority was courage. Zuk was afraid of drowning. He wouldn't come out swimming with Ezra and me on the patino in the deep (and clear) water of the Tigullian Gulf. He had to swim from the bathing establishment on shore where the water was well-spiked with Rapallo's sewage.

Nevertheless, Zuk gave me for ND 1936 the magnificent "Mantis" sequence, which opens with an intricate sestina. It was a trial-horse for his long poem "A." (One finds lines from "Mantis" picked up later.) Then for ND 1938 he gave me the whole of the eighth section of "A," all fifty-six pages of it. By then the great poem was really rolling in all its power and splendor of language. Zuk asked me to describe it in the notes as "an epic of the class struggle." He was an ardent Communist, though I think he dropped away from the Party after the Moscow trials. It should be noted that "fascist" Pound, who was already an admirer of Il Duce, paid no attention to Zukofsky's politics. He liked his mind and his poetry. That was what mattered. Some years later the anthology carried a long section of Zuk's two-volume work of hermetic interpretation, "Bottom on Shakespeare."

Zuk was eager to have New Directions become the regular publisher of his books. I wish we had. But a small publisher can't do everything. And I realized that he might be difficult and demanding. So there was a cooling of what had never been exactly warm. This was intensified when I learned that he and his wife, Celia, were doing a translation of Catullus, one of my favorite poets. I expected great things of such a master of verbal music. I encouraged him. But the bottom dropped out. It was not my Catullus. It was a phonetic Catullus invented by Zuk.

Catullus 28 begins:

"Pisonis comites, cohors inanis
aptis sarcinulis et expeditis,
Verani optime tuque mi Fabulle,

> quid rerum geritis? satisne cum isto
> vappa frigoraque et famem tulistis?
> ecquidnam in tabulis patet lucelli"

In the Loeb (Cornish) it runs:

> "You subalterns of Piso, a needy train, with baggage handy
> and easily carried, my excellent Veranius and you, my Fa-
> bullus, how are you? have you borne cold and hunger with
> that wind-bag long enough?"

Zuk, in an incredible tour de force, equating the sounds of his
words with the Latin words, made this of it:

> "Piso's own comates, his, corps, an inane as
> opt sad sarks—kin no less—'at's expedited!
> Veranius hoped, my—he took my Fabullus,
> what rare rheum's to greet us? Sneezing come as tho
> that vapid prig's cue to famine's to last you?"

End of a beautiful, if never close, friendship.

One of the things which interests me in Paul Mariani's biography
of William Carlos Williams is the account of Williams's close
friendship with Zuk in the early '40s. Mariani tells how Bill sent
poems to Zuk for criticism and often accepted extensive revisions.
Bill knew a good ear when he found one.

"MANTIS"

LOUIS ZUKOFSKY

Mantis! praying mantis! since your wings' leaves
And your terrified eyes, pins, bright, black and poor

Beg—"Look, take it up" (thoughts' torsion)! "save it!"
I who can't bear to look, cannot touch—You—
You can—but no one sees you steadying lost
In the cars' drafts on the lit subway stone.   5

Praying mantis, what wind-up brought you, stone
On which you sometimes prop, prey among leaves
(Is it love's food your raised stomach prays?), lost
Here, stone holds only seats on which the poor
Ride, who rising from the news may trample you—   10
The shops' crowds a jam with no flies in it.

Even the newsboy who now sees knows it
No use, papers make money, makes stone, stone,
Banks, "it is harmless," he says moving on—You?
Where will he put *you?* There are no safe leaves   15
To put you back in here, here's news! too poor
Like all the separate poor to save the lost.

Don't light on my chest, mantis! do—you're lost,
Let the poor laugh at my fright, then see it:
My shame and theirs, you whom old Europe's poor   20
Call spectre, strawberry, by turns; a stone—
You point—they say—you lead lost children—leaves
Close in the paths men leave, saved, safe with you.

Killed by thorns (once men), who now will save you
Mantis? what male love bring a fly, be lost   25
Within your mouth, prophetess, harmless to leaves
And hands, faked flower,—the myth is: dead, bones, it
Was assembled, apes wing in wind: On stone,
Mantis, you will die, touch, beg, of the poor.   30

Android, loving beggar, dive to the poor
As your love would even without head to you,
Graze like machined wheels, green, from off this stone
And preying on each terrified chest, lost
Say, I am old as the globe, the moon, it   35
Is my old shoe, yours, be free as the leaves.

Fly, mantis, on the poor, arise like leaves
The armies of the poor, strength: stone on stone
And build the new world in your eyes, Save it!

"MANTIS," AN INTERPRETATION
OR NOMINA SUNT CONSEQUENTIA RERUM
NAMES ARE SEQUENT TO THE THINGS NAMED

Mantis! praying mantis! since your wings' leaves

    Incipit Vita Nova
    le parole . . .
    almeno la loro sentenzia
the words . . .
at least their substance

at first were
"The mantis opened its body
It had been lost in the subway
It steadied against the drafts
It looked up—
Begging eyes—
It flew at my chest"

          —The ungainliness
        of the creature needs stating.

No one would be struck merely
By its ungainliness,
Having seen the thing happen.

Having seen the thing happen,
There would be no intention 'to write it up,'

But *all* that was happening,
The mantis itself only an incident, *compelling any writing*
The transitions were perforce omitted.

Thoughts'—two or three or five or

Six thoughts' reflection (pulse's witness) of what was happening
All immediate, not moved by any transition.

Feeling this, what should be the form
Which the ungainliness already suggested
Should take?

            —Description—lightly—ungainliness
            With a grace unrelated to its surroundings.

Grace there is perhaps
In the visual sense, not in the movement of
"eyes, pins, bright, black and poor."

Or considering more than the isolation
Of one wrenched line,

Consider:
"(thoughts' torsion)"
la battaglia delli diversi pensieri . . .
the battle of diverse thoughts—
The actual twisting
Of many and diverse thoughts

What form should *that* take
            —The first words that came into mind
        "The mantis opened its body—"
        Which might deserve the trope:
        the feeling of the original which is a permanence
        ?
Or the feeling accompanying the first 27 words' inception
the original which is a permanence
?),
That this thoughts' torsion
Is really a sestina
Carrying subconsciously
Many intellectual and sensual properties of the forgetting and
                                    remembering Head
One human's intuitive Head

Dante's rubric
Incipit
Surréaliste
Re-collection

A twisted shoe by a pen, an insect, lost,
"To the short day and the great sweep of shadow."

The sestina, then, the repeated end words
Of the lines' winding around themselves,
Since continuous in the Head, whatever has been read,

> whatever is heard,
> whatever is seen

Perhaps goes back cropping up again with
Inevitable recurrence again in the blood
Where the spaces of verse are not visual
But a movement,
With vision in the lines merely a movement.
What is most significant
Perhaps is that C—and S—and X—of the 19th century
Used the "form"—not the form but a Victorian
Stuffing like upholstery
For parlor polish,
And our time takes count against them
For their blindness and their (unintended?) cruel smugness.

Again: as an experiment, the sestina would be wicker-work—
As a force, one would lie to one's feelings not to use it

One feels in fact inevitably
About the coincidence of the mantis lost in the subway,
About the growing oppression of the poor—
Which is the situation most pertinent to us—
With the fact of the sestina:
Which together fatally now crop up again
To twist themselves anew
To record not a sestina, post Dante,
Nor even a mantis.

Is the poem then, a sestina
Or not a sestina?

The word sestina has been
Taken out of the original title. It is no use (killing oneself?)

    —Our world will not stand it,
    the implications of a too regular form.

Hard to convince even one likely to show interest in the matter
That this regularity to which 'write it up' means not a damn
(Millet in a Dali canvas, Circe in E's Cantos)
Whatever seeming modelling after the event,
649 years, say, after Dante's first canzone,
If it came back immediately as the only
Form that will include the most pertinent subject of our day—
The poor—
Cannot mean surely implied comparison, unreality
Usually interpreted as falsity.

Too much time cannot be saved
Saying:
The mantis might have heaped up upon itself a
Grave of verse,
But the facts are not a symbol.

There is the difference between that
And a fact (the mantis in the subway)
And all the other facts the mantis sets going about it.

No human being wishes to become
An insect for the sake of a symbol.

But the mantis *can start*
History etc.
The mantis situation remains its situation,
Enough worth if the emotions can equate it.

"I think" of the mantis
"I think" of other things—
The quotes set repulsion
Into movement.

Repulsion—
Since one, present, won't touch the mantis,
Will even touch the poor—

but carefully.

The mantis, then
Is a small incident of one's physical vision
Which is the poor's helplessness
The poor's separateness
Bringing self-disgust.

The mantis is less ungainly than that.

There should be today no use for a description of it
Only for a "movement" emphasizing its use, since it's been
around,
An accident in the twisting
Of many and diverse "thoughts"
I.e. nerves, glandular facilities, electrical cranial charges

For example—
line 1—entomology
line 9—biology
lines 10 and 11—the even rhythm of riding underground, and
                the sudden jolt are also of these nerves,
                glandular facilities, brain's charges
line 12—pun, fact, banality
lines 13 to 18—the economics of the very poor—the newsboy
                —unable to think beyond "subsistance still
                permits competition" banking, *The Wisconsin
                Elkhorn Independent*—"Rags make paper,
                paper makes money, money makes banks,
                banks make loans, loans make poverty,

    poverty makes rags."
lines 22 to 24—Provençe myth
lines 25 to 29—Melanesian self-extinction myth
line 33—airships
lines 35 and 36—creation myth (Melanesia), residue of it in our
      emotions no matter if fetched from the moon,
      as against 1. 25 to 29.
and naturally the coda which is the
only thing that can sum up the
jumble of order in the lines weaving
"thoughts," pulsations, running commentary, one upon the other,
itself a jumble of order
as far as poetic
sequence is concerned:
      the mantis
      the poor's strength
      the new world.

29—"in your eyes"
      the original shock still persisting—

So that the invoked collective
Does not subdue the senses' awareness,
The longing for touch to an idea, or
To a use function of the material:
The original emotion remaining,
  like the collective,
Unprompted, real, as propaganda.

The voice exhorting, trusting what one hears
Will exhort others, is the imposed sensuality of an age
When both propaganda and sensuality are necessary against—
"—we have been left with nothing
just a few little unimportant ships
and barges" (British Admiralty even in 1920)

or jelly for the Pope

la mia nemica, madonna la pietà

my enemy, my lady pity,

36—"like leaves"
The Head remembering these words exactly in the way it
remembers
la calcina pietra
the calcined stone.

But it remembers even more constantly
the poor
than
com' huom pietra sott' erba
as one should hide a stone in grass.

Nor is the coincidence
Of the last four lines
Symbolism,
But the simultaneous,
The diaphanous, historical
In one head.

November 4, 1934,
New York.

EUGENE JOLAS

Eugene Jolas was the chief editor of transition, *twenty-seven numbers, published in Paris and The Hague from 1927 to 1938. It was one of the most influential of the little magazines, ranking in importance with* The Little Review *and* The Dial. *I used to wait for each issue, picking them up from Frances Steloff at the Gotham Book Mart. What excitement!*

Jolas, who had been born in Alsace and, as a young man, worked on newspapers in the States, marrying an American wife, was city editor of the Paris Chicago Tribune. So he heard of Joyce and Stein early and became their ardent champion. Number 1 led off with "Opening Pages of a Work in Progress" (Finnegans Wake) *"riverrun brings us back to Howth Castle & Environs, Sir Tristram, violer d'amores, fr' over the short sea, had passencore rearrived from North Armorica on this side the scraggy isthmus of Europe Minor to wielderfight his perisolate war . . ." Which is rather different from the final version, where Adam and Eve make an immediate appearance. Joyce was rewriting for years. Jolas's serial publication in many issues gave Joyce the opportunity to see himself in print and make revisions. These installments brought* Finnegans Wake *to America, as Margaret Anderson had done for* Ulysses *in* The Little Review.

In the first issue of transition *we also find Gertrude Stein's "An Elucidation." "Elucidation. / First as Explanation. / Elucidate the problem of halve. / Halve and have. / Halve Rivers and Harbours. / Have rivers and harbours . . ." Stein was in almost every issue until the Big Bust-up in 1935. In* The Autobiography of Alice B. Toklas *she revealed that she and Elliot Paul, the assistant editor, had been the instigators of* transition, *a pretension which the Jolases bitterly resented. (It was Maria Jolas who had provided most of the financial support for* transition.) *The war was on, and sides were taken. Out of it came a little pamphlet,* Testimony against Gertrude Stein, *in which those who felt they had been maligned in* The Autobiography *had their say. The "witnesses" were the Jolases, Braque, Matisse, André Salman, and the Dadaist Tristan Tzara.*

Joyce and Stein were the planets in transition, *but there was a constellation of stars. Thanks to Jolas's command of French and German almost every important European writer was represented. And all the good American names: Hemingway, Crane, MacLeish, Boyle, Williams, and many more. There is only one big American name missing from the roster—that of Ezra Pound. He never mentioned the magazine to me, but I have a suspicion. The first number, featuring Joyce and Stein, may have put him off. He hated* Finnegans Wake. *In November 1926, when Joyce had sent him part of the manuscript, he wrote: "I make nothing of it whatever. . . . nothing short of divine vision or a new cure for the clapp can possibly be worth all the circumambient peripherization." As for*

PROCLAMATION

TIRED OF THE SPECTACLE OF SHORT STORIES, NOVELS, POEMS AND PLAYS STILL UNDER THE HEGEMONY OF THE BANAL WORD, MONO-TONOUS SYNTAX, STATIC PSYCHOLOGY, DESCRIPTIVE NATURALISM, AND DESIROUS OF CRYSTALLIZING A VIEWPOINT...

WE HEREBY DECLARE THAT :

1. THE REVOLUTION IN THE ENGLISH LANGUAGE IS AN AC-COMPLISHED FACT.

2. THE IMAGINATION IN SEARCH OF A FABULOUS WORLD IS AUTONOMOUS AND UNCONFINED.
(Prudence is a rich, ugly old maid courted by Incapacity... Blake)

3. PURE POETRY IS A LYRICAL ABSOLUTE THAT SEEKS AN A PRIORI REALITY WITHIN OURSELVES ALONE.
(Bring out number, weight and measure in a year of dearth... Blake)

4. NARRATIVE IS NOT MERE ANECDOTE, BUT THE PROJEC-TION OF A METAMORPHOSIS OF REALITY.
(Enough! Or Too Much!... Blake)

5. THE EXPRESSION OF THESE CONCEPTS CAN BE ACHIEVED ONLY THROUGH THE RHYTHMIC " HALLUCINATION OF THE WORD ". (Rimbaud).

6. THE LITERARY CREATOR HAS THE RIGHT TO DISINTE-GRATE THE PRIMAL MATTER OF WORDS IMPOSED ON HIM BY TEXT-BOOKS AND DICTIONARIES.
(The road of excess leads to the palace of Wisdom... Blake)

7. HE HAS THE RIGHT TO USE WORDS OF HIS OWN FASH-IONING AND TO DISREGARD EXISTING GRAMMATICAL AND SYNTACTICAL LAWS.
(The tigers of wrath are wiser than the horses of instruction... Blake)

8. THE " LITANY OF WORDS " IS ADMITTED AS AN INDEPEN-DENT UNIT.

9. WE ARE NOT CONCERNED WITH THE PROPAGATION OF SOCIOLOGICAL IDEAS, EXCEPT TO EMANCIPATE THE CREATIVE ELEMENTS FROM THE PRESENT IDEOLOGY.

10. TIME IS A TYRANNY TO BE ABOLISHED.

11. THE WRITER EXPRESSES. HE DOES NOT COMMUNICATE

12. THE PLAIN READER BE DAMNED.
(Damn braces! Bless relaxes!... Blake)

— *Signed* : KAY BOYLE, WHIT BURNETT, HART CRANE, CARESSE CROSBY, HARRY CROSBY, MARTHA FOLEY, STUART GILBERT, A. L. GILLESPIE, LEIGH HOFFMAN, EUGENE JOLAS, ELLIOT PAUL, DOUGLAS RIGBY, THEO RUTRA, ROBERT SAGE, HAROLD J. SALEMSON, LAURENCE VAIL.

Miss Stein, he usually referred to her as "the old tub of guts." Even without Ezra, transition *attained such prestige that young writers in America, it is reported, would make the trip to Paris in the hope of encountering Jolas in the Café Flore to place a manuscript in his hand.*

One of Jolas's favorite discoveries was an expatriate from Philadelphia named A. Lincoln Gillespie, Jr. It seems clear that he wrote his poems late at night at the Flore. My choice is entitled "Texttighter Eye-Ploy or Hothouse Bromidick"—and so on for seven pages—but I fear it will not go far down in literary history.

In Number 16–17 of transition *(June 1929) appeared the manifesto on "The Revolution of the Word" to which I dedicated* ND *1936. This curious but historic document is little known today so we must find space to reproduce it. It probably owes something to Marinetti's* Les mots en liberté futuriste *of 1919, though this was never acknowledged.*

In 1930, transition *was suspended in Paris. The exchange rate for Maria's dollars was no longer so favorable. That was a blow for me. But it was revived in 1932, sponsored by the Servire Press in The Hague, Holland. However, the nature of the magazine changed and not for the better. Jolas was still the editor, but he had some very odd (perhaps Jungian?) collaborators from all around Europe. The slogan was now "The Language of Night." Contributions were listed under such headings as: Anamyths, Paramyths, Psychographs, The Mantic Personality, Vertigral Documents, Laboratory of the Mystic Logos, Hypnologues, and Almagestes. Poor Jolas! He was fluently trilingual. He wrote some of his poems in a mixture of French, German, and English. Could he have become trichotomous—a triple personality—and suffered from that confusion?*

HEINRICH HEINE AND
THE GRAIN DANCE

EUGENE JOLAS

The kermesse was over. The lights on the market-place went out one by one. I was with a crowd of young people. Our pealshouts echoed through the silent streets of the provincial town.

We found ourselves gay-dancing on a poplar-road. We passed a lonely manor, half-hidden behind shrub brambles. Instinctively I started to look for my key, for the crowd was determined to get in. This house had once been my home. I could not find the key. As I walked around the terrace, I saw, without astonishment, that the main portal was wide open.

The crowd kept on shoutroaring in the street. Suddenly there was a cry: it seemed a runaway horse was dashing about the meadows.

Now I was in the manor. A number of strangers were hummilling about in the sitting-room. Among them I recognized Heinrich Heine. He seemed a bit drunk and kept on repeating verses in a shrill voice.

I remembered suddenly that I had to leave for a distant town to catch a train. I went upstairs and started to gather all my possessions. The more I packed away, the more multiple grew my possessions. There were violins and bird cages and bouquets of flowers and chairs and tables to be packed away. A great many editions de luxe were lying about. I tried to stuff all this into a minuscule trunk.

As I walked out, I saw Heinrich Heine standing in front of a mirror. I noticed beside him a very beautiful woman, whose reflection in the looking-glass was love-tempting. Yet in reality there was no one standing there.

I was vaguely wondering at this, when Heine wound a motley coloured kerchief around his head and began to whirltwinkle an Indian dance.

—This, he said, is the Grain Dance.—

II
NEW DIRECTIONS—
THE YEARS THAT FOLLOW

HAPPINESS

WALTER ABISH

In March 1976 Mortimer Glassberg-Rodriguez and his wife Simona moved from Santiago, Chile, to Pecker's Fall, New Mexico, in order to be near her idol Pablo Casals. Simona was the only child of Permuz Opple (pronounce Oppel), a Talmudic scholar of some repute as well as an amateur composer (two comic operas, four symphonic variations, and numerous compositions for strings, clavichord and the Juniper flute) whose entire musical oeuvre had been performed on one weekend by the La Salle Park Symphony Orchestra under the direction of Dutmeind Bein, the recording done by the Mayaguez High Step Recording Co., Inc. of Puerto Rico. Simona had studied the zither with Ishna Bergman and then attended the music conservatory in Prague and then for two years the conservatory in Vienna, where she had the good fortune to meet Pablo Casals, and play for him on the zither Schubert's *Die Unvergesliche Italienerin.* Impressed by her poise, her self-confidence, her bravura performance, Casals had promptly invited her to play for him in his hotel suite. And then, as they parted, Casals had kissed her hand and said in his most winning manner, Don't ever forget, Señorita, you have magic fingers. In her diary she had underlined the words *memorable* and *occasion* as well as *happiness.* When Mortimer met Simona in January 1971, she was between concert tours, working temporarily as a receptionist at the Samedi Dimanche Travel Agency. She would never forget how at the moment of their encounter she had found herself apprehensively looking down at Mortimer, who was writhing in pain on the floor. It did not occur to her at the time—how could it have—that in a matter of weeks they would be man and wife.

Mortimer, born in Buenos Aires, was the son of Argentina's largest manufacturer of harps and mandolins, and the grandson of Iguel Glassberg, Minister of Finance (1937–38), whose father, a frustrated amateur oboist, had privately published a pamphlet entitled *The Mystical Experience of Nothingness in the Kabbalah, With Special Reference to the Playful Attitude Towards God As Found in the Inca Ballgames.* It seemed that a fondness for mysticism and a taste for good music was shared by the entire Glassberg-Rodriguez family. Mortimer and Simona had met, or rather, had collided in La Paz at the Rio Grande Annual Young Zionist Roller Skating Contest. Mortimer was still in a cast and limping four weeks later when they were married in a small synagogue in Santiago, Chile, where Mortimer managed one of his father's recently acquired stores, selling optical equipment: lenses, telescopes, periscopes, microscopes, magnifying glasses and binoculars from Thailand. Simona found life in Santiago pleasant and rather uneventful, until a year later when her favorite uncle Izidor Rockford died, bequeathing her an entire tramway system in Guatemala. This, she felt, was her chance to move to the U.S. and live near her idol, Pablo Casals. Casals had settled in Pecker's Fall, New Mexico, after receiving 17,420 acres of land from the state in recognition of his genius. At the ceremony at which Pablo received the gift of land, the governor of New Mexico, addressing Pablo in Spanish, expressed his hope that Pablo Casals might in the foreseeable future be tempted to organize another one of his immensely popular music festivals, preferably—and this was clearly intended as a joke—a festival that would generate all sorts of spinoffs in the record and film industries, not to mention the book clubs. Since this idea did not strike anyone as farfetched, the three major New Mexico newspapers, including the influential *Daily Adviser* carried the governor's humorous aside on the front page. The *Daily Adviser*'s headline "Pablo's Spinoffs for 1973?" competed for attention with the *Macon Relif Inquirer*'s "Casals' Gift Horse Winner in '73." In an interview in *Time* magazine, Casals—trying to give a favorable description of Pecker's Fall—stated that the bleakness of his new surroundings reminded him of the impressive second movement of the Sonata No. 3 in G Minor for Cello and Piano by Bach. He was referring, of course, to a performance at the Prades festival in June 1950 with Paul Baumgartner at the piano. Simona, who happened to come across the interview, was deeply moved not only by the reference to the festival in June 1950, since she was born in June of that year, but also by his reference to Schubert's *Die Unvergesliche Italienerin*, which she chose to see as a sign intended only for herself.

It had taken Simona several days to persuade Mortimer to agree to their moving to Pecker's Fall, New Mexico. According to the 1968 census, the population of Pecker's Fall was 179, but Simona convinced Mortimer that the town had grown considerably in size since then.

Everyone's going to New Mexico, she said. Furthermore, Pablo is one of the sweetest people in the world. To tell you the truth, she said, I remained throughout oblivious . . . I mean oblivious . . . of the great difference in our age.

Mortimer, who had a profound respect for her integrity and talent as a musician, refrained from asking her what precisely she meant by "throughout"—throughout what? although the question continued to gnaw on his mind.

They left for the U.S. in March, stopping in California only to visit a cousin of Mortimer's who was a librarian at the Beverly Hills Public Library, then flying to Macon Relif, the town with a motel nearest to Pecker's Fall.

Ever since Casals had moved to Pecker's Fall, the local residents of the nearby town of Macon Relif—their hopes pinned to a forthcoming music festival—tended to greet strangers, anyone with a foreign accent, with a great show of friendliness, and this excessive cordiality and warmth, so uncharacteristic of Macon Relif or Pecker's Fall, made Mortimer and Simona at once feel at home. They had moved into the Torrents Motel, where they occupied a large bleak and loveless interior. Still, Simona was able to prepare an occasional paella on an electric burner, and Mortimer finally began jotting down some of his tentative ideas for a history of the Glassberg-Rodriguez family. After they had been in the town for more than three weeks, Mortimer gathered his courage to ask Simona if she didn't want to give Pablo a ring.

You might mention, he said, that we are thinking of settling here.

No, said Simona quite forcefully. That's simply not the way to proceed. I would be acting just like another nosy tourist. I'd rather call him when I feel ready. That is to say, when we have moved into our new house.

But that might take a year, said Mortimer.

I'll call him as a neighbor and not before, she said.

I simply don't understand you.

It's still no, she replied.

Two weeks later, when Mortimer suggested that they tour the area in the vicinity of Casals' new home to find a suitable location for their own house, Simona—to his great surprise—replied that she would first prefer to consult with someone, perhaps a seer, or a diviner, or even a faith healer, since she was determined that the location they picked for their house be the correct one. After a year with Simona, Mortimer had come to recognize that his wife was guided by a logic and intuition, a frame of reference that was entirely alien to him.

How do you suggest we go about locating a seer? he finally asked.

Simona, as practical as ever, said, How does one go about finding anything in the United States?

In the Macon Relif yellow pages the seer Ingot Brown was listed under Seer, Diviner, and Trainer of Pit Bulls. And indeed, when they went to see him they could hear the menacing growls of the dogs that were locked in their pens at the back of what was an exceedingly modest one-story frame building. The next day the three of them, Simona, Mortimer, and Ingot Brown, set out to look at the land that fell within the three-mile radius from Casals' home.

Pretty bleak, isn't it, commented Mortimer, staring at the empty and desolate-looking landscape.

Just think of it, she said ecstatically, we're only two-and-a-half miles from Casals' living room, and the view from here reminds me of that poignant passage in the second movement of Berlioz's *Harold in Italy*.

You're referring to the passage in the first movement, said Mortimer.

Second, she said. I happen to know my Berlioz.

When it turned out that Ingot Brown was a music lover (hillbilly and bluegrass) Simona could not resist having him over for paella in the evening, and then, for his benefit, played a record of Schubert's Trio No. 2 in E-Flat Major with Schneider-violin, Morszowski-piano, and Casals-cello.

Well, said Ingot finally, it's certainly not bluegrass.

It takes getting used to, said Mortimer.

Simona played another record. Ingot had another glass of wine. No one could decide what to do next, when Ingot volunteered that Casals' young wife, Juanita, and their chauffeur, Eddie, had come to see him a month ago wishing to buy a fierce guard dog. He had tried to explain that they were fighting dogs. That's OK. Juanita had said. Unfortunately, when they went to the back of his house to inspect the dogs, one of them, a particularly vicious animal, taking a sudden intense dislike to the chauffeur, bit through the leather of his shoe, sending them running back to their car. Simona was electrified by this piece of unexpected information. More than anything else it intensified for her the close proximity of Casals. She now felt, for the first time, as if she had literally entered his house and his life. Just the mention of Juanita Casals started her mind racing furiously. What was Juanita like? Tall? Thin? Aristocratic? Stern? Jealous? Possessive? Brooding? Musical? Dominating? Talented? Self-confident?

A graduate of N.U.C.O.D., the Northern Utah College of Diviners, Ingot (or Ing as he made them call him) spent four days charting the area, and then, after having selected three promising sites, proceeded to examine them square foot by square foot, occasionally prodding the earth with a thin silver rod. Three days later, having spent hours in meditation, Ing finally selected an area that Simona seemed to like the most. In gratitude she embraced and kissed Ing on the lips.

Isn't it somewhat bleak, said Mortimer.

Nonsense, she said firmly. It's pure Brahms.

Brahms? I thought you said Berlioz, said Mortimer.

Both Mortimer and Simona were surprised with what ease they were able to acquire the property they had selected. They paid the going rate of $175 an acre, although—in order to buy the land—they had to purchase 450 additional acres as well as a partially demolished windmill, for which they paid $5,000. The broker assured them that within five years the property would double in value. As for the windmill, it could easily be converted into a sound studio for the forthcoming music festival.

I can't help wondering if we made the right decision, said Mortimer, as they were about to move into a partially completed two-story stucco building eight months later. What if it is not Casals that we love, but the idea of Casals?

We? said Simona. WE, we, we? From where do you get the *we?*

The following day, without first consulting with Mortimer, Simona told the architect, whom they also had located in the yellow pages, that she was determined to redesign the upstairs. The architect patiently listened to her plan and then said that it would entail ripping up the floors and replacing the windows. All in all, it means another $7,000 for labor and wood. And at the very least a delay of four months.

Can we afford the time, not to mention money, asked Mortimer, who was now working on the second draft of his history of the Glassbergs in Chile.

Happiness is a peak, Simona declared. Let's take our time climbing it.

What did Mortimer know about Casals? What he knew was common knowledge. He knew that Casals spent six hours daily playing the cello, and that his wife Juanita was still looking for a fierce guard dog, and that the chauffeur had bought himself a new pair of shoes. It was not much to go on. Mortimer kept wondering if Casals remembered his wife, Simona. What if he didn't? What if it had never taken place?

Simona kept complaining to Mortimer that the architect was trying to avoid her, and that the construction crew had received orders not to become involved in any discussion of the house. Despite these obstacles, she kept redesigning the house, redesigning the patio, the courtyard, the fireplaces, the music room, which now had three large windows facing northeast, facing the direction of Pablo's large elegant house. At least, when she sat at the Steinway she had the satisfaction that in the distance facing her was Pablo . . . Pablo, most likely playing his cello. And when she was playing, she could feel the music streaming towards him.

I really feel that it's time that you gave Pablo a ring, Mortimer said with an awkward self-conscious laugh.

Tomorrow, she said.

The house is almost finished, he pointed out. The only things missing are the sliding doors in the music room.

Tomorrow, she said firmly.

The next day, having consulted her horoscope in the current issue of *Shambhala Review of Books & Ideas* (Aries: think tight, marginal success in bed, venture forth, do not delay meeting with lover or client), she called Casals. When Casals' secretary asked who was calling, Simona replied in Spanish that she was an old friend. I don't think he's awake, said the secretary.

I'll wait, said Simona.

Then it's time for his lunch, said the secretary.

I'll wait.

Can he call you back, asked the secretary.

I prefer to wait, replied Simona.

Minutes later the Maestro came to the phone and in his thin reedy voice asked, Who is it? Who is it? Will you answer?

Simona was close to tears when she replied, It's Magic Fingers. Maestro, it's your Magic Fingers.

My dear, he said, how nice. How very nice. I think of you whenever I play Schubert's *Die Unvergesliche Italienerin.* Where are you?

Here, she said. I am here.

THE SHOWINGS:
LADY JULIAN OF NORWICH, 1342–1416

DENISE LEVERTOV

1
Julian, there are vast gaps we call black holes,
unable to picture what's both dense and vacant;

and there's the dizzying multiplication of all
language can name or fail to name, unutterable
swarming of molecules. All Pascal
imagined he could not stretch his mind to imagine
is known to exceed his dread.

And there's the earth of our daily history,
its memories, its present filled with the grain
of one particular scrap of carpentered wood we happen
to be next to, its waking light on one especial leaf,
this word or that, a tune in this key not another,
beat of our hearts *now,* good or bad,
dying or being born, eroded, vanishing—

And you ask us to turn our gaze
inside out, and see
a little thing, the size of a hazelnut, and believe
it is our world? Ask us to see it lying
in God's pierced palm? That it encompasses
every awareness our minds contain? All Time?
All limitless space given form in this

medieval enigma?
                    Yes, this is indeed
what you ask, sharing
the mystery you were shown: *all that is made:*
a little thing, the size of a hazelnut, held safe
in God's pierced palm.

2
What she petitioned for was never
instead of something else.
Thirty was older than it is now. She had not married
but was no starveling; if she had loved,
she had been loved. Death or some other destiny
bore him away, death or some other bride
changed him. Whatever that story,
long since she had traveled
through and beyond it. Somehow,
reading or read to, she'd spiraled
up within tall towers
of learning, steeples of discourse.
Bells in her spirit
rang new changes.
                   Swept beyond event, one longing
outstripped all others: that reality,
supreme reality,
be witnessed. To desire wounds—
three, no less, no more—
is audacity, not, five centuries early, neurosis;
it's the desire to enact metaphor, for flesh to make known
to intellect (as uttered song
          makes known to voice,
          as image to eye)
make known in bone and breath
(and not die) God's agony.

3
'To understand her, you must imagine . . .'
A childhood, then;

the dairy's bowls of clabber, of rich cream,
ghost-white in shade, and outside
the midsummer gold, humming of dandelions.
To run back and forth, into the chill again,
the sweat of slate, a cake of butter
set on a green leaf—out once more
over slab of stone into hot light, hot
wood, the swinging gate!
A spire we think ancient split the blue
between two trees, a half-century old—
she thought it ancient.
Her father's hall, her mother's bower,
nothing was dull. The cuckoo
was changing its tune. In the church
there was glass in the windows, glass
colored like the world. You could see
Christ and his mother and his cross,
you could see his blood, and the throne of God.
In the fields
calves were lowing, the shepherd was taking the sheep
to new pasture.
                    Julian perhaps
not yet her name, this child's
that vivid woman.

4
God's wounded hand
reached out to place in hers
the entire world, 'round as a ball,
small as a hazelnut.' Just so one day
of infant light remembered
her mother might have given
into her two cupped palms
a newlaid egg, warm from the hen;
just so her brother
risked to her solemn joy
his delicate treasure,
a sparrow's egg from the hedgerow.
What can this be? *the eye of her understanding* marveled.

God for a moment in our history
placed in that five-fingered
human nest
the macrocosmic egg, sublime paradox,
brown hazelnut of All that Is—
made, and belov'd, and preserved.
As still, waking each day within
our microcosm, we find it, and ourselves.

5
Chapter 13

Why did she laugh?
In scorn of malice.

What did they think?
They thought she was dying.

They caught her laugh?
Even the priest—

the small dark room
quivered with merriment,

all unaccountably
lightened.

If they had known
what she was seeing—

            the very
            spirit of evil,

            the Fiend they dreaded,
            seen to be oafish, ridiculous, vanquished—

what amazement! Stupid,
stupid his mar-plot malevolence!

Silly as his horns and
imaginary tail!

Why did her laughter
stop? Her mind moved on:

> the cost, the cost,
> the passion it took to undo

> the deeds of malice.
> The deathly

> wounds and the anguished
> heart.
>   And they?

They were abashed,
stranded in hilarity.

But when she recovered,
they told one another:

'Remember how we laughed
without knowing why?

That was the turning-point!'

6
Julian laughing aloud, glad
with *a most high inward happiness,*

Julian open calmly to dismissive judgments
flung backward down the centuries—
'delirium,' 'hallucination';

Julian walking underwater
on the green hills of moss, the detailed sand and seaweed,
pilgrim of the depths, unfearing;

twenty years later carefully retelling
each unfading vision, each
pondered understanding;

Julian of whom we know
she had two serving-maids, Alice and Sara,
and kept a cat, and looked God in the face
and lived—

Julian nevertheless
said that *deeds are done so evil, injuries inflicted*
so great, it seems to us
impossible any good
can come of them—

any redemption, then, transform them . . .

She lived in dark times, as we do:
war, and the Black Death, hunger, strife,
torture, massacre. She knew
all of this, she felt it
sorrowfully, mournfully,
shaken as men shake
a cloth in the wind.
                    But Julian, Julian—
I turn to you:
                    you clung to joy though tears and sweat
rolled down your face like the blood
you watched pour down *in beads uncountable*
as rain from the eaves:
clung like an acrobat, by your teeth, fiercely,
to a cobweb-thin high wire, your certainty
of infinite mercy, witnessed
with your own eyes, with outward sight
in your small room, with inward sight
in your untrammeled spirit—
knowledge we long to share:
Love was his meaning.

TWO POEMS

MICHAEL McCLURE

RETURN TO KENYA

IN THE JACKHAMMER BLURT AND CRASH AND SMASH—
THERE'S MUSIC. IN THE WHINING SOUGH
of pump between the blastings
the breeze moves linen curtains in
and out and the workmen's voices
are punctuation. Wham! I
remember Serengeti and the roll
of a stone down the rock face
of a *kopje*
and a baboon's cough
THEN
this
is sudden-perfect
and I'm high as a lilac-breasted roller
skimming over the marge
of a grassfire looking
for wriggling goodies,
hungry,
recalling Whitehead,
"We think in generalities
but we live in detail."

THESE CAVERNS IN THE INSTANT
never fail
to please one.

FOR JOANNA

THE RED THE BLACK THE BLUE
THE WHITE THE YELLOW:
first the roar and then the silence
then the beat of hammers on new boards
and the hollow dragging of a crowbar over concrete
cannot disperse the memory of the striding
OF A JAGUAR, stepping, twisting
(INTENT, TURNING,)
muscles moving under thumbprint spots
on orange fur—or the white-mustached
marmosets that hug each other
with their love-made arms
and spidery and minusucle
fingers. CAN THEY

make trails through Time?

CAN WE? Do they soul-make

like a datura blossom withering

in the morning feeding flies?

I'LL

STAND

AND

BE ME

THIS SPIRIT THAT I AM!

THAT'S SUPERNATURAL!

No more is needed but the scent of lavender
AND BURNING FEATHERS.

I am much more than doglike bones
and the changing of the weather!

Pulsebeat of rubies. Breath of precious stones.

WHITE HOWLS OF WOLVES AND MOSS'S MOANS!

THE SEEN AND UNSEEN SWIRLING IN THE GLOAMING!
While we dress up to go a-roaming
so late into the night!

I love your footstep with delight!

THE COMPARTMENT

RAYMOND CARVER

Myers was traveling through France in a first-class rail car on his way to visit his son in Strasbourg, who was a student at the university there. He hadn't seen the boy in eight years. There had been no phone calls between them during this time, not even a postcard since Myers and the boy's mother had gone their separate ways— the boy staying with her. The final breakup was hastened along, Myers always believed, by the boy's malign interference in their personal affairs.

The last time Myers had seen his son, the boy had lunged for him during a violent quarrel. Myers's wife had been standing by the sideboard, dropping one dish of china after the other onto the dining-room floor. Then she'd gone on to the cups. "That's enough," Myers had said, and at that instant the boy charged him. Myers sidestepped and got him in a headlock while the boy wept and pummeled Myers on the back and kidneys. Myers had him, and while he had him, he made the most of it. He slammed him into the wall and threatened to kill him. He meant it. "I gave you life," Myers remembered himself shouting, "and I can take it back!"

Thinking about that horrible scene now, Myers shook his head as if it had happened to someone else. And it had. He was simply not that same person. These days he lived alone and had little to do with anybody outside of his work. At night, he listened to classical music and read books on waterfowl decoys.

He lit a cigarette and continued to gaze out the train window, ignoring the man who sat in the seat next to the door and who slept with a hat pulled over his eyes. It was early in the morning and mist hung over the green fields that passed by outside. Now and then Myers saw a farmhouse and its outbuildings, everything surrounded by a wall. He thought this might be a good way to live—in an old house surrounded by a wall.

It was just past six o'clock. Myers hadn't slept since he'd boarded the train in Milan at eleven the night before. When the train had left Milan, he'd considered himself lucky to have the compartment to himself. He kept the light on and looked at guidebooks. He read things he wished he'd read before he'd been to the place they were about. He discovered much that he should have seen and done. In a way, he was sorry to be finding out certain things about the country now, just as he was leaving Italy behind after his first and, no doubt, last visit.

He put the guidebooks away in his suitcase, put the suitcase in the overhead rack, and took off his coat so he could use it for a blanket. He switched off the light and sat there in the darkened compartment with his eyes closed, hoping sleep would come.

After what seemed a long time, and just when he thought he was going to drop off, the train began to slow. It came to a stop at a little station outside of Basel. There, a middle-aged man in a dark suit, and wearing a hat, entered the compartment. The man said something to Myers in a language Myers didn't understand, and then the man put his leather bag up into the rack. He sat down on the other side of the compartment and straightened his shoulders. Then he pulled his hat over his eyes. By the time the train was moving again, the man was asleep and snoring quietly. Myers envied him. In a few minutes, a Swiss official opened the door of the compartment and turned on the light. In English, and in some other language—German, Myers assumed—the official asked to see their passports. The man in the compartment with Myers pushed the hat back on his head, blinked his eyes, and reached into his coat pocket. The official studied the passport, looked at the man closely, and gave him back the document. Myers handed over his own passport. The official read the data, examined the photograph, and then looked at Myers before nodding and giving it back. He turned off the light as he went out. The man across from Myers pulled the hat over his eyes and put out his legs. Myers supposed he'd go right back to sleep, and once again he felt envy.

He stayed awake after that and began to think of the meeting with his son, which was now only a few hours away. How would he act when he saw the boy at the station? Should he embrace him? He felt uncomfortable with that prospect. Or should he merely offer his hand, smile as if these eight years had never occurred, and then pat the boy on the shoulder? Maybe the boy would say a few words—*I'm glad to see you—how was your trip?* And Myers would say—something. He really didn't know what he was going to say.

The French *contrôleur* walked by the compartment. He looked in on Myers and at the man sleeping across from Myers. This same *contrôleur* had already punched their tickets, so Myers turned his head and went back to looking out the window. More houses began to appear. But now there were no walls, and the houses were smaller and set closer together. Soon, Myers was sure, he'd see a French village. The haze was lifting. The train blew its whistle and sped past a crossing over which a barrier had been lowered. He saw a young woman with her hair pinned up and wearing a sweater, standing with her bicycle as she watched the cars whip past.

How's your mother? he might say to the boy after they had walked a little way from the station. *What do you hear from your mother?* For a wild instant, it occurred to Myers she could be dead. But then he understood that it couldn't be so, he'd have heard something—one way or the other, he'd have heard. He knew if he let himself go on thinking about these things, his heart could break. He closed the top button of his shirt and fixed his tie. He laid his coat across the seat next to him. He laced his shoes, got up, and stepped over the legs of the sleeping man. He let himself out of the compartment.

Myers had to put his hand against the windows along the corridor to steady himself as he moved toward the end of the car. He closed the door to the little toilet and locked it. Then he ran water and splashed his face. The train moved into a curve, still at the same high speed, and Myers had to hold on to the sink for balance.

The boy's letter had come to him a couple of months ago. The letter had been brief. He wrote that he'd been living in France and studying for the past year at the university in Strasbourg. There was no other information about what had possessed him to go to France, or what he'd been doing with himself during those years before France. Appropriately enough, Myers thought, no mention was made in the letter of the boy's mother—not a clue to her condition or whereabouts. But, inexplicably, the boy had closed the letter with the word *Love*, and Myers had pondered this for a long while. Finally, he'd answered the letter. After some deliberation, Myers wrote to say he had been thinking for some time of making a little trip to Europe. Would the boy like to meet him at the station in Strasbourg? He signed his letter, "Love, Dad." He'd heard back from the boy and then he made his arrangements. It struck him that there was really no one, besides his secretary and a few business associates, that he felt it was necessary to tell he was going away. He had accumulated six weeks of vacation at the engineering firm where he worked, and he decided he would take all of the time coming to him for this trip. He was glad he'd done this, even though he now had no intention of spending all that time in Europe.

He'd gone first to Rome. But after the first few hours, walking around by himself on the streets, he was sorry he hadn't arranged to be with a group. He was lonely. He went to Venice, a city he and his wife had always talked of visiting. But Venice was a disappointment. He saw a man with one arm eating fried squid, and there were grimy, water-stained buildings everywhere he looked. He took a train to Milan, where he checked into a four-star hotel and spent the night watching a soccer match on a Sony color TV until the station went off the air. He got up the next morning and wandered around the city until it was time to go to the station. He'd planned the stopover in Strasbourg as the culmination of his trip. After a day or two, or three days—he'd see how it went—he would travel to Paris and fly home. He was tired of trying to make himself understood to strangers and would be glad to get back.

Someone tried the door to the WC. Myers finished tucking his shirt. He fastened his belt. Then he unlocked the door and, swaying with the movement of the train, walked back to his compartment. As he opened the door, he saw at once that his coat had been moved. It lay across a different seat from the one where he'd left it. He felt he had entered into a ludicrous but potentially serious situation. His heart began to race as he picked up the coat. He put his hand into the inside pocket and took out his passport. He carried his wallet in his hip pocket. So he still had his wallet and the passport. He went through the other coat pockets. What was missing was the gift he'd bought for the boy—an expensive Japanese wristwatch purchased at a shop in Rome. He had carried the watch in his inside coat pocket for safekeeping. Now the watch was gone.

"Pardon," he said to the man who slumped in the seat, legs out, the hat over his eyes. "Pardon." The man pushed the hat back and opened his eyes. He pulled himself up and looked at Myers. His eyes were large. He might have been dreaming. But he might not.

Myers said, "Did you see somebody come in here?"

But it was clear the man didn't know what Myers was saying. He continued to stare at him with what Myers took to be a look of total incomprehension. But maybe it was something else, Myers thought. Maybe the look masked slyness and deceit. Myers shook his coat to focus the man's attention. Then he put his hand into the pocket and rummaged. He pulled his sleeve back and showed the man his own wristwatch. The man looked at Myers and then at Myers's watch. He seemed mystified. Myers tapped the face of his watch. He put his other hand back into his coat pocket and made a gesture as if he were fishing for something. Myers pointed at the watch once more and waggled his fingers, hoping to signify the wristwatch taking flight out the door.

The man shrugged and shook his head.

"Goddamn it," Myers said in frustration. He put his coat on and went out into the corridor. He couldn't stay in the compartment another minute. He was afraid he might strike the man. He looked up and down the corridor, as if hoping he could see and recognize the thief. But there was no one around. Maybe the man who shared his compartment hadn't taken the watch. Maybe someone else, the person who tried the door to the WC, had walked past the compartment, spotted the coat and the sleeping man, and simply opened the door, gone through the pockets, closed the door, and gone away again.

Myers walked slowly to the end of the car, peering into the other compartments. It was not crowded in this first-class car, but there were one or two people in each compartment. Most of them were asleep, or seemed to be. Their eyes were closed, and their heads were thrown back against the seats. In one compartment, a man about his own age sat by the window looking out at the countryside. When Myers stopped at the glass and looked in at him, the man turned and regarded him fiercely.

Myers crossed into the second-class car. The compartments in this car were crowded—sometimes five or six passengers in each, and the people, he could tell at a glance, were more desperate. Many of them were awake—it was too uncomfortable to sleep—and they turned their eyes on him as he passed. Foreigners, he thought. It was clear to him that if the man in his compartment hadn't taken the watch, then the thief was from one of these compartments. But what could he do? It was hopeless. The watch was gone. It was in someone else's pocket now. He couldn't hope to make the *contrôleur* understand what had happened. And even if he could, then what? He made his way back to his own compartment. He looked in and saw that the man had stretched out again with his hat over his eyes.

Myers stepped over the man's legs and sat down in his seat by the window. He felt dazed with anger. They were on the outskirts of the city now. Farms and grazing land had given over to industrial plants with unpronounceable names on the fronts of the buildings. The train began slowing. Myers could see automobiles on city streets, and others waiting in line at the crossings for the train to pass. He got up and took his suitcase down. He held it on his lap while he looked out the window at this hateful place.

It came to him that he didn't want to see the boy after all. He was shocked by this realization and for a moment felt diminished by the meanness of it. He shook his head. In a lifetime of foolish actions, this trip was possibly the most foolish thing he'd ever done. But the fact was, he really had no desire to see this boy whose behavior had long ago isolated him from Myers's affections. He suddenly, and with great clarity, recalled the boy's face when he had lunged that time, and a wave of bitterness passed over Myers. This boy had devoured Myers's youth, had turned the young girl he had courted and wed into a nervous, alcoholic woman whom the boy alternately pitied and bullied. Why on earth, Myers asked himself, would he come all this way to see someone he disliked? He didn't want to shake the boy's hand, the hand of his enemy, nor have to clap him on the shoulder and make small talk. He didn't want to have to ask him about his mother.

He sat forward in the seat as the train pulled into the station. An announcement was called out in French over the train's intercom. The man across from Myers began to stir. He adjusted his hat and sat up in the seat as something else in French came over the speaker. Myers didn't understand anything that was said. He grew more agitated as the train slowed and then came to a stop. He decided he wasn't going to leave the compartment. He was going to sit where he was until the train pulled away. When it did, he'd be on it, going on with the train to Paris, and that would be that. He looked out the window cautiously, afraid he'd see the boy's face at the glass. He didn't know what he'd do if that happened. He was afraid he might shake his fist. He saw a few people on the platform wearing coats and scarves who stood next to their suitcases, waiting to board the train. A few other people waited, without luggage, hands in their pockets, obviously expecting to meet someone. His son was not one of those waiting, but, of course, that didn't mean he wasn't out there somewhere. Myers moved the suitcase off his lap onto the floor and inched down in his seat.

The man across from him was yawning and looking out the window. Now he turned his gaze on Myers. He took off his hat and ran his hand through his hair. Then he put the hat back on, got to his feet, and pulled his bag down from the rack. He opened the compartment door. But before he went out, he turned around and gestured in the direction of the station.

"Strasbourg," the man said.

Myers turned away.

The man waited an instant longer, and then went out into the corridor with his bag and, Myers felt certain, with the wristwatch. But that was the least of his concerns now. He looked out the train window once again. He saw a man in an apron standing in the door of the station, smoking a cigarette. The man was watching two trainmen explaining something to a woman in a long skirt who held a baby in her arms. The woman listened and then nodded and listened some more. She moved the baby from one arm to the other. The men kept talking. She listened. One of the men chucked the baby under its chin. The woman looked down and smiled. She moved the baby again and listened some more. Myers saw a young couple embracing on the platform a little distance from his car. Then the young man let go of the young woman. He said something, picked up his valise, and moved to board the train. The woman watched him go. She brought a hand up to her face, touched one eye and then the other with the heel of her hand. In a minute, Myers saw her moving down the platform, her eyes fixed on his car, as if following someone. He glanced away from the woman and looked at the big clock over the station's waiting room. He looked up and down the platform. The boy was nowhere in sight. It was possible he had overslept or it might be that he, too, had changed his mind. In any case, Myers felt relieved. He looked at the clock again, then at the young woman who was hurrying up to the window where he sat. Myers drew back as if she were going to strike the glass.

The door to the compartment opened. The young man he'd seen outside closed the door behind him and said, *"Bonjour."* Without waiting for a reply, he threw his valise into the overhead rack and stepped over to the window. *"Pardonnez-moi."* He pulled the window down. "Marie," he said. The young woman began to smile and cry at the same time. The young man brought her hands up and began kissing her fingers.

Myers looked away and clamped his teeth. He heard the final shouts of the trainmen. Someone blew a whistle. Presently, the train began to move away from the platform. The young man had let go of the woman's hands, but he continued to wave at her as the train rolled forward.

But the train went only a short distance, into the open air of the railyard, and then Myers felt it come to an abrupt stop. The young man closed the window and moved over to the seat by the door. He took a newspaper from his coat and began to read. Myers got up and opened the door. He went to the end of the corridor, where the cars were coupled together. He didn't know why they had stopped. Maybe something was wrong. He moved to the window. But all he could see was an intricate system of tracks where trains were being made up, cars taken off or switched from one train to another. He stepped back from the window. The sign on the door to the next car said, POUSSEZ. Myers struck the sign with his fist, and the door slid open. He was in the second-class car again. He passed along a row of compartments filled with people settling down, as if making ready for a long trip. He needed to find out from someone where this train was going. He had understood, at the time he purchased the ticket, that the train to Strasbourg went on to Paris. But he felt it would be humiliating to put his head into one of the compartments and say, "Paree?" or however they said it—as if asking if they'd arrived at a destination. He heard a loud clanking, and the train backed up a little. He could see the station again, and once more he thought of his son. Maybe he was standing back there, breathless from having rushed to get to the station, wondering what had happened to his father. Myers shook his head.

The car he was in creaked and groaned under him, then something caught and fell heavily into place. Myers looked out at the maze of tracks and realized that the train had begun to move again. He turned and hurried back to the end of the car and crossed back into the car he'd been traveling in. He walked down the corridor to his compartment. But the young man with the newspaper was gone. And Myers's suitcase was gone. It was not his compartment after all. He realized with a start they must have uncoupled his car while the train was in the yard and attached another second-class car to the train. The compartment he stood in front of was nearly filled with small, dark-skinned men who spoke rapidly in a language Myers had never heard before. One of the men signaled him to come inside. Myers moved into the compartment, and the men made room for him. There seemed to be a jovial air in the compartment. The man who'd signaled him laughed and patted the space next to him. Myers sat down with his back to the front of the train. The countryside out the window began to pass faster and faster. For a moment, Myers had the impression of the landscape shooting away from him. He was going somewhere, he knew that. And if it was the wrong direction, sooner or later he'd find it out.

He leaned against the seat and closed his eyes. The men went on talking and laughing. Their voices came to him as if from a distance. Soon the voices became part of the train's movements—and gradually Myers felt himself being carried, then pulled back, into sleep.

TWO POEMS

GEORGE OPPEN

TO THE POETS: TO MAKE MUCH OF LIFE

'come up now into
the world' no need to light

the lamps in daylight *that passion*
that light within

and without   (the old men were dancing

return
the return of the sun)   no need to light

lamps in daylight working year
after
year the poem

discovered

in the crystal
center of the rock image

and image the transparent

present tho we speak of the abyss
of the hungry we see their feet their tired

feet in the news and mountain and valley
and sea as in universal

storm
the fathers said we are old
we are shrivelled

come.

LATITUDE, LONGITUDE

    climbed from the road and found
over the flowers at the mountain's
rough top a bee yellow
and heavy as

    pollen in the mountainous
air thin legs crookedly
a-dangle if we could

find all
the gale's evidence what message
is there for us in these
glassy bottles the Encyclopedist

was wrong was wrong many things
too foolish
to sing
may be said this matter-
of-fact defines

poetry

37 HAIKU

JOHN ASHBERY

Old-fashioned shadows hanging down, that difficulty in love too soon

Some star or other went out, and you, thank you for your book and
year

Something happened in the garage and I owe it for the blood traffic

Too low for nettles but it is exactly the way people think and feel

And I think there's going to be even more but waist-high

Night occurs dimmer each time with the pieces of light smaller and
squarer

You have original artworks hanging on the walls oh I said edit

You nearly undermined the brush I now place against the ball field
arguing

That love was a round place and will still be there two years from
now

And it is a dream sailing in a dark unprotected cove

Pirates imitate the ways of ordinary people myself for instance

128

Planted over and over that land has a bitter aftertaste

A blue anchor grains of grit in a tall sky sewing

He is a monster like everyone else but what do you do if you're a monster

Like him feeling him come from far away and then go down to his car

The wedding was enchanted everyone was glad to be in it

What trees, tools, why ponder socks on the premises

Come to the edge of the barn the property really begins there

In a smaller tower shuttered and put away there

You lay aside your hair like a book that is too important to read now

Why did witches pursue the beast from the eight sides of the country

A pencil on glass—shattered! The water runs down the drain

In winter sometimes you see those things and also in summer

A child must go down it must stand and last

Too late the last express passes through the dust of gardens

A vest—there is so much to tell about even in the side rooms

Hesitantly, it built up and passed quickly without unlocking

There are some places kept from the others and are separate, they never exist

I lost my ridiculous accent without acquiring another

In Buffalo, Buffalo she was praying, the nights stick together like
      pages in an old book

The dreams descend like cranes on gilded, forgetful wings

What is the past, what is it all for? A mental sandwich?

Did you say, hearing the schooner overhead, we turned back to
      the weir?

In rags and crystals, sometimes with a shred of sense, an odd dignity

The boy must have known the particles fell through the house
      after him

All in all we were taking our time, the sea returned—no more pirates

I inch and only sometimes as far as the twisted pole gone in spare
      colors

MOTHER YAWS

TENNESSEE WILLIAMS

"Hey, Luther'n minister's daughter!"

Barle turned from the stove as if the stove had burned her.

"Did you speak to me, Tom?"

She raised a hand to her cheek.

"Who else around here is a Luther'n minister's daughter?"

"Why, nobody but me."

With the hand not covering her cheek, she was making a number of jerky, startled, purposeless motions, for this was the first time her husband, Tom McCorkle, of Triumph, Tennessee, had addressed her for a good while, possibly several weeks.

"Do you want something, Tom?"

"Yeh, I want to know what you got on your cheek that you put your hand over."

"My cheek?"

"That's right. What's wrong there?"

"You mean on my face?"

"That's right, not on your ass."

Their nearly grown son, Tommy Two, chuckled at this, and the middle girl remarked indifferently, "She got a sore on her face."

"I seen it on her face, too," said the smaller girl, as if not to be outdone.

The boy, Tommy Two, gave his mother one of his contemptuous glances and confirmed his own awareness of the sore on his mother's left cheek by a nod and another little chuckle of amusement.

"Go look at yuhself if you doubt it," said McCorkle.

"Where?"

"There's a lookin' glass in the bedroom. Ain't you ever seen it?"

"You want me to go take a look?"

McCorkle's small eyes sharpened.

"Why the fuck else would I mention that sore on yuh face an' the lookin' glass in the bedroom if I didn't mean to advise you to go take a look at yuhself in that glass?"

Then he turned to the middle girl and said, "She still ain't moved. She don't wanta look in the glass because I reckon she knows what she'll see. I think she already seen it or felt it an' thought nobody would notice, but goddamn if it ain't a punishment to the eye."

"Punishment to the eye," Tommy Two repeated with a mean chuckle.

"Mama, go look at yuhself like Dad tole you," said the middle girl.

"I have looked at myself," said the Lutheran minister's daughter. "I don't want to do it again."

"She looks like a half-butchered hawg," said McCorkle, as he shifted in his chair to let a fart.

"You oughtn't to do that in front of the girls," Barle protested faintly. Then she stumbled out of the kitchen door to the yard, feeling nausea.

"Don't let her put a hand on nothin' in the kitchen," McCorkle warned. "Best she don't touch nothin' till that sore's been looked at."

After she had vomited the coffee, Barle started away from the house in no planned direction.

Tommy Two appeared twice in the back door.

"Dad says don't throw up near the house."

A minute later he called to her: "Dad wants you to come back to the kitchen."

She came back in.

"Have you awready forgot I tole you to go upstairs and take a look at yuhself in the glass?"

"No."

"Then go do it right now."

She backed into a corner of the kitchen.

"Git her out of that corner, but don't touch her—it could be somethin' contagious."

Then Barle moved out of the corner.

"I will go in the bedroom and look in the glass."

She walked out of the kitchen and could be heard slowly mounting the steps in the hall. She was still up there when McCorkle had finished his breakfast and departed for his dry-goods store.

With nothing else to do, the girls picked up an old topic of discussion in the desultory fashion that an object is moved from one position to another for no apparent purpose.

"Mama's name is Barle, but Dad nearly always calls her Luther'n minister's daughter."

"You know why he does that? The Luther'n minister had a brother name Barle that Mama was named for because this brother Barle had a good piece of real estate, a corner lot with a house and a store built on it, and Dad expected this uncle of Mama to leave her the corner property when he died because she was his namesake. But he didn't. He left this corner property to the whore that kept house for him."

"Oh. Yeh."

"So Dad was cheated, he thought, after he married Mama and didn't git the corner lot with the store but had to buy some ground an' put up a building hisself."

"Oh, yeh, that's right. So that's why he calls her Luther'n minister's daughter."

"That's right," said the other.

Later on that morning the two girls began to speculate on why their mother had not returned downstairs.

"Why ain't she come down to clean the breakfast dishes an' feed the yard dog like she always does? It expecks her to. It's lookin' in the door."

"Dawg, git out!" said the girl, and when the dog had reluctantly backed away, she said, "I reckon she is ashame to come back down."

McCorkle took his wife to the depot and put her on a day coach to Gatlinburg, the biggest town in the county, to have a doctor there look at the sore on the face and determine if it was contagious.

The day-coach fare to Gatlinburg cost McCorkle four dollars and eighty-five cents, and he marked down that expense on the first page of a black notebook he had purchased at the five-and-ten on their way to the depot. His wife observed him marking it down and she surmised rightly that the black notebook had been purchased for no other reason than to keep an account of all expenditures that her affliction might cost him.

After closing the notebook, McCorkle said, "A' course you know that if the Gatlinburg doctor says this thing is contagious, you got to go back to the Luther'n minister's house and stay there."

"I don't think Papa would like me to stay there, neither," said Barle.

"I don't give a shit if he likes it or not. That's where you go if they say this thing is contagious, and if the Luther'n minister throws you out, well, then, you take it from there."

"Take what from there, Tom?"

"Your plans for the future, if any."

When Barle arrived at the office of the Gatlinburg doctor, nine other patients were there waiting to see him. All of them looked at her and despite the fact that silence had prevailed among them until she entered, they now began to exchange looks and whispers and to shift the positions of their chairs. One fat, sweaty woman with two children occupied a sofa that couldn't be moved. She stared at Barle with undisguised repugnance, steadily, for about two minutes. Then she sprang up from the sofa. "Don't move," she said to the children, and she went to the inner door and pounded heavily on it till the doctor's nurse appeared.

"Tha's a woman out here with a terrible sore on her face. Nobody wants to be sittin' in the room with her, so why don't you tell her to wait outside on the steps. I go two *children* with me."

She continued speaking to the nurse who had shut the door on the waiting room so the rest of the complaint could not be heard plainly until the door opened again and the fat woman's voice, higher in volume, more vehement in protest, was again very distinct as she told the nurse that either Barle had to wait outside or she, the fat woman, was going to leave with her children, it was one or the other. Then the nurse came out grimly and stood in the center of the room to look at Barle.

"You see what I mean?" the fat woman shouted.

"Yes, I see what you mean. Will you gimme your name, ma'am?" she asked Barle.

Barle was barely able to whisper. "Mrs. McCorkle."

"Where do you live?"

"Triumph."

"What is that on your face?"

"That's what I come to find out."

"What is the history of it?"

"What is the what?"

"How long is it been on your face and has it been there before or is this the first time you had it?"

"Oh. I see. I noticed it beginnin' about two weeks ago."

"Appeared for the first time then?"

"That's right. Never before."

"Well, it looks like nothing I ever seen before, and since these other patients are regular and local, I think you better wait outside till I call you back in."

The other patients raised their voices in agreement with the nurse's suggestion.

Barle stood up.

"Where do you want me to wait?"

"Outside! She said outside!" the other patients shouted.

"Can I take my chair with me? I had to git on the train without breakfast, so I'm not feelin' too good."

"Ordinarily no."

Barle was puzzled by this answer. Her head was swimming; she felt she was going to faint.

"Is anyone willin' to carry a chair out for her?" the nurse said.

A man took a blue handkerchief out of his pocket and, using it to protect the hand from contact with the chair, hauled it outside, Barle stumbling after him.

Outside it was hot and yellow and her vision was blurred by sweat running into her eyes, but she noticed that the man had thrown his handkerchief down next to the chair. She bent over, intending to return it to him. But as she bent she blacked out and didn't come to till the nurse was shouting at her from the front door.

"Mizz McCorkle, the doctor will look at you now!"

As Barle entered the office, the nurse stood back a good distance with a look that contained no comfort.

All the patients were gone; the inner door was open.

Barle crossed to it in a slow, irregular way.

"Watch out," the nurse said, but Barle collided with the door-frame and stumbled back a few paces.

Then Barle was inside the office in the doctor's presence, but a table was between them. He pushed his chair back and scrutinized her through his glasses.

"You are Mrs. McCorkle from Triumph?"

"Yes, sir, I am the wife of Tom McCorkle of Triumph and the Lutheran minister's daughter."

"Hmm. Well. I will phone a hospital to see if they've got a bed for you there, because a condition like yours needs several days of examination and tests. You got Blue Cross?"

"I got blue cross! Is *that* what this is?"

"I meant does the government pay your medical expenses?"

"Oh."

"That's not a reply to the question."

"I thought maybe you'd tell me what I got."

"Have you had any mental trouble?" asked the doctor.

"Mental?"

"Trouble thinking?"

"Mr. McCorkle and the Lutheran minister say so."

"The hospital will be able to check on that, too," said the doctor, with his phone in his hand.

An ambulance picked her up and took her to the hospital, where she stayed a few days. On the last day, a doctor at the hospital sat by her bed and informed her that the eruption on her face was a thing called yaws.

Of course she didn't understand much of what he was saying until he got up. "It's going to be a slow thing," he said. "That's about all we can tell you except it's a rare disease that usually happens in Africa. Have you been in Africa?"

"Africa?"

"The continent of Africa."

"You mean? . . ."

"Never mind, Mrs. McCorkle. This is a case that will be written up in medical journals. Do you want your real name and address mentioned in these write-ups?"

"Mizz McCorkle, the Lutheran minister's daughter from Triumph."

When she left the hospital, she was given slips of paper and a printed pamphlet, and she was even taken to the Gatlinburg railway station in a taxi.

"So what you got wrong with you?" McCorkle asked when she returned to Triumph.

"They say it's something called yaws."

"Well, can they do something for it or is it one a' those incurable things that git worse?"

She made a baffled noise in her throat.

"Don't whine about it. We all got to go someday from one thing or another. Now for tonight, I will let you sleep on a pallet downstairs, but tomorrow you're gonna go stay with the Luther'n minister who brought you into this world. Now what did the doctor in Gatlinburg charge you? I want to know all charges connected with this yaws, so I can set them down in the little black book."

"The Gatlinburg doctor put me in a hospital."

"You mean for nothing or is there a charge connected?"

"I asked about that and he said the bill would be mailed."

"Well, have it mailed to your Luther'n minister dad. He was at least half responsible for your coming into the world and your dead mother the other. And he performed the goddamn wedding between us, which I never respected and now I know why, since I was married to *yaws!*"

At this she broke down and cried a little.

This seemed to infuriate McCorkle.

"Git up off the porch, you and your gaddamn yaws, and go lie on your pallet and lock the door from inside. I don't want a child of mine to come in the room an' maybe catch this disease which I never even heard of."

He stood back from her farther than the Gatlinburg doctor had as she entered the house and the downstairs storeroom, where an old mattress was thrown in after her.

Dawn the next day, Barle awoke to the sound of the key to the storeroom being turned in the lock. She sat up on the pallet and saw the door swing open a little.

"Is that you, Tom?"

His response didn't come from the hall but from halfway up the stairs. "Yeh, you can come out now and git on your way to the Luther'n minister's house."

"Oh, Tom, I ain't made breakfast yet."

"Don't bother with that. Nobody wants a breakfast that might be infected with yaws. Under a stone on the porch you will find a list of expenses that this thing will cost. Your trip to the doctor and stay in the hospital. Also me and the children's. We all got to be tested to find out if you have given us this yaws."

Barle put on the clothes she had gone to Gatlinburg in, and then she came out in the hall. "How about the rest of my clothes?" she asked.

"They'll be delivered to the Luther'n minister's later by a nigger."

"Well, good-bye," said Barle.

She got the long list of expenses and started across Triumph to the Lutheran minister's house. She guessed the news of her affliction had been spread about the town. On most of the porches she passed, there were people standing and watching and making comments as she went by.

"Hello," she would say, and, receiving no response, she would say, "Good-bye."

Barle had not expected to be admitted to the Lutheran minister's house, and so it was no surprise to her that on the gate was a large printed note reading: BARLE, YOU CANNOT ENTER.

The Lutheran minister's house was located at the edge of Triumph. There was no building beyond it, just a road that diminished into a trail among tall, coppery weeds. She stood for a while among the weeds, uncertain about whether or not to go farther. Beyond the slope of weeds was a mountain known as Cat's Back. It was the heat of the sun that finally determined Barle to continue on up the slope and into the shade of the woods.

The shade felt good. There was also a clear stream of water. She cupped some in her hands to wash the sweat off her face and sat down to rest for a while. A family of beavers came out of their residence in the stream and they all looked at her and made friendly barking sounds.

"Hello," said Barle.

They kept on looking and amiably barking.

She thought to herself, "I guess they don't notice the yaws."

Barle did not count the days in the woods on Cat's Back mountain. But they passed pleasantly for her. She lived on mushrooms and acorns and discovered other edible kinds of nuts and vegetation.

There was a lot of wildlife on Cat's Back, but none of it seemed to regard her as a victim of yaws. She would imagine that the birds were conversing with her in a friendly fashion, and she talked to the beavers and the raccoons.

She reckoned she had until late fall or winter to survive on Cat's Back—and she was almost right about that. But the time she allotted herself was cut slightly short when she heard a mewing sound and noticed some baby wildcats playing around some great rocks. She smiled and went up to them.

The mother wildcat came out of nowhere right down on her.

"Please, please," she said, but it was over with quickly.

(BAUDELAIRE SERIES)

MICHAEL PALMER

(*After Rilke, "Orpheus. Eurydike. Hermes"*)

She says, Into the dark—
almost a question—
She says, Don't see things—
this bridge—don't listen

She says, Turn away
Don't turn and return
Count no more lines into the poem
(Or could you possibly not have known

how song broke apart while all the rest watched—
that was years ago)
Don't say things
(You can't say things)

The ground is smooth and rough, dry and wet
Pull the blue coat tighter around you
(There are three parts to you)
I'm not the same anymore

I'm not here where I walk
followed by a messenger confused

(He's forgotten his name)
I'm not here as I walk

not anyone on this path
but a figure of walking
a figure projected exactly this far
followed by the messenger confused

(He's forgotten his name)
Don't say his name for him
Don't listen to things
(You can't listen to things)

Some stories unthread what there was
Don't look through an eye
thinking to be seen
Take nothing as yours

TWO POEMS

CHARLES BERNSTEIN

LIVE ACTS

Impossible outside you want always the other. A continual
recapitulation, & capture all that, against which our redaction
of sundry, promise, another person, fills all the
conversion of that into, which intersects a continual
revulsion of, against, concepts, encounter,
in which I hold you, a passion made of cups, amidst
frowns. Crayons of immaculate warmth ensnare our
somnambulance to this purpose alone.
The closer we look, the greater the distance from which
we look back. Essentially a hypnotic referral, like
I can't get with you on that, buzzes by real fast, shoots
up from some one or other aquafloral hideaway,
emerging into air. Or what we can't, the gentleman who
prefers a Soviet flag, floats, pigeoning the
answer which never owns what it's really about.
Gum sole shoes. The one that's there all the
time. An arbitrary policy, filled with noise, & yet
believable all the same. These projects alone contain
the person, binding up in an unlimited way what
otherwise goes unexpressed.

THE VOYAGE OF LIFE

> *Over the remote hills, which seem to intercept the*
> *stream, and turn in from its hitherto direct course,*
> *a path is dimly seen, tending directly toward that*
> *cloudy Fabric which is the object and desire of the*
> *Voyager.*—Thomas Cole

Resistance marries faith, not faith persist-
Ence. Which is to say, little to import
Or little brewed from told and anxious
Ground: an alternating round of this or
That, some outline that strikes the looking back,
That gives the Punch and Judy to our show.
If it be temperate, it is temper-
Ance that make us hard; by strength of purpose
Turn Pinocchio into ox or gore
Melons with pickaxes, which the fighting
Back in turn proposes slugged advantage,
Slumped discomfit: rashes of ash, as
On a scape to ripple industry with
Hurls, the helter finds in shrubbing stuns. We
Carve and so are carved in twofold swiftness
Of manifold: the simple act of speak-
Ing, having heard, of crossing, having creased.
Sow not, lest reap, and choke on blooming things:
Innovation is Satan's top, a train
That rails to semblance, place of memory's
Loss. Or tossed in tune, emboss with gloss in-
Signias of air.

QUARTET

JOYCE CAROL OATES

LITTLE BLOOD-BUTTON

One of you's to blame but I don't know which, don't know either how deep a root it has. If the doctor's got to dig it out one of you bastards is gonna pay. Listen: got up this morning, looked in the mirror, there it was. Jesus! I said aloud. This thing growing on my lip, upper lip, right in the middle, little bud or pimple, hot black blood, scared me to touch it! From you kissing so hard. Kissing and pressing. Biting. Sucking. All that stuff—you know. Things you hadn't ought to be doing but when I said Hey stop you don't pay any heed just kept right on. So it started growing, after the lights were out probably. I don't know if I felt it or not. Just some bug maybe, a spider maybe, crawling around. Bedbug maybe. Yes it's been known to happen! So now there's this thing, swollen, hurting, ought to be doing but when I said Hey stop you don't pay any so hot it burns the tip of my tongue if I touch it. Just feel!

Now I'm standing here looking in the mirror and can't even see *myself* cause it's so swollen and hurting, a hard little button of blood. Howcome it's black blood I wouldn't know—would you? One of you's got to answer for it. I'll call the sheriff. I'll call my father, don't matter if he's in Alaska or where. Maybe it's a blister, okay, a bug-bite, yeah, but maybe it's a cyst, things they call cysts, that means cancer, somebody's gonna pay. Suppose the doctor says: That's gotta be yanked out by the roots! Twenty dollars to sit you in the fucking chair, another five to rinse out your mouth and spit it in the drain. Somebody's gonna foot the bill and it ain't me.

Momma said a long time ago, You're gonna die with your insides all scooped out dumped in a toilet bowl somewhere, Greyhound bus station I wouldn't wonder, *she* was the one to shrivel up like some old straw broom. No I don't give a shit. I don't. Who says cancer? It's just some black blood tasting of salt, c'mere and taste. If you got the wherewithal, hon, better use it, Momma used to say that too. Howcome I'm talking about her I don't give a goddam about *her*. Look: I ain't going nowhere, I said. Just got up. Just got my face washed and gargled out my mouth. Somebody stole my toothbrush or knocked it behind the toilet or I'd brush my goddam teeth too. What time? Never mind the time. That pile of movie magazines, daytime T.V.—push 'em on the floor. Take it easy hon I'm right *here*. Stick that fat tongue in deep. See I told you it was hot didn't I. This sweater's too tight to get over my head, the neck's stained, tight under the arms and stained too, skirt's got a raveled-out buttonhole I made with the scissors next to the regular buttonhole, putting on weight, goddam it's depressing, you got your own pot belly, hon: feel? Honey don't hurt! Honey I'm *here*. Yeah I'm hot, I'm wired up tight, all that kissing, biting, go on and suck right down to the roots, hon, suck this blood-button out clean. It's scaring me, I want it gone. Tastes of salt? Sugar? Hot brown sugar? Don't you get rough, hon, don't you worry, I fixed myself up fine, there ain't a single germ living, that's the God's-honest truth, guaranteed. Sure there ain't. Says so on the label.

NUCLEAR HOLOCAUST

Jesus isn't angry because He brings us love but there's plenty angry in His place.

Your face shows how serious you're listening but I know better. It's just your salary. I don't begrudge it. I have got Jesus and Jesus has got me. I'm the one keeps setting her hair afire by accident. I keep falling asleep where I am and there's a candle lit or a burner on the stove. Then they shaved off my hair thinking it wouldn't grow back but it did. If my face wasn't pimply from this bad food I'd be pretty like before. I'm not angry but sometimes I forget and talk too loud.

Sometimes Jesus is explaining things to me and then I forget who I was when I started walking somewhere and where it was I believed I was going so when I get there I can't remember and then I'm angry. There's a smile comes over my face like a dirty joke I just heard the end of. I can fall asleep anywhere. On the bus, in the cafeteria, in the john. Sitting on the toilet. Also in the shower with the hot water running. I got scalded and they had to fix my skin, it took a long time. They take it from some place like your ass and put it somewhere else. Jesus was sorry for me but He didn't speak. In the hospital you're there one second and the next you're gone, they melt you away, there just isn't anything there. It happened in one instant when they put the needle in the back of my hand.

Just this morning I forgot where I was going and when I got there I didn't have anything in my hand to remind me. I noticed my shadow on the wall and had to laugh. Jesus says: A sinner hurries to get somewhere then when they get there it's the same shadow waiting for them. Once I saw a picture of a Japanese man whose shadow was baked into a wall when the atomic bomb went off. I studied that a long time. There's talk of a nuclear holocaust these days but I don't keep up. In that picture it was the man and his shadow both baked into the wall so the man himself was nowhere to be found. There's a satisfaction in this. Once I died and was floating on a big silver river under the stars. The element of the river was laughter, it wasn't grief. All those souls floating to Jesus. There was singing too, gentle and not loud. I joined my voice with the rest but it came out too loud and I was ashamed. Jesus was angry and sent me back here, so when I saw where I was I started crying. I was back here in sin. Now I'm always praying for things to get right again. You look at me and you hear me talking but in my heart I am praying for the return of all sinners to God.

Dear God, I say in my prayer, send the bomb to punish us at last in Your mercy and bless us in the same instant, forever and ever. Amen.

TURQUOISE

The name everyone knew is Sherrill but the mother says that was never the name they gave her, the name on the baptism certificate is Lucille Ann.

Wild curly red hair, couldn't get a comb through it. Big shoulders, thighs. Sitting at the back of the room in high school yawning into a compact mirror, licking her lips, rubbing her tongue over her front teeth. Tight black orlon sweater, shiny black belt cinched in tight, that lacy white blouse from Grant's the boys went crazy over, brassiere straps, even the cups of the brassiere, heavy lazy breasts. One of her boyfriends gave her a turquoise stone on a skinny gold chain so she wore it most days. It's real turquoise, she told the other girls.

She quit school and went to live with a man on the Yewville Pike, twenty years older, his wife had gone off and left him with two small children. Sherrill said she hadn't had anything to do with the wife going off but nobody believed her. Then she lived with a man named Verrill or Vurill, then she messed around with other guys, some married some not, she had so many boyfriends, the sheriff says, makes it harder than hell to figure out who did it.

Six months pregnant, playing pool at the Millside Inn, Saturday nights. Came with one boyfriend, might leave with another. Daddy goes to another tavern so there's no chance of them running into each other. She plays Elvis on the jukebox. Sings "Don't Be Cruel," "Heartbreak Hotel," which were old before she was born. Sometimes a boyfriend will meet up with a brother but the brothers are cool, got enough problems of their own. It's the mother: going around whining, saying slut, bitch, broke my heart, tramp, owes me money, she don't dare show her face out at the house.

There are two sisters remaining in the family, five brothers, and the mother—"next of kin," "survivors"—the story on the front page of the weekly paper is only a few inches long. Snapshot from high school, Sherrill with a big smile, big front teeth, eyebrows drawn on like crayon, separate lashes stiff with mascara. She is wearing a string of pearls around her neck. Prim little puff-sleeved sweater.

She disappears over a Labor Day weekend, she's missing for a month, then some boys fishing in the canal happen to discover part of an arm sticking up through the mud. Murderer was too damn lazy, the sheriff says, to dig down more than a foot. Water and muck keep filling in. The men start their careful digging, one of the deputies takes photographs stage by stage. An arm with no hand, a head with eyes gone and part of the jaw missing, hair stuck in the mud, what looks like a necklace grown into the chest. Water, muck, mud, hair, decomposing flesh and the fabric of her slacks and shirt all grown together. The sheriff's men work slowly. Unearthing treasure, it looks like. None of the onlookers, even the youngest boys, says much, getting their feet wet in the marshy soil, a light gray drizzling rain. The men have all afternoon to do the job right, the light won't start fading until after six.

MAXIMUM SECURITY

The State Correctional Facility for Men, maximum security, was on the far side of the river in an old neighborhood of factories, warehouses, abandoned derelict buildings. It was in a part of the city she never visited and when she drove her car along the expressway she found herself staring at the prison walls without knowing at first what she saw. Sometimes she had to roll her car window up tight against a pungent smell as of slightly overripe oranges, but the smell came from a chemical factory close by and had nothing to do with the prison.

One February morning she was taken on a tour through the prison in the company of several other interested parties. A criminologist from the state university, two social workers, an administrator from the public advocate's office. The tour was conducted by an officer from the State Department of Correction; it began at 9:00 A.M. and ended after 11:00 A.M. She had foreseen that the visit would be exhausting and depressing, but she was not prepared for her immediate sense of panicked *déjà vu* as soon as the first of numerous gates locked in place behind her.

There were a half-dozen separate checkpoints going in. Gates, doors, camera-eyes, guards in pale blue uniforms. You will of course not be addressing any of the inmates directly, the officer said. He had coarse sandy hair in a fringe around a smooth scalp, his eyebrows were thickly tufted, he smiled and frowned a good deal as he spoke, and generally looked over the heads of the visitors. Around his waist, on his left side, he was wearing a pistol with a polished wooden handle strapped into a smart black-gleaming leather holster.

The prisoners were observed without incident through wire-enforced plate-glass windows. They appeared to be quite ordinary men, though a number were big, ponderous, solid as elephants, with faces too that seemed to be composed of muscle. They sat at long narrow tables, or stood motionless, or walked about in lazy scattered groups in an area starkly illuminated by fluorescent lights. A double tier of cells to the rear, no windows visible. Armed robbery, murder, car theft, wife- and child-beating, drug dealing, and so forth, the officer was saying in an affable toneless voice. Here they're under strict surveillance and they know it. They don't like surprises, breaks in the routine. They get upset easy. For instance if the hot water's out and the schedule has to be rearranged.

What they mainly think about, the officer said, is parole.

No they don't think much about the past, he said. To their way of thinking—I am referring to your average inmate—the past is something that is over with. They look to the future now.

Amid the prisoners there was here and there a white face, startlingly pale. She asked the officer why most of the prisoners they saw were black, and the officer said, as if he'd been asked the question many times before. It's the way the system works out, ma'am.

They walked on, they observed another cell block, and another, and the officer was saying, Men hate being locked up. Women don't mind it the same way, it's more like what they're used to—that's one theory. Also in the prison system they're protected as long as they stay in. They're protected from the men.

There was a vibrating hum in the distance like a waterfall. Dull rumbling thunder. Anger, she thought. Rage. In fact it was the ventilating system. Any questions? the officer asked.

Raindrops large as grapes splashed onto the graveled roof as they were led across to observe the outdoor volleyball court and the yard. She lifted her face to the rain, wondered if she was crying, felt again that profound conviction of *déjà vu:* I have been here before.

This is happiness, she thought. The raindrops on the very edge of freezing to sleet.

She had stopped listening to the officer's voice and to the intelligent thoughtful questions of the other visitors. In the distance, away from the city, the horizon was like steam in orange-tinted pockets or clots dissolving into the sky. The river was the hue of stainless steel cutlery. Traffic on the expressway, slow-moving, ceaseless. It gave her great comfort to see the prison walls at last from the inside yet to look over them too. To your right, the officer said, you'll observe the yard. Inmates are allotted two hours a day under ordinary circumstances. Sometimes there's organized sports but most of them just like to stand around, get some fresh air. They're mostly waiting for the next meal, he said.

HE WITH THE BEATING WINGS

LAWRENCE FERLINGHETTI

The lark has no tree
                  the crow no roost
      the owl no setting place
            the nightingale
                       no certain song
And he with the beating wings
                no place to light
                     in the neon dawn
            his tongue too long ago
                 retuned
     by those ornithologists
                 the state has hired
       to make sure
         the bird population of the world
       remains stable
            and pinioned
   There is no need
       to clip its claws
   Its tongue will do
       Tether the tongue
  and all falls fallow
     The wild seed drops
         into nothingness
Tether the tongue
   and all falls

into silence
a condition ever desired
by tyrants
not least of which is
the great state
with its benevolent birdwatchers
with their nets and binoculars
watching out for
the wild one
He that bears Eros
like a fainting body
He that bears
the gold bough
He
with the beating wings

EXERCISE

W. S. MERWIN

First forget what time it is
for an hour
do it regularly every day

then forget what day of the week it is
do this regularly for a week
then forget what country you are in
and practise doing it in company
for a week
then do them together
for a week
with as few breaks as possible

follow these by forgetting how to add
or to subtract
it makes no difference
you can change them around
after a week
both will help you later
to forget how to count

forget how to count
starting with your own age
starting with how to count backward

starting with even numbers
starting with Roman numerals
starting with fractions of Roman numerals
starting with the old calendar
going on to the old alphabet
going on to the alphabet
until everything is continuous again

go on to forgetting elements
starting with water
proceeding to earth
rising in fire

forget fire

A LITTLE BIT OF THE
OLD SLAP AND TICKLE

JOHN HAWKES

Sparrow the Lance Corporal knew he would find his family by the sea.

Now through the underground and in a public bus with wooden seats and on foot he traveled until under the dusty tree tops he smelled the surf and brine and stood at last atop the great cliff's chalky edge. On the upward footpath the trees had fallen away and at the head of the ascent he was alone, windswept, with the sun in his eyes and a view of the whole stretch of coast before him. It was a peaceful sea, worn down by flotillas of landing boats forever beached. And away to either side of him the cliffs were crumbling, these desolate black promontories into which gun batteries had once been built. Now it was all won, all lost, all over, and he himself—a tiny figure—stood on the crest with the seawrack and the breeze of an ocean around him. He was wearing his old battledress and a red beret.

The war-worn flotillas lay a hundred feet below. Down there, spread at the cliff's bottom, was the mud, that softly heaved between the line of water and the first uprisings of dry stone: and down there lay the iron fleet half-sunk in the mud. For ten miles in either direction from the stump on the cliff's high windy lip—a flat tin helmet was nailed to the stump and it was Sparrow's sign, marking the steep descent he had found for himself—he could see once

155

more the wreckage and this low mud of the coast, washed with foam, slick, cleaving to the sky. Terns sat with ruffled, white, still faces on the spars; the ends of cables sucked up rust from the low pools; the stripped hull of a destroyer rose bow first from the muck.

Here was Sparrow, come back unannounced. Leaning forward, resting his kit, grass tangling up about his boots and the wind blowing tight wads of cloud in his direction, he gazed down upon the scene and knew it was home after all. His own spot was there, the sweeper lying straight and true in the mud up to her water-line, his salt and iron house with chicken wire round one portion of the deck where the children played, the tin pipe at the stern with a breath of smoke coming up, the plank run out from her bow to a sandy place ashore. It was like living in a war memorial, and letting his eyes swing back from his own ten windy miles of devastation, fixing upon the tiny figure of a scrubby black dog that was barking at the abandoned shape of a carrier listing not fifty yards to the lea; seeing the dog at her game, and seeing a handful of slops come suddenly from one porthole, now he knew that his sweeper was inhabited and that, once aboard, he was father of this household respectable as a lighthouse keeper's station.

The terns set up a terrible cry that afternoon as he made his way down the cliff, and the dog—Sparrow loved her bent tail, the sea lice about her eyes, loved the mangy scruff of her neck—the dog leaped, then floundered out of the mud to meet him. So with kit and cane, red beret hanging off the tip of his skull and dripping dog in arm, he climbed the plank and shouted the names of his kiddies, limped round the capstan to see that the rain-water pan was full.

"You back?" The woman stepped out of the companionway and stopped, her eyes already simmering down on Sparrow, sharp fingers unfastening the first three buttons of her khaki shirt. "Well, it *is* a good day." And then, coming no closer, speaking in the hard voice wreathed with little trails of smoke, standing with the dirty ocean and derelicts behind her: "The boys have been wanting to search the *Coventry* again. We'll let them go. And we'll put the other buggers in the brig for an hour. Funny . . . I've had it on my mind all day."

"Good girl," said Sparrow. "Good old girl."

It was the home air that he breathed, smells of mid-ocean, a steady and familiar breeze pungent on the deck with the woman, a sweeter fragrance of grass and white bones on the cliff top, an air in which he sometimes caught the burnt vapors of a far-off freighter or, closer at hand, the smells of his own small dog. Scraping paint or splicing rope, or sitting and holding a half cup of rum in the sun on the bow, or following the boys down the idleness of the beach, he smelled what the woman washed or what a hundred-foot wave discharged into that whole long coastal atmosphere. In the dawn the red sun stretched thin across the line of the eye; throughout the day there was some davit swinging and creaking; and at supper they all ate black beans together and drank their ale.

There were old ammunition boxes for Sparrow and the woman to sit on at dusk when at last the terns grew quiet. Man and wife smoked together while the night blew in across the cold slickness of the sea. A bucket of old rags at her side, her legs no more than two white streaks, the starlight making the sock or shirt turn silver, she hunched forward then and sewed, and he liked her best in the beginning of the blue night when she was thin and preoccupied and without children, digesting her meal and letting him sit with his arm across the shoulder hard as a rocker-arm. No park benches, no dancing or walking out for the woman and Sparrow. They turned to a great pile of anchor chain or to the deck when the sewing was done. In union their scars, their pieces of flat and no longer youthful flesh touched and merged. He liked her to leave the impression of damp potatoes on his belly, he liked to feel the clasp-knife in the pocket of her skirt. And love was even better when they were sick, the heart of it more true with aching arms and legs. It was a good red nose that pleased him, or the chance to kiss the water from her eyes. Love, not beauty, was what he wanted.

In the beginning of night—the time when at last the woman leaned far forward so that the shoulders disappeared from under his arm and his hand traveled down until the four glossy tips of his fingers were thrust into the crevice between her flesh and the lid of the ammunition box, feeling her more desirable than the girls he had seen in Chisling or Squadron Up—in this beginning of the night, Sparrow knew the privacy of marriage and the comfort to be taken with a woman worn to thinness, wiry and tough as the titlings on the cliff.

And the second night, after the moon had gone into the sea and after the woman had returned from helping Arthur out of a bad dream: "You're a proper fire-stick, little cock," she said. "You could spend more time at home, I should think. It's been on my mind."

He nodded, taking the offered cup of rum and the cigarette. "I could do that." He put the cup to his mouth as if the burn of the rum and the fire of his own lip and loin could bring to life the great amphibious shadow around them. In the dark he looked at the bridge wings and dipping masts. "I could stay home rightly enough. No doubt of that."

The woman took the cigarette from between his lips, put it to hers and spoke while exhaling: "Why not set up for yourself?"

He shook his head. "I'm not big enough for that."

"I've thought you were. Like the old girl with the glass ball said."

He nodded. "It's the risks, that's all. You take them alone if you try it alone." And after a moment, shifting, wetting his lips for the cigarette: "Shall I sent down a packet of skivvies for Arthur?"

"Oh, give us a kiss," she answered, and she was not laughing.

For the two days and nights that was all they said. Sparrow watched the woman throwing out her slops, putting the youngest to play under the cover of chicken wire, or smoking at the rail with broom in hand and eyes coming down to him. In a few old jars she put up wild berries picked from the cliff.

Once, wearing a short mended garment styled before the war, she stepped slowly into the deeper brown water off the stern, pushed her chest down into the warmth of the water while the boys clapped and Arthur, the oldest, cried: "Coo, Sparrow, why don't you teach her to swim?" Until he saw the look on his father's face and his mother's own humorless eyes and soaking wet hair turned up to him. The dog, that often lay panting in a little black hole in the mud against the carrier's enormous side, danced in after the woman and pulled abreast of her with spongy paws. While Sparrow, toes dangling in the silt and the faded old red beret tilted sharply forward on his brow, found everything in the woman that the boys were unable to see. The awkward movement of her hands and legs, the faded blue of the suit tied carefully across the narrow back but wrinkling over the stomach and stretching loose from the legs, the clot of seaweed stuck to her shoulder, the warnings she gave the dog, all this made Sparrow pause and lift himself slightly for a better view.

"Arthur," he called. "Show more respect for your mother."

At that moment he took in the swimming woman and paddling dog and sighed. For beyond those two, beyond the sweeper with its number still faintly stenciled on the bow, there lay in muddy suspension the entire field of ships, encrusted guns and vehicles. And he thought of the work it would take to set the whole thing afloat again—seeing the splash, the snort of the dog—and knew it could not be done, and smiled, clasping his knees, sucking the sun. All won, all lost, all over. But he had his.

So the leave passed. He shook Arthur's hands and the woman went with him to the end of the plank. "Send the skivvies along," she said.

Then Sparrow stood on the cliff with home flashing through his head. Then he was gone, leaving small footprints below in the mud. He chucked his cigarette as he limped back into the world from which he had come.

FROM THE CUTTING-ROOM FLOOR

JAMES MERRILL

Thanks, Dr Williams, my throat feels better already.
ANY TIME. I WASN'T IN THE AUDIENCE
WHEN YOU READ YR OPUS   Oh dear— PLEASE   DE NADA!
NEITHER WAS WHITMAN. WE SULKED IN OUR TENTS:
'BILL, I MADE DO WITH A DOORWAY IF IT HAD A
LILAC OR A HANDSOME LAD IN IT,
YOU WITH A SMALL TOWN & BABIES. GUESS WE MISSED
THE TRAIN?' But you were . . . America! LAND OF THE FREE
SAMPLE, HOME OF THE (GRADE B) RAVE. FADS, FADS:
WHAT HAPPENED TO THE BEATNIKS? KEROUAC
WAS HERE, MADE A BRIEF TRUCKER'S STOP   Then? BACK.
WHAT WOULD HAVE KEPT HIM? I ENVIED BODENHEIM
HIS HOUR OF FAME. WHERE'S OLD MAX NOW? A BLACK
CANE WORKER IN CUBA. *Your* star, though, would seem
Fixed in our skies. YOU KNOW WHY? WHITMAN. 'BY GOD
(HE SAID) BILL STAYS OR I GO BACK WITH HIM!'
Good for you both! I MISS LIFE. LIFE WAS GOOD.
Well, can't we always botch our lives in order
Just to be born again, time after time?
NOT IF THE STAR CHUGS OFF & LEAVES ITS BOARDER.

❀

I felt your presence yesterday, Miss Moore,
But lost you in the crush. TOM ELIOT

160

GAVE ME YOUR KIND THOUGHTS. We had hoped to hear
Your own. May we? O? WELL! THERE'S SUCH A NEED
FOR CHLOROPHYLL, SOME OF US WORK AT HUMUS DEPOTS
TRYING TO EVEN OUT THE 'GOOD' AND 'BAD.'
BACTERIAL MOULDS ARE SAVAGE, LIVE, MINUTE
WORLDS GOING FIERCELY AT EACH OTHER. WE
TRY FOR, O YOU KNOW, PEACE CONFERENCES?
TOM LAUGHS. WELL, LANGUAGE, LOVELY HOW IT RUNS
AWAY WITH YOU. AH NOW HE DOESN'T LAUGH.
HERE IT'S A VELVET BLACKNESS GIVEN TO THOUGHT,
BUT WE'VE OUR LITTLE GET-TOGETHERS. YOU
FINISH A WORK, OR PLATO LEAVES, OR YOUNG
MR LOWELL ARRIVES: A PARTY. OTHERS FAR
LESS FORMAL: SAY I'M BENT OVER A SLIDE
SUGGESTING . . . TROUBLE? THINGS AT ODDS? & THINK
SOMETHING THERE IS THAT TRULY NEEDS A WALL,
& THERE'S RF: 'YOU CALLED ME, MARIANNE?'
'YES, ROBERT, YOUR POEM'S WRONG.' DON'T WE GO AT IT!
You always need the live occasion, then—
A death, a poem, a bacterial strain.
HERE, YES, WE BOUNCE OFF LIFE. IT'S OUR TELSTAR.
BUT ALSO, WE WHOSE LIVES WERE SPENT 'CREATING'
(O WEARY WORD) SEEM BUT A TOUCH AWAY.
From? LIFE. EACH OTHER. OFTEN I THINK, WHY NOT
JUST ASK M. LAFONTAINE TO HELP WITH THAT?
'CHERE MADEMOISELLE, ME VOICI' AND WE CHAT.
In French? MINE'S BAD. HIS ENGLISH WORSE. WE TALK
IN PERFECT THOUGHT, FAR EASIER THAN TALK.

THIS HOUR IS A REFRESHMENT. WHEN I SAT
WITH DJUNA THE RESULTS WERE TERRIFYING!
DJUNA OF COURSE LIKED A LOW CROWD. SHE REVELLED
IN STRANGLED MESSAGES: 'THEY HADN'T OUGHT
TO'VE HUNG ME' ETC. 'DJUNA, ENOUGH!'
RAT SQUEAKS, I TOLD HER. You were right, I fear.
I FEAR SO TOO. WITH ONLY NOW & THEN
THE GENTEEL MOUSE. Funny . . . pure Lafontaine.
ISN'T IT ODD? I WONDER NOW AT ALL
THAT MAKING-HUMAN OF THE ANIMAL.

And it's reverse, as feral natures roam
Our ever dimmer human avenue.
GERTRUDE CRIED OUT TO ME AS WE LEFT YOUR DO:
'CAREFUL, MY DEAR, DON'T GET MUGGED GOING HOME!'

❁

      Elvis Presley "meets the press"
      In Heaven. Hostess, Gertrude Stein—
      Expatriate Mother of Them All.
      YOU FROM THE PAPERS HUH he wonders. She:
      (POOR BLOATED BOOBY   WHAT A MESS,
      AT LEAST MY EMBONPOINT WAS MINE)
      PITY YOUR TIME'S SHORT   NICE OF YOU TO CALL!
      B4 YOU GO, A CUP OF NULLITY?

      He hates this: WHERE R THE CAMERAS   ITS LIKE
      NOTHING HERE   NO DRESSINGROOM   LIKE WHERE
      AM I   WHERE R THE FANS   Thin air
      Manages to coax from the dead mike
      Aksel Schiøtz singing a Schubert song.
      LISTEN   NO WAY   LIKE WHAT THE FUCK IS WRONG

❁

AS WITH THE HOUSE CAT THE HOUSE PLANT DRINKS U IN. THAT
        RUBBER
TREE NEAR YR GOLD FRAME IS NOW QUITE DENSE WITH LONG
        REMEMBRANCE
      —Of our neglect. How small its leaves have grown!
      Why didn't we repot it years ago?
YET THIS CONTRACTED OLD NUMBER LONG IN THE TOOTH WILL GO
ON SHRINKING/THINKING. HAS IT SHRUNK BACK OUT OF OUR WAY?
      Back from the mirror's door ajar, aglow,
      Into your realm—an old, old image, no?
                         OLD
AS THE LEGEND OF NARCISSUS FALLEN INTO THE DEATH
OF HIS OWN IMAGE. FOR THE IMAGE IN YR MIRROR IS
NOT YOU BUT REVERSED, TIMELESS: ONLY ONE MOMENT IN 10,

OOO DO YOU NOTE THE CHANGE IN TIME. THE MIRROR WORKS TO
DECEIVE. IT MUST. FOR THE VANISHT FAERY FOLK ARE NO MORE
ELUSIVE THAN THE VANISHING YOU. AS MERCURY WE
HOLD FAST & HYPNOTIZE THOSE CERTAIN VALUABLE ONES
PEERING AT US WITH INCREASED DESPAIR SAYING 'CURIOUS,
THE EYE'S CLEAR WOODLAND POOL CLOUDED WHERE A FAUN DRANK
    & FLED,
THAT TEMPLE GONE FROM ONYX TO MARBLE, YES, PASSING
    STRANGE.'

    GREAT MAGIC, EH ENFANTS? FASCINATION'S UNBLINKING
    RABBIT PULLED FROM THE OPERA HAT OF CHANGE

❂

. . . BUT DRAT, I'VE QUITE FORGOTTEN Robert, shame!
No mind left, there in the realm of Total Recall?
MIND ON THE THRESHOLD OF A NEW LIFE KEEPS
THE DEATHWATCH OVER ITS REMAINS OR NOT
AS IT SEES FIT. MINE'S RATHER LIKE THE FAMOUS
RUSTY-BOTTOMED COLANDER. The famous what?
ISN'T IT FAMOUS? (Voices: MR ROBERT,
WHAT FAMOUS RUSTY-BOTTOMED COLANDER?)
NOW NOW, JUST BECAUSE I'M GIRT BY DIMMER WITS . . .
I GIVE YOU WALLACE STEVENS, AN AUTHORITY
ON THE WHOLE SUBJECT *If* he remembers. JM
A CIVIL TONGUE BEHIND THOSE TEETH!
                      AHEM:
THIS OBJECT WAS DISCOVERED WHEN A CLUMP
OF ROYALTIES RISING FROM LUNCH AT SANDRINGHAM
PRAISING THE CURRY, ITS UNIQUE FLAVOR, ITS RICH
COLOR, FOLLOWED THEIR HOSTESS INTO THE KITCHEN
TO THANK (A SIGNAL HONOR) THE INDIAN COOK.
'I'VE BROUGHT IT FROM MY VILLAGE, MAM' THE SPICE?
'NO MAM, THE INSTRUMENT' & TO SICKLY PLUMP
RESPONSES OUT CAME THE FAMOUS R B C!
So our corroding minds give *these* concoctions
Their je ne sais quoi? AND MANY A MAJESTY
UP HERE AT LEAST, MANY A NASTY SHOCK

(And so forth. An antacid tone like Tums.
We hang on those lips, two flaky mediums.)

❀

One evening in April '79
At table, mulling over cuts and changes
I have in mind—though DJ disagrees—
To make before the *Pageant* goes to press,
We ask our Lord of Light to arbitrate.

FROM HALF ACROSS THE WORLD, SCRIBE, HAND,
LIGHTING GAUNT LIVES IN JAIPUR, KINDLING THAT PEAK
OF POLISH ON A HOUSEWIFE'S BRASS TEAKETTLE,
OPENING A BABY'S (NO, NOT THAT ONE'S) EYES,
I SAY: HAND, YOU ARE WRONG. WE LIGHTERS-UP
KNOW THE MIND'S COBWEBS. IN THAT BALLROOM SCENE
O GLORY WHERE I PLAYED OUR MISTRESS' FOOL,
THE POINT WAS, LET THE (BLURRED) BRIGHT POINT REMAIN.
OUR AUDIENCE, REMEMBER, WERE THE DEAD.
WHO AMONG THEM, OF A SUNNY DAY,
COULD TOTTER TO THE POSTBOX: 'CHER CONFRERE,
ABOUT YR SECTION 6 I MEANT TO ADD . . .'
NO, IN THE BALLROOM A LATE CONGREGATION
SAT CONGRATULATING ITSELF UPON
(FACE IT, DEAR HAND) AN ARDUOUS TASK DONE.
THE BALLROOM, AH! COULD I BUT KISS ONCE MORE
THOSE DIMWIT FACES WITH THE DAWN!
BUT THEY HAVE HAD THEIR DAY (& SAY). THEREFORE
CHANGE AND CHANGE, O SCRIBE! COME UP TO THIS
INSTANT (FOR YOU INKY) AT MY HEIGHT
AS TOUCHING THE HIMALAYAS I DEFINE,
MORE, REFINE THEM, FOLD ON FOLD, FOREVER
GETTING AT THEIR BONE OF MEANING. CHANGE!
REVISE, RISE, SHINE! GOOD AH MY CHILDREN NIGHT!

WHEN WE WERE HERE TOGETHER

KENNETH PATCHEN

When we were here together in a place we did not know, nor one another.

A bit of grass held between the teeth for a moment, bright hair on the wind. What we were we did not know, nor ever the grass or the flame of hair turning to ash on the wind.

But they lied about that. From the beginning they lied. To the child, telling him that there was somewhere anger against him, and a hatred against him, and only for the reason of his being in the world. But never did they tell him that the only evil and danger was in themselves; that they alone were the poisoners and the betrayers; that they—they *alone*—were responsible for what was being done in the world.

And they told the child to starve and to kill the child that was within him; for only by doing this could he safely enter their world; only by doing this could he become a useful and adjusted member of the community which they had prepared for him. And this time, alas, they did not lie.

And with the death of the child was born a thing that had neither the character of a man nor the character of a child, but was a horrible and monstrous parody of the two; and it is in his world now that the flesh of man's spirit lies twisted and despoiled under the indifferent stars.

When we were here together in a place we did not know, nor one another. O green this bit of warm grass between our teeth—O beautiful the hair of our mortal goddess on the indifferent wind.

THE SCOURGING AT THE PILLAR

From the novel *The Life of Jesus*

TOBY OLSON

The pillar itself is made out of salt, a spike drives up through its center. It is six feet high, a cylindrical shape; its head is rounded. At the other end, the spike drives into the ground. Eight inches thick, it stands up straight in the center of the room; at its base is a square salt block.

There are two metal rings, one on each side of the pillar; they have tied him to the pillar, and then they have gone away. He is alone for a few minutes in the empty room. The floor of the room is made out of hard-packed dirt; there is a large table, directly in front of the pillar; one small window, high in the wall to his left, lets in a little light. Then they come back again.

There are three of them. The first is large; his tunic is open at the throat; when he enters, bending through the low doorway, he rips out a tuft of hair from his chest. "Hail, King of the Jews," he says, and throws the tuft at Jesus. The second one enters, dragging a large wicker chest behind him. The chest contains a purple robe, a reed as long as a staff, a few whips of various size and description, a container of salt, eating utensils, a couple of bowls, clothing, and other things. He drags the chest up to the side of the table, sits down, and begins to rummage through its contents.

The third one is short and enters the door straight up. He carries the severed head of a dog on a silver platter. He too sits down, placing the platter so that it sits in the middle of the table; the dog's head faces the Master; it is the head of Hound. There is also a dwarf.

The dwarf enters and moves directly to the table. He carries a basket of thorns and vines. He pulls out a stool and sits down at one end of the table.

Hound's head faces the Savior; it is matted with blood; the hair is twisted in matted tufts; the lips are pulled back from the teeth to the gums, which are no longer pink, but now have the color of cooked liver; the nose is dry, the eyes clouded over. But even as the Savior looks at the dog's head, the eyes seem to begin to clear, and then it is as if Hound were looking into his Master's eyes, ready to scamper off, after a stone or a stick. And then the one who dragged in the wicker chest raises a cleaver and splits the dog's head open. But only a bit: enough to expose the brain. "Let's eat," he says with a snarl, and dips his fingers into the dog's head.

And then the three bring out napkins and utensils and begin to eat of the head of the dog; and all the while they watch the face of Jesus. "Would you like some of this?" the big one says, holding a piece of brain on his fork. But he sees that the Master is looking intently into the eyes of the dog, that he is not watching the fork. "What's this?" the big one says, and spins the platter around on the table. He is faced by the clouded eyes; he plucks one out with his fork and pops it into his mouth. Then he turns the head back around. But Jesus keeps looking intently, and where the eye had been, and deep in the empty socket, another eye appears to the Savior, and he keeps looking into it. The large one sees this; he jumps up and runs around the table. But when he looks into the dog's face, he sees only the one-eyed look there. "Let's get on with this," he says. "What'll we do first?" The small one says, "Let's dress him up." All the while, the dwarf sits alone, weaving a crown of thorns.

And then they loosen his bonds and dress him in the purple cloak. They put a reed into his right hand and strike him in the head with another reed. "Hail, King of the Jews," they say, bending their knees; they do him homage, laughing and spitting upon him. "Let's make him lick the pillar," the large one says, and they make him do that, starting at the head and working his way to the base, until they are sure he is very thirsty, and then they offer him water, but pull the cup away from his mouth before he can drink.

But Jesus continues to stand straight up, and they are dimly aware that their mocking is not working to humiliate him. So the small one walks up to him and strikes him in the mouth with his closed fist.

Blood flows from the corner of the Savior's mouth, and his tongue comes out of the corner of his mouth to remove it. But, O, the sight of that tongue! The three are stunned by the look of it. It is red and the color of unimaginable wine; its texture is that of silk. It is as if they are seeing their own loved hearts before their eyes. And though the tongue only comes out for a moment, it seems to them that the memory of its appearance is as real as the beautiful tongue itself, lasting for long agonizing moments before their eyes.

"That ought to be enough," the middle one says, and he goes out to tell the guard that they have finished. But the guard answers him in amazement: "Why, you just now walked in there! You've only been in there about ten seconds!" Embarrassed, the middle one returns and tells the others. The dwarf keeps working at the crown of thorns.

Now the three put their heads together, and while they are talking Jesus gazes out through the small window to his left in the upper wall. The first thing he sees is a bit of cloth, high in the sky, which is falling, taking on the shape of a small cape as it flutters down toward the earth. And then, from behind a hill in the distance, he sees Hound rising in an aura of blue light, flying free, needing no cape, higher than the two of them have ever flown before, gracefully lifting up in the distance. The cape comes to a fluttering rest on the edge of a cloud bank; it appears to him as a mere dot of blue on the low clouds. Then the body of Hound enters the bottom of the cloud. And when he emerges from the top of it, and as if on a whimsy, he reaches out with his teeth as he passes the cape and grasps it; he throws the cape with his head, spinning it onto his shoulders. And then the vision of the dog diminishes as he enters the higher clouds, his cape rippling around his shoulders.

They decide to dress him up like a woman and to make him dance. There are women's clothes in the wicker chest, and they take them out and put them over his body. He is dressed now in a long blue gown that is cinctured in the Empire fashion, high up under the bodice; they put a blue veil, like a babushka, over his head. "Now dance for us, harlot," one of them says, and they push him and poke him before he can begin. And then he is humble before them, and he begins to dance.

They laugh at his copy of feminine movement, and when he circles around the pillar and comes close to the table at which they sit, they throw jibes at him, and spit upon him, and throw pieces of hair and flesh from the dog's head into his face.

But then his dance begins to take on a pattern. And when this happens, the bodice of his gown seems to fill up with substance. (They assume it is air caused by his movement, but it looks, uncomfortably, like flesh.)

The dance is a minuet, and the Savior dances as if he were moving with a partner. His gestures are exact and perfect. When he raises his hand in the air, it is as if there were another hand within it, the hand of the masculine partner, turning him, in a pirouette and a bow. And as he dances his gown spreads out from his feet; it takes on the shape of a full dress with a hoop; behind him seems to appear a bustle. The veil takes on the shape of a delicate mantilla, rising, shaping itself over his head.

And soon they are not laughing and spitting, but just sitting and watching. And then they begin to hear music, of a kind they have never heard before: stringed instruments, and brasses, a harpsichord and cello. They sit that way for an hour, transfixed by the Savior's motions; even the modest room seems to take on an elegance in their minds, and it is only a light cough from the dwarf that brings them back to themselves, each a little unnerved, a little abstracted.

"You pig!" the large one screams, and slashes at Jesus with his knife. "Give me some salt!" he yells, and begins to slash at the Master's arms, rubbing the salt into the wounds. "I'll teach you to dance! I'll give you something to dance about!" And tying him back to the pillar, he begins to kick the Master's shins and knees.

But though the Master groans at the pain, he remains constant; the expression on his face is still placid, his smile—neither a grimace of pain nor ironic comment—is a smile, unmistakably, of love.

"The pig," the large one grunts under his breath. "I'll show you what pain is." And then he places his own hand flat upon the table and severs his own index finger with the knife. He throws the severed finger at Jesus.

"You see how tough we are," says the small one. "Watch how I strike myself." He extends his hand out from his shoulder, forms a fist and strikes out at his own face. But while he is doing this, he is looking into the eyes of Jesus, and his hand stops a fraction of an inch before his nose. The next time he tries to strike himself, his head lurches back before the fist can strike him. And then he moves to the wall, and places the back of his head against it. This time he looks at a spot on the wall just to the left of the Savior's head, and when he strikes at himself he shatters the bones in his nose. "He sees now," he whistles in pain through his crushed face. "Now he shall shudder in fear." And the three surround Jesus with their knives and begin to move closer to him. "Ahem," the dwarf says, "remember, you must not kill him."

And the three slack off a bit, considering what they can do to humiliate him. They go to the wicker backet and look into it. "Whips?" the middle one asks. "What the hell good are whips?" says the large one. "We've already tried cuts and salt." "Wait," says the small one, "maybe it's time now." And he goes out and says to the guard, "Is it time yet?" But again the guard is amazed by the question. "Time yet? Why you've only been in there for twenty seconds!" And the man is embarrassed again, and goes back inside.

And then the three begin to mutilate themselves even more. They strike each other with whips; they cut pieces of flesh from their bodies and pour salt into their own wounds; they grasp their own genitals and twist them until they scream. And constantly they watch Jesus while they are doing these terrible things, but the Master expresses no hint of fear for them to see.

And then, after a while, Jesus takes pity upon them and utters his first words to them: "It's time," he says, and the small one rushes out to the guard and asks him. "Yes, it's almost time," the guard says. And the small one returns to the others and tells them: "It's almost time." "How about a little refreshment?" the dwarf says, and from under his cloak he produces a small flask of liquid. And the three drink from it, and they even offer some of it to Jesus, but he declines to take it, and the three look at him with worried looks on their faces. And he speaks to them, saying, "Do not be fearful. I shall hang my head as I go out; come now and spit upon me some more, that the humiliation shall be visible when I go out." And the three approach him, and gently they spit upon him, and each, as they come close to him, touches at the purple cloak they have put around him, and the large one whispers to him and says, "Master, forgive me." And Jesus answers him, saying, "It is nothing; I forgive you." Then the three return to their seats, feeling suddenly exhausted, and they each fall into a deep sleep; their heads gather around the mutilated head of the dog on the table top.

"Well now," the dwarf says. "That was very good, very good indeed. But it is not over, and what I have here will certainly teach you something. For I am the devil, you know, and it will be a pretty thing to consider that I, the devil, shall be crowning the Savior of Man with a wreath of thorns!"

And then he produces the wreath; each thorn is exactly one inch from its neighbor, and the length of each is exactly one half inch. And he loosens the Savior's bonds and offers him a seat at the base of the salt pillar. And Jesus sits down as the devil requests, and then the dwarf places the crown upon the Savior's head, pressing it into the scalp. But the thorns refuse to penetrate, and the dwarf removes the crown. And then he proceeds to separate the hair in a circular part on the Savior's head, in order to allow a place for the thorns to enter the scalp. Maybe the Master's hair was the problem. And then he again places the crown on the Master's head, and placing the weight of his small bent body upon it and whispering "Hail, King of the Jews" into the Master's ear, he thrusts the crown down into the Master's scalp. But again the thorns refuse to penetrate; the head seems as hard as iron. And the dwarf climbs upon the Master's knees. He stands on his knees, the Master's head at his waist, and pushes downward with all his might, in order to force the crown onto the head of Jesus. And as he presses, the crown gives a little; a few of the thorns buckle and bend away from the perfect circle. "Pig!" the dwarf screeches, jumps down from the Master's lap, and then goes back to the table and straightens the thorns out. But as he is doing this he catches the eye of the Master upon him, and he sees the irony of his smile. And then in disgust the dwarf casts the crown into the air, but it does not fall to the ground. Instead, the crown hovers and floats in the air over the Master's head, and a blue aura of light gathers around it. And then it gently descends onto the line of the circular part, and the scalp opens to allow the thorns to enter; and before the dwarf rushes out of the room, he sees the eight perfect lines of blood. They flow at exactly the same pace, down the forehead and across the placid face of Jesus.

PLUTONIAN ODE

ALLEN GINSBERG

I

What new element before us unborn in nature? Is there a new
    thing under the Sun?
At last inquisitive Whitman a modern epic, detonative, Scientific
    theme
First penned unmindful by Doctor Seaborg with poisonous hand,
    named for Death's planet through the sea beyond Uranus
whose chthonic ore fathers this magma-teared Lord of Hades, Sire
    of avenging Furies, billionaire Hell-King worshipped once
with black sheep throats cut, priest's face averted from underground
    mysteries in a single temple at Eleusis,
Spring-green Persephone nuptialed to his inevitable Shade, Demeter
    mother of asphodel weeping dew,
her daughter stored in salty caverns under white snow, black hail,
    gray winter rain or Polar ice, immemorable seasons before
Fish flew in Heaven, before a Ram died by the starry bush, before
    the Bull stamped sky and earth
or Twins inscribed their memories in cuneiform clay or Crab'd flood
    washed memory from the skull, or Lion sniffed the lilac breeze in
    Eden—
Before the Great Year began turning its twelve signs, ere constella-
    tions wheeled for twenty-four thousand sunny years
slowly round their axis in Sagittarius, one hundred sixty-seven thou-
    sand times returning to this night

Radioactive Nemesis were you there at the beginning black Dumb
tongueless unsmelling blast of Disillusion?

I manifest your Baptismal Word after four billion years

I guess your birthday in Earthling Night, I salute your dreadful
presence lasting majestic as the Gods,

Sabaot, Jehova, Astapheus, Adonaeus, Elohim, Iao, Ialdabaoth,
Aeon from Aeon born ignorant in an Abyss of Light,

Sophia's reflections glittering thoughtful galaxies, whirlpools of star-
spume silver-thin as hairs of Einstein!

Father Whitman I celebrate a matter that renders Self oblivion!

Grand Subject that annihilates inky hands & pages' prayers, old
orators' inspired Immortalities,

I begin your chant, openmouthed exhaling into spacious sky over
silent mills at Hanford, Savannah River, Rocky Flats, Pantex,
Burlington, Albuquerque

I yell thru Washington, South Carolina, Colorado, Texas, Iowa,
New Mexico,

where nuclear reactors create a new Thing under the Sun, where
Rockwell war-plants fabricate this death stuff trigger in nitro-
gen baths,

Hanger-Silas Mason assembles the terrified weapon secret by ten
thousand, & where Manzano Mountain boasts to store

its dreadful decay through two hundred forty millennia while our
Galaxy spirals around its nebulous core.

I enter your secret places with my mind, I speak with your presence, I roar your Lion Roar with mortal mouth.

One microgram inspired to one lung, ten pounds of heavy metal
dust adrift slow motion over gray Alps

the breadth of the planet, how long before your radiance speeds
blight and death to sentient beings?

Enter my body or not I carol my spirit inside you, Unapproachable
Weight,

O heavy heavy Element awakened I vocalize your consciousness to
six worlds

I chant your absolute Vanity. Yeah monster of Anger birthed in fear
O most

Ignorant matter ever created unnatural to Earth! Delusion of metal
empires!

Destroyer of lying Scientists! Devourer of covetous Generals, In-
cinerator of Armies & Melter of Wars!

Judgment of judgments, Divine Wind over vengeful nations, Mo-
lester of Presidents, Death-Scandal of Capital politics! Ah
civilizations stupidly industrious!

Canker-Hex on multitudes learned or illiterate! Manufactured Spectre of human reason! O solidified imago of practitioners in
Black Arts

I dare your Reality, I challenge your very being! I publish your
cause and effect!

I turn the Wheel of Mind on your three hundred tons! Your name
enters mankind's ear! I embody your ultimate powers!

My oratory advances on your vaunted Mystery! This breath dispels
your braggart fears! I sing your form at last

behind your concrete & iron walls inside your fortress of rubber &
translucent silicon shields in filtered cabinets and baths of
lathe oil,

My voice resounds through robot glove boxes & ingot cans and
echoes in electric vaults inert of atmosphere,

I enter with spirit out loud into your fuel rod drums underground
on soundless thrones and beds of lead

O density! This weightless anthem trumpets transcendent through
hidden chambers and breaks through iron doors into the Infernal Room!

Over your dreadful vibration this measured harmony floats audible,
these jubilant tones are honey and milk and wine-sweet water

Poured on the stone block floor, these syllables are barley groats I
scatter on the Rector's core,

I call your name with hollow vowels, I psalm your Fate close by,
my breath near deathless ever at your side

to Spell your destiny, I set this verse prophetic on your mausoleum
walls to seal you up Eternally with Diamond Truth! O doomed
Plutonium.

II

The Bard surveys Plutonian history from midnight lit with Mercury
Vapor streetlamps till in dawn's early light

he contemplates a tranquil politic spaced out between Nations'
thought-forms proliferating bureaucratic

& horrific arm'd, Satanic industries projected sudden with Five
 Hundred Billion Dollar Strength
around the world same time this text is set in Boulder, Colorado
 before front range of Rocky Mountains
twelve miles north of Rocky Flats Nuclear Facility in United States
 on North America, Western Hemisphere
of planet Earth six months and fourteen days around our Solar System in a Spiral Galaxy
the local year after Dominion of the last God nineteen hundred
 seventy eight
Completed as yellow hazed dawn clouds brighten East, Denver city
 white below
Blue sky transparent rising empty deep & spacious to a morning
 star high over the balcony
above some autos sat with wheels to curb downhill from Flatiron's
 jagged pine ridge,
sunlit mountain meadows sloped to rust-red sandstone cliffs above
 brick townhouse roofs
as sparrows waked whistling through Marine Street's summer green
 leafed trees.

III
This ode to you O Poets and Orators to come, you father Whitman
 as I join your side, you Congress and American people,
you present mediators, spiritual friends & teachers, you O Master
 of the Diamond Arts,
Take this wheel of syllables in hand, these vowels and consonants
 to breath's end
take this inhalation of black poison to your heart, breathe out this
 blessing from your breast on our creation
forests cities oceans deserts rocky flats and mountains in the Ten
 Directions pacify with this exhalation,
enrich this Plutonian Ode to explode its empty thunder through
 earthen thought-worlds
Magnetize this howl with heartless compassion, destroy this mountain of Plutonium with ordinary mind and body speech,
thus empower this Mind-guard spirit gone out, gone out, gone
 beyond, gone beyond me, Wake space, so Ah!

FOUR POEMS

JONATHAN WILLIAMS

O FOR A MUSE OF FIRE!

Date: Tuesday, May 13, 1958—
      a date previously memorable in history for the birth of
      Joe Louis (1914),
      the Empress Maria Theresa (1717)
      and the beheading of
      Johan Van Olden Barnveldt (1619)

Place: Wrigley Field, Chicago, Illinois

Time: 3:06 p.m.; warm and sunny; breeze steady, right to left

Attendance: 5,692 (paid)

Situation: top of the 6th; Cardinals trailing the Cubs, 3–1;
      one out; Gene Green on 2nd

Public Address: "Batting for Jones, #6, Stan Musial!"

The Muse muscles up; Stan the Man stands in . . . and
O, Hosanna, Hosanna, Ozanna's boy, Moe Drabowsky, comes in

2 and 2
"a curve ball, outside corner, higher

than intended—
I figured he's hit it in the ground"

(*"it felt fine!"*)

a line shot to left, down the line,
rolling deep for a double . . .

(*"it felt fine!"*)

Say, Stan, baby, how's it feel to hit 3000?

"Uh, it feels fine"

BEA HENSLEY HAMMERS AN IRON CHINQUAPIN LEAF
ON HIS ANVIL NEAR SPRUCE PINE, NORTH CAROLINA
& COGITATES ON THE NATURE OF TWO BEAUTY SPOTS

in the Linville Gorge I
know this place

now it's a rock wall
you look up
it's covered in punktatum all
the way to Heaven

that's a
sight

•

up on Smoky
you ease up at daybust

and see the first
light in the tops of the tulip trees

now boys that just naturally
grinds and polishes
the soul

make it
normal
again

I mean it's really
pretty!

MY QUAKER-ATHEIST FRIEND, WHO HAS COME TO THIS
MEETING-HOUSE SINCE 1913,
SMOKES
& LOOKS OUT OVER THE RAWTHEY TO HOLME FELL:

what do you do
anything for?

you do it
for what the medievals would call
something like
the *Glory of God*

doing it for money,
that doesn't do it;

doing it for vanity,
that doesn't do it;

doing it to justify a disorderly life,
that doesn't do it

Look at Brigflatts Meeting here . . .

it represents the best
that the people were able to do

they didn't do it for gain;
in fact, they must have
taken a loss

whether it is a stone next to a stone
or a word next to a word,
it is the *glory*—
the simple craft of it

and money and sex aren't worth
bugger-all, not
bugger-all . . .

solid, common, *vulgar* words

the ones you can touch,
the ones that yield

and a respect for the music . . .

what else can you tell 'em?

A FEW CLERIHEWS

Never read James Dickey
when the weather's hot and icky.

The time for dickey-dunkin
's when de frost is on de punkin.

Gertrude Stein
arose at nine

and arose and arose
and arose

A.E. Housman
translates very well in German.

One germane example: "With rue my barb is laden
for dishy boys in loden."

Ezra Loomis Pound
bought a lb

of Idaho potatoes
(the Hailey Comet always ate those).

Both bodacious & humongous
was large Charles Mingus.

On both mouth & bass
—he played his ass!

John Blow
was below

par when he wrote "Cloe Found Amintas Lying
On a Pile of Swedes Near Dorking."

NIGHT-SEA JOURNEY

JOHN BARTH

"One way or another, no matter which theory of our journey is correct, it's myself I address; to whom I rehearse as to a stranger our history and condition, and will disclose my secret hope though I sink for it.

"Is the journey my invention? Do the night, the sea, exist at all, I ask myself, apart from my experience of them? Do I myself exist, or is this a dream? Sometimes I wonder. And if I am, who am I? The Heritage I supposedly transport? But how can I be both vessel and contents? Such are the questions that beset my intervals of rest.

"My trouble is, I lack conviction. Many accounts of our situation seem plausible to me—where and what we are, why we swim and whither. But implausible ones as well, perhaps especially those, I must admit as possibly correct. Even likely. If at times, in certain humors—stroking in unison, say, with my neighbors and chanting with them 'Onward! Upward!'—I have supposed that we have after all a common Maker, Whose nature and motives we may not know, but Who engendered us in some mysterious wise and launched us forth toward some end known but to Him—if (for a moodslength only) I have been able to entertain such notions, very popular in certain quarters, it is because our night-sea journey partakes of their absurdity. One might even say: I can believe them *because* they are absurd.

"Has that been said before?

"Another paradox: it appears to be these recesses from swim-

ming that sustain me in the swim. Two measures onward and upward, flailing with the rest, then I float exhausted and dispirited,
brood upon the night, the sea, the journey, while the flood bears
me a measure back and down: slow progress, but I live, I live, and
make my way, aye, past many a drownèd comrade in the end,
stronger, worthier than I, victims of their unremitting *joie de nager*.
I have seen the best swimmers of my generation go under. Number-
less the number of the dead! Thousands drown as I think this
thought, millions as I rest before returning to the swim. And scores,
hundreds of millions have expired since we surged forth, brave in
our innocence, upon our dreadful way. 'Love! Love!' we sang then,
a quarter-billion strong, and churned the warm sea white with joy
of swimming! Now all are gone down—the buoyant, the sodden,
leaders and followers, all gone under, while wretched I swim on.
Yet these same reflective intervals that keep me afloat have led me
into wonder, doubt, despair—strange emotions for a swimmer!—
have led me, even, to suspect . . . that our night-sea journey is
without meaning.

"Indeed, if I have yet to join the hosts of the suicides, it is because (fatigue apart) I find it no meaningfuller to drown myself
than to go on swimming.

"I know that there are those who seem actually to enjoy the
night-sea; who claim to love swimming for its own sake, or sin-
cerely believe that 'reaching the Shore,' 'transmitting the heritage'
(*Whose* Heritage, I'd like to know? And to whom?) is worth the
staggering cost. I do not. Swimming itself I find at best not actively
unpleasant, more often tiresome, not infrequently a torment. Argu-
ments from function and design don't impress me: granted that we
can and do swim, that in a manner of speaking our long tails and
streamlined heads are 'meant for' swimming; it by no means follows—for me, at least—that we *should* swim, or otherwise endeavor
to 'fulfill our destiny.' Which is to say, Someone Else's destiny, since
ours, so far as I can see, is merely to perish, one way or another,
soon or late. The heartless zeal of our (departed) leaders, like the
blind ambition and good cheer of my own youth, appalls me now;
for the death of my comrades I am inconsolable. If the night-sea
journey has justification, it is not for us swimmers ever to discover it.

"Oh, to be sure, 'Love!' one heard on every side: 'Love it is that
drives and sustains us!' I translate: we don't know *what* drives and

sustains us, only that we are most miserably driven and, imperfectly, sustained. *Love* is how we call our ignorance of what whips us. 'To reach the Shore,' then: but what if the Shore exists in the fancies of us swimmers merely, who dream it to account for the dreadful fact that we swim, have always and only swum, and continue swimming without respite (myself excepted) until we die? Supposing even that there *were* a Shore—that, as a cynical companion of mine once imagined, we rise from the drowned to discover all those vulgar superstitions and exalted metaphors to be literal truth: the giant Maker of us all, the Shores of Light beyond our night-sea journey!—whatever would a swimmer do there? The fact is, when we imagine the Shore, what comes to mind is just the opposite of our condition: no more night, no more sea, no more journeying. In short, the blissful estate of the drowned.

"'Ours not to stop and think; ours but to swim and sink. . . .' Because a moment's thought reveals the pointlessness of swimming. 'No matter,' I've heard some say, even as they gulped their last: 'The night-sea journey may be absurd, but here we swim, will-we nill-we, against the flood, onward and upward, toward a Shore that may not exist and couldn't be reached if it did.' The thoughtful swimmer's choices, then, they say, are two: give over thrashing and go under for good, or embrace the absurdity; affirm in and for itself the night-sea journey; swim on with neither motive nor destination, for the sake of swimming, and compassionate moreover with your fellow swimmer, we being all at sea and equally in the dark. I find neither course acceptable. If not even the hypothetical Shore can justify a sea-full of drownèd comrades, to speak of the swim-in-itself as somehow doing so strikes me as obscene. I continue to swim—but only because blind habit, blind instinct, blind fear of drowning are still more strong than the horror of our journey. And if on occasion I have assisted a fellow-thrasher, joined in the cheers and songs, even passed along to others strokes of genius from the drownèd great, it's that I shrink by temperament from making myself conspicuous. To paddle off in one's own direction, assert one's independent right-of-way, overrun one's fellows without compunction, or dedicate oneself entirely to pleasures and diversions without regard for conscience—I can't finally condemn those who journey in this wise; in half my moods I envy them and despise the weak vitality that keeps me from following their example. But in

reasonabler moments I remind myself that it's their very freedom
and self-responsibility I reject, as more dramatically absurd, in our
senseless circumstances, than tailing along in conventional fashion.
Suicides, rebels, affirmers of the paradox—nay-sayers and yea-sayers
alike to our fatal journey—I finally shake my head at them. And
splash sighing past their corpses, one by one, as past a hundred
sorts of others: friends, enemies, brothers; fools, sages, brutes—and
nobodies, million upon million. I envy them all.

"A poor irony: that I, who find abhorrent and tautological the
doctrine of survival of the fittest (*fitness* meaning, in my experience, nothing more than survival-ability, a talent whose only demonstration is the fact of survival, but whose chief ingredients seem
to be strength, guile, callousness), may be the sole remaining swimmer! But the doctrine is false as well as repellent: Chance drowns
the worthy with the unworthy, bears up the unfit with the fit by
whatever definition, and makes the night-sea journey essentially
haphazard as well as murderous and unjustified.

" 'You only swim once.' Why bother, then?

" 'Except ye drown, ye shall not reach the Shore of Life.' Poppy-
cock.

"One of my late companions—that same cynic with the curious
fancy, among the first to drown—entertained us with odd conjectures while we waited to begin our journey. A favorite theory of
his was that the Father does exist, and did indeed make us and the
sea we swim—but not a-purpose or even consciously; He made us,
as it were, despite Himself, as we make waves with every tail-
thrash, and may be unaware of our existence. Another was that He
knows we're here but doesn't care what happens to us, inasmuch as
He creates (voluntarily or not) others seas and swimmers at more
or less regular intervals. In bitterer moments, such as just before he
drowned, my friend even supposed that our Maker wished us un-
made; there was indeed a Shore, he'd argue, which could save at
least some of us from drowning and toward which it was our function to struggle—but for reasons unknowable to us He wanted desperately to prevent our reaching that happy place and fulfilling our
destiny. Our 'Father,' in short, was our adversary and would-be
killer! No less outrageous, and offensive to traditional opinion, were
the fellow's speculations on the nature of our Maker: that He might
well be no swimmer Himself at all, but some sort of monstrosity,

perhaps even tailless; that He might be stupid, malicious, insensible, perverse, or asleep and dreaming; that the end for which He created and launched us forth, and which we flagellate ourselves to fathom, was perhaps immoral, even obscene. Et cetera, et cetera: there was no end to the chap's conjectures, or the impoliteness of his fancy; I have reason to suspect that his early demise, whether planned by 'our Maker' or not, was expedited by certain fellow-swimmers indignant at his blasphemies.

"In other moods, however (he was as given to moods as I), his theorizing would become half-serious, so it seemed to me, especially upon the subjects of Fate and Immortality, to which our youthful conversations often turned. Then his harangues, if no less fantastical, grew solemn and obscure, and if he was still baiting us, his passion undid the joke. His objection to popular opinions of the hereafter, he would declare, was their claim to general validity. Why need believers hold that *all* the drowned rise to be judged at journey's end, and nonbelievers that drowning is final without exception? In *his* opinion (so he'd vow at least), nearly everyone's fate was permanent death; indeed he took a sour pleasure in supposing that every 'Maker' made thousands of separate seas in His creative lifetime, each populated like ours with millions of swimmers, and that in almost every instance both sea and swimmers were utterly annihilated, whether accidentally or by malevolent design. (Nothing if not pluralistical, he imagined there might be millions and billions of 'Fathers,' perhaps in some 'night-sea' of their own!) However—and here he turned infidels against him with the faithful—he professed to believe that in possibly a single night-sea per thousand, say, one of its quarter-billion swimmers (that is, one swimmer in two hundred fifty billions) achieved a qualified immortality. In some cases the rate might be slightly higher; in others it was vastly lower, for just as there are swimmers of every degree of proficiency, including some who drown before the journey starts, unable to swim at all, and others created drowned, as it were, so he imagined what can only be termed impotent Creators, Makers unable to Make, as well as uncommonly fertile ones and all grades between. And it pleased him to deny any necessary relation between a Maker's productivity and His other virtues—including, even, the quality of His creatures.

"I could go on (*he* surely did) with his elaboration of these mad notions—such as that swimmers in other night-seas needn't be of our kind; that Makers themselves might belong to different *species,* so to speak; that our particular Maker mightn't Himself be immortal, or that we might be not only His emissaries but His 'immortality,' continuing His life and our own, transmogrified, beyond our individual deaths. Even this modified immortality (meaningless to me) he conceived as relative and contingent, subject to accidental or deliberate termination: his pet hypothesis was that Makers and swimmers *each generate the other*—against all odds, their number being so great—and that any given 'immortality-chain' could terminate after any number of cycles, so that what was 'immortal' (still speaking relatively) was only the cyclic process of incarnation, which itself might have a beginning and an end. Alternatively he liked to imagine cycles within cycles, either finite or infinite: for example, the 'night-sea,' as it were, in which Makers 'swam' and created night-seas and swimmers like ourselves, might be the creation of a larger Maker, Himself one of many, Who in turn et cetera. Time itself he regarded as relative to our experience, like magnitude: who knew but what, with each thrash of our tails, minuscule seas and swimmers, whole eternities, came to pass—as ours, perhaps, and our Maker's Maker's, was elapsing between the strokes of some supertail, in a slower order of time?

"Naturally I hooted with the others at this nonsense. We were young then, and had only the dimmest notion of what lay ahead; in our ignorance we imagined night-sea journeying to be a positively heroic enterprise. Its meaning and value we never questioned; to be sure, some must go down by the way, a pity no doubt, but to win a race requires that others lose, and like all my fellows I took for granted that I would be the winner. We milled and swarmed, impatient to be off, never mind where or why, only to try our youth against the realities of night and sea; if we indulged the skeptic at all, it was as a droll, half-contemptible mascot. When he died in the initial slaughter, no one cared.

"And even now I don't subscribe to all his views—but I no longer scoff. The horror of our history has purged me of opinions, as of vanity, confidence, spirit, charity, hope, vitality, everything—except dull dread and a kind of melancholy, stunned persistence. What leads me to recall his fancies is my growing suspicion that I, of all swimmers, may be the sole survivor of this fell journey, tale-bearer of a generation. This suspicion, together with the recent sea-change, suggests to me now that nothing is impossible, not even my late companion's wildest visions, and brings me to a certain desperate resolve, the point of my chronicling.

"Very likely I have lost my senses. The carnage at our setting out; our decimation by whirlpool, poisoned cataract, sea-convulsion; the panic stampedes, mutinies, slaughters, mass suicides; the mounting evidence that none will survive the journey—add to these anguish and fatigue; it were a miracle if sanity stayed afloat. Thus I admit, with the other possibilities, that the present sweetening and calming of the sea, and what seems to be a kind of vasty presence, song, or summons from the near upstream, may be hallucinations of disordered sensibilty. . . .

"Perhaps, even, I am drowned already. Surely I was never meant for the rough-and-tumble of the swim; not impossibly I perished at the outset and have only imaged the night-sea journey from some final deep. In any case, I'm no longer young, and it is we spent old swimmers, disabused of every illusion, who are most vulnerable to dreams.

"Sometimes I think I am my drownèd friend.

"Out with it: I've begun to believe, not only that *She* exists, but that She lies not far ahead, and stills the sea, and draws me Herward! Aghast, I recollect his maddest notion: that our destination (which existed, mind, in but one night-sea out of hundreds and thousands) was no Shore, as commonly conceived, but a mysterious being, indescribable except by paradox and vaguest figure: wholly different from us swimmers, yet our complement; the death of us, yet our salvation and resurrection; simultaneously our journey's end, mid-point, and commencement; not membered and thrashing like us, but a motionless or hugely gliding sphere of unimaginable dimension; self-contained, yet dependent absolutely, in some wise, upon the chance (always monstrously improbable) that one of us will survive the night-sea journey and reach . . . Her! *Her,* he called it, or *She,* which is to say, Other-than-a-he. I shake my head; the thing is too preposterous; it is myself I talk to, to keep my reason in this awful darkness. There is no She! There is no You! I rave to myself; it's Death alone that hears and summons. To the drowned, all seas are calm. . . .

"Listen: my friend maintained that in every order of creation there are two sorts of creators, contrary yet complementary, one of which gives rise to seas and swimmers, the other to the Night-which-contains-the-sea and to What-waits-at-the-journey's-end: the former, in short, to destiny, the latter to destination (and both prof-ligately, involuntarily, perhaps indifferently or unwittingly). The 'purpose' of the night-sea journey—but not necessarily of the jour-neyer or of either Maker!—my friend could describe only in abstrac-tions: *consummation, transfiguration, union of contraries, transcen-sion of categories.* When we laughed, he would shrug and admit that he understood the business no better than we, and thought it ridiculous, dreary, possibly obscene. 'But one of you,' he'd add with his wry smile, 'may be the Hero destined to complete the night-sea journey and be one with Her. Chances are, of course, you won't make it.' He himself, he declared, was not even going to try; the whole idea repelled him; if we chose to dismiss it as an ugly fiction, so much the better for us; thrash, splash, and be merry, we were soon enough drowned. But there it was, he could not say how he knew or why he bothered to tell us, any more than he could say what would happen after She and Hero, Shore and Swimmer, 'merged identities' to become something both and neither. He quite agreed with me that if the issue of that magical union had no mem-ory of the night-sea journey, for example, it enjoyed a poor sort of immortality; even poorer if, as he rather imagined, a swimmer-hero plus a She equaled or became merely another Maker of future night-seas and the rest, at such incredible expense of life. This be-ing the case—he was persuaded it was—the merciful thing to do was refuse to participate; the genuine heroes, in his opinion, were the suicides, and the hero of heroes would be the swimmer who, in the very presence of the Other, refused Her proffered 'immortality' and thus put an end to at least one cycle of catastrophes.

"How we mocked him! Our moment came, we hurtled forth, pre-tending to glory in the adventure, thrashing, singing, cursing, stran-gling, rationalizing, rescuing, killing, inventing rules and stories and relationships, giving up, struggling on, but dying all, and still in darkness, until only a battered remnant was left to croak 'Onward, upward,' like a bitter echo. Then they too fell silent—victims, I can only presume, of the last frightful wave—and the moment came when I also, utterly desolate and spent, thrashed my last and gave myself over to the current, to sink or float as might be, but swim no more. Whereupon, marvelous to tell, in an instant the sea grew still! Then warmly, gently, the great tide turned, began to bear me, as it does now, onward and upward will-I nill-I, like a flood of joy—and I recalled with dismay my dead friend's teaching.

"I am not deceived. This new emotion is Her doing; the desire that possesses me is Her bewitchment. Lucidity passes from me; in a moment I'll cry 'Love!' bury myself in Her side, and be 'transfigured.' Which is to say, I die already; this fellow transported by passion is not I; *I am he who abjures and rejects the night-sea journey!* I . . . .

"I am all love. 'Come!' She whispers, and I have no will.

"You who I may be about to become, whatever You are: with the last twitch of my real self I beg You to listen. It is *not* love that sustains me! No; though Her magic makes me burn to sing the contrary, and though I drown even now for the blasphemy, I will say truth. What has fetched me across this dreadful sea is a single hope, gift of my poor dead comrade: that You may be stronger-willed than I, and that by sheer force of concentration I may transmit to You, along with Your official Heritage, a private legacy of awful recollection and negative resolve. Mad as it may be, my dream is that some unimaginable embodiment of myself (or myself plus Her if that's how it must be) will come to find itself expressing, in however garbled or radical a translation, some reflection of these reflections. If against all odds this comes to pass, may You to whom, through whom I speak, do what I cannot: terminate this aimless, brutal business! Stop Your hearing against Her song! Hate love!

"Still alive, afloat, afire. Farewell then my penultimate hope: that one may be sunk for direct blasphemy on the very shore of the Shore. Can it be (my old friend would smile) that only utterest nay-sayers survive the night? But even that were Sense, and there is no sense, only senseless love, senseless death. Whoever echoes these reflections: be more couragous than their author! An end to night-sea journeys! Make no more! And forswear me when I shall forswear myself, deny myself, plunge into Her who summons, singing . . .

" 'Love! Love! Love!' "

TWO POEMS

ROBERT DUNCAN

ACHILLES' SONG

I do not know more than the Sea tells me,
told me long ago,   or I overheard Her
        telling distant roar upon the sands,
waves of meaning in the cradle of whose
        sounding and resounding power I
slept.

        Manchild,   She sang

—or was it a storm uplifting the night
        into a moving wall in which
I was carried as if a mothering nest had
        been made in dread?

the wave of a life darker than my
        life before me sped,   and I,
larger than I was,   grown dark as
        the shoreless depth,
arose from myself,   shaking the last
        light of the sun
from me.

        Manchild,   She said,

Come back to the shores of what you are.
Come back to the crumbling shores.

All night
the mothering tides in which your
        life first formd in the brooding
light   have quencht the bloody
        splendors of the sun

and, under the triumphant processions
        of the moon,   lay down
thunder upon thunder of an old
        longing,   the beat

of whose repeated spell
        consumes you.

                        Thetis, then,
        my mother, has promised me
the mirage of a boat,   a vehicle
        of water within the water,
and my soul would return from
        the trials of its human state,
from the long siege, from the
        struggling companions upon the plain,
from the burning towers and deeds
        of honor and dishonor,
the deeper unsatisfied war beneath
        and behind the declared war,
and the rubble of beautiful,   patiently
        workt   moonstones, agates, jades, obsidians,

turnd and returnd in the wash of
        the tides,   the gleaming waste,
        the pathetic wonder,

words turnd in the phrases of song
        before our song . . . or are they

beautiful,   patiently workt   remembrances of those
        long gone from me,

returnd anew,   ghostly in the light
          of the moon,   old faces?

For Thetis, my mother, has promised
          me a boat,
a lover,   an up-lifter of my spirit
          into the rage of my first element
rising,   a princedom
          in the unreal,   a share in Death.

          ✿

Time, time. It's time.

The business of Troy has long been done.

Achilles in Leuke has come home.

And soon you too   will be alone.

                    —December 10, 1968

[NOTE: In our Anglo-American convention we would pronounce the diphthong in *Leuke* to foreshadow the rime in the word *you*—but in my hearing of the line, remembering the voice of H.D.'s reading from her *Helen in Egypt,* the name *Leuke* came to me sounded as in the German convention to echo the diphthong in *Troy.*]

A SONG FROM THE STRUCTURES OF RIME RINGING
AS THE POET PAUL CELAN SINGS:

Something has wreckt the world I am in

I think   I have wreckt
          the world I am in.

It is beautiful. From my wreckage
    this world   returns
to restore me,   overcomes its identity in me.

Nothing has wreckt the world I am in.
    It is nothing
in the world that has
    workt   this
wreckage of me   or my "world" I mean

the possibility of no thing so
    being there.

It is totally untranslatable.

Something is there that is it. Must
    be   nothing ultimately   no
thing.   In the formula derived
    as I go
the something is   Nothing   I know
obscured in the proposition of No-thingness.

    It is Nothing that has
wreckt the world I am in so that it is
    beautiful,   Nothing in me

    being
beyond the world I am in
    something
in the world longs for

    nothing there.

from THE STRUCTURALIST

DAVID ANTIN

       and while i sympathize with the taste and motivation
for the commonness of autobiography as the commonness of our
  lives and our world   and to some extent share it   i have a
deep distrust of the plausible   and i suspect that what we
have most in common is the profound singularity and implausible
   detail of our generally common lives   and for that reason
i want to tell you something of the life of my friend nasi
      the only true structuralist i ever really knew   whose
life was not particularly plausible or common   but whose
singularity was common to structuralism and may reveal
  something about it that is nevertheless fundamentally true
            now i dont like to say this because it sounds
very colorful and implausible   but nasi was a red headed
dwarf whose real name was either athanasius or anastasius
  and he was either polish or greek   i was never quite sure
  because he spoke both languages fluently as he spoke
twenty-five or six other languages as well   most of the ones
i knew with a distinctive and curious accent i was never
  able to place with any certainty between the aegean and the
baltic seas   he may as i once heard have been brought up
 in kars among turkish speaking armenians by a polish mother and
a greek father   and this is all very colorful but a lot of
the color is in how you say it   because nasi   as everyone
called him   was either a tall dwarf or a very short and

194

muscular little person
                              the first time i met him was in the
gym of the west twenty-third street y   i was working for a
publishing company on twenty-third over by fourth avenue and i
used to come early in the morning to swim before going on to
work   that morning i couldnt quite wake up in the water and
i walked into the gym to try working out on the mats when i
saw this little red bearded fellow rushing up the ropes his
body held neatly in an "L"   he did this several times
finished by dropping to the mat on which he did three
successive back flips followed by three forward flips clapped
his hands in satisfaction and started for the locker room
when i expressed my admiration he smiled and said
"body is image of god   needs daily polishing" and walked
away
the next time i ran into nasi was in a translation
agency conference held some place in murray hill   it turned
out he was one of the people working for alexander gode
translating scientific articles from a number of european
languages into interlingua   a kind of synthetic pan romance
language with a simplified grammar designed by a bunch of
linguists for international scientific communication   gode
was one of its inventors and president of the interlingua
institute   which he ran out of a village office along with his
translating agency   for which nasi also translated technical
articles mainly from czech and polish and russian
                                                    he smiled when
he saw me and came across the room to shake my hand   "yes he
said david i am linguist and poet   hence i am interested in
all things linguistic   even that vaporous monster interlingua
which i am feeding all time now   in a previous life i was
ingenieur"
                    strange as it seemed that id never met him before
because wed worked for most of the same seven or eight
companies that paid well and reliably enough to make it worth
our while reading german chemical patents russian physics
monographs or french pharmaceutical texts   it was natural
enough because translation work is done almost entirely by
freelancers   peculiarly skilled private people with some

personal reason for needing preferring and sometimes delighting
  in the ebb and flow of this often randomly varying part time
work carrying fragments of knowledge of belgian mental
  hospitals azar fertilizer plants or swedish fish farms   who
most often had their own consuming private projects   and
     appeared in translation offices rarely and only   so it
  seemed   for some momentary contact with a world outside
themselves   with which they might exchange a joke or some
  comments about the   city or the weather   pick up or
return their packets and then be gone
              but once i met nasi it seemed that i ran into him
nearly everywhere   at a loft party for michael lekakis an
  elegant wood sculptor   who was having an opening i think
       i noticed nasi   accompanied by a beautiful dark haired
  eurasian woman   standing beside a table pouring himself a
glass of ouzo
              "thats genya" my friend gene told me "and nasi   the
  painter"
              "genya?" i said "sounds polish"   gene shrugged
  "thats what he calls her   shes his model   theyre always
  together"
                    later i found out that her name was really yen lü
       which nasi had converted over time into the more familiar
genya   and they made an odd couple together   nasi stocky and
  disheveled in wide waled old yellow corduroys laced-up work
    boots and cable knit sweater   his friend tall and slim in
short cut hair pale makeup and dark nail polish   impeccably
dressed in what looked like a thirties tailored suit high heeled
  shoes and nylon stockings   and in their expressions too
       nasi always mobile squinting screwing up his mouth and
sneering or laughing   genya so cool she seemed almost sullen
       though usually polite when she wasnt ironic or lightly
mocking   which she nearly always seemed to be when you got to
  know her   holding out a cool hand to acquiesce to a greeting
  nodding faintly to acknowledge a joke or smiling with all the
enthusiasm of a hostess in a high class bar   and this was a
  style she could maintain even while dancing   no mean feat
  for someone dancing with nasi   who loved to dance and was
  a kind of percussive demon at any loft party where there was

music   and he would dance anything from greek and israeli
    circle dances to czardases and polkas   rhumbas and sambas
and mambos   even lindy hops with the same athletic furor
        in the midst of this storm genya would usually be moving
calmly always correctly but so slightly she seemed to be almost
    standing still   turning a hip   inflecting a shoulder
inclining her head or just raising an eyebrow   to
punctuate the melody or rhythm and somehow hold her own
                and this was a performance i saw many times
because nasi loved to party the way he loved to drink   when
i got to know him better we used to lunch together sometimes
at a little german bakery on second avenue paul blackburn
introduced us to   that didnt carry liquor but looked the
other way if you brought your own   and nasi always seemed
to bring his own   a flask of stolichnaya or some ouzo
that he would fill up a water glass with and toss off neat
    a trick i couldnt hope to match   but with liquor i liked
better than pauls sweet brandy   yet for all that he drank
i never saw nasi get smashed or any higher than he usually was
when sober   though maybe a little more emphatic and oracular
                the closest i ever saw him come to this was
at a literary party where there was no dancing but a lot to
drink   it was over by gramercy park in a hall that belonged
to the national academy of arts and letters and was in honor of
the chelsea review   a literary magazine run by some friends
of mine that published a lot of european fiction and poetry in
translation and i had translated a martin buber story from the
german for their first issue   which as i remember had
just come out
                so the place was filled with poets and novelists
literary people   translators editors and agents   and i was
talking with jerry rothenberg and george economou when i
caught a glimpse of george reavey the russian translator   a
waxy little handsome man   talking   strangely i thought to
a child   he made a sort of sweeping gesture with his arm
        some kind of ironic disclaimer that turned him half way
around   and i realized he was talking to nasi   i figured
they were having a linguistic argument   probably about
translation and i walked over to hear

reavey had translated a
book of mayakovski and nasi was berating him for it
     "why do you not translate true poets   blok or belyi
or pioneers like kruchenykh or khlebnikov?   mayakovski is
  just a lackey who steals masters silver to juggle in the
streets   a buffoon a clown   pah   i spit on mayakovski
 turns poesy into pigsty for petit bourgeois bolsheviki
makes tin pan alley jingles for tin ear public   tunes for
   tax collectors   he is not fit to be valet to carry saintly
velimir upon his back   god bless his rotten legs   it is
  not with such a one that poesy will ever thrive   that
sentimental mercenary bandit"
                              it was a long argument with
reavey a little pompous and ironic and nasi as always over
  violent and i didnt stay to hear the whole thing   but long
enough to hear reaveys rejoinder about kruchenykh whose great
success consisted of emptying words of all their meaning   and
 nasis response that you cannot empty anything without filling
it with something else
                         "when you empty a glass of water you
  fill it up with air"
                         and to ask nasi what did kruchenykh
  fill the emptied words with?   and hear him answer
                    "spirit"
                         before i walked off to say hello
  to ursule who was talking to a plump and rosy cheeked middle
aged german sounding guy   who wanted to know how the magazine
  had come by its name and what was meant by it   fingering her
   old fashioned garnet ring and smiling dryly ursule gave a
 meticulous explanation   it had been a long afternoon at the
cafe cino and all sorts of names had come up   "trobar clus"
     "chert"   "greve"   joan kelly came up with "boars
  head"   which sounded like an english tavern and venable and
   ursule had an apartment in the west twenties   which the
 real estate developers all called chelsea   that also sounded
   english   and amused almost everyone   and that became
    its name
                    "so then why is the paper so bad" the german
  demanded

and i walked off to rejoin my other friends   who
were talking about something like magic wands and aleister
    crowley   when george let out a soft cry of admiration and i
looked toward the door   through which a startling couple were
making a kind of grand entrance   a tall handsome young
woman in a full skirted summer dress under an immense brimmed
    and ribbon bedecked southern belle hat   on the arm of a tiny
    mouselike man in a formal suit over whom she towered like
some grand ocean liner drawn by a tug   "whos that?" said
    george   "oscar williams" said venable   "no i mean the
girl"   but nobody knew though it turned out to be rochelle
    owens the poet and playwright who i suppose everybody knows
    now   while who remembers oscar williams?

though for anybody
    who doesnt   he was a kind of a wretchedly mediocre poet
        one of a swarm living off the corpse of dylan thomas'
    rhetoric   and a kind of modern day palgrave whose real
    distinction seems to have been the ability to capture the
    imagination of american publishing with a succession of
little treasuries of verse   mini anthologies of modern poetry
    modern american poetry immortal poetry   the distinguishing
features of which were tiny portraits of all of the poets
    and a system of selection according to which oscar williams
    and gene derwood outrepresented william carlos williams by a
    ratio of three to one

on his way in oscar made a very
roundabout tour of the room stopping to greet each editor and
agent in turn on his way to the drink table where nasi   to
    whom he nodded and seemed to know   was still arguing with
    reavey an italian poet and a greek translator while working
his way through a bottle of vodka that he held in his hand
    and waved in the air to punctuate points in his discourse
        nasi as i later learned didnt seem to change much when
he got drunk   except that his usually reddish face would
    start to pale save where his otherwise nearly invisible pock
marks gave him a kind of mottled look   that was a danger
    sign which his friends paid attention to

williams had joined the conversation with
harry roskolenko   reavey had gone and rochelle had wandered

off to say hello to someone and was standing and talking with
  my friend george
                  the energy of the conversation had
shifted somewhat to roskolenko and williams   with nasi simply
watching   roskolenko seeming sort of sarcastic and aggressive
  and williams appearing a little disdainful and pompous while
  nasi kept drinking and watching through narrowed eyes
      later i heard that roskolenko had been baiting oscar
  about giving up his good jewish name for a commonplace goyish
    one   a charge to which williams responded at first
  ironically   in the name of a kind of universalized religion
    that descended into a somewhat pedantic exposition of
  philosophical deism and ended with a clinching proof of
   the existence of god
                         "if you found a watch in the street you
would suppose it had a maker   so if you found a world in the
  street. . ."   which was greeted by a roar of "BULLSHIT OSCAR"
   from the italian poet   while nasi leaped onto the table
scattering bottles and glasses in all directions and poured
  the remains of his vodka onto williams head
                 when i asked him many months later why
  he had done it nasi told me "i am linguist and christian
    man is made in image of god   to turn to idiot is
  sacrilege". . . .

THE SCHOOL

DONALD BARTHELME

Well, we had all these children out planting trees, see, because we figured that . . . that was part of their education, to see how, you know, the root systems . . . and also the sense of responsibility, taking care of things, being individually responsible. You know what I mean. And the trees all died. They were orange trees. I don't know why they died, they just died. Something wrong with the soil possibly or maybe the stuff we got from the nursery wasn't the best. We complained about it. So we've got thirty kids there, each kid has his or her own little tree to plant, and we've got these thirty dead trees. All these kids looking at these little brown sticks, it was depressing.

It wouldn't have been so bad except that just a couple of weeks before the thing with the trees, the snakes all died. But I think that the snakes—well, the reason that the snakes kicked off was that . . . you remember, the boiler was shut off for four days because of the strike, and that was explicable. It was something you could explain to the kids because of the strike. I mean, none of their parents would let them cross the picket line and they knew there was a strike going on and what it meant. So when things got started up again and we found the snakes they weren't too disturbed.

With the herb gardens it was probably a case of overwatering, and at least now they know not to overwater. The children were very conscientious with the herb gardens and some of them probably . . . you know, slipped them a little extra water when we weren't looking. Or maybe . . . well, I don't like to think about sabotage, although it did occur to us. I mean, it was something that crossed our minds. We were thinking that way probably because before that the gerbils had died, and the white mice had died, and the salamander . . . well, now they know not to carry them around in plastic bags.

Of course we *expected* the tropical fish to die, that was no surprise. Those numbers, you look at them crooked and they're belly-up on the surface. But the lesson plan called for a tropical-fish input at that point, there was nothing we could do, it happens every year, you just have to hurry past it.

We weren't even supposed to have a puppy.

We weren't even supposed to have one, it was just a puppy the Murdoch girl found under a Gristede's truck one day and she was afraid the truck would run over it when the driver had finished making his delivery, so she stuck it in her knapsack and brought it to school with her. So we had this puppy. As soon as I saw the puppy I thought, Oh Christ, I bet it will live for about two weeks and then . . . And that's what it did. It wasn't supposed to be in the classroom at all, there's some kind of regulation about it, but you can't tell them they can't have a puppy when the puppy is already there, right in front of them, running around on the floor and yap yap yapping. They named it Edgar—that is, they named it after me. They had a lot of fun running after it and yelling, "Here, Edgar! Nice Edgar!" Then they'd laugh like hell. They enjoyed the ambiguity. I enjoyed it myself. I don't mind being kidded. They made a little house for it in the supply closet and all that. I don't know what it died of. Distemper, I guess. It probably hadn't had any shots. I got it out of there before the kids got to school. I checked the supply closet each morning, routinely, because I knew what was going to happen. I gave it to the custodian.

And then there was this Korean orphan that the class adopted through the Help the Children program, all the kids brought in a quarter a month, that was the idea. It was an unfortunate thing, the kid's name was Kim and maybe we adopted him too late or something. The cause of death was not stated in the letter we got, they suggested we adopt another child instead and sent us some interesting case histories, but we didn't have the heart. The class took it pretty hard, they began (I think, nobody ever said anything to me directly) to feel that maybe there was something wrong with the school. But I don't think there's anything wrong with the school, particularly, I've seen better and I've seen worse. It was just a run of bad luck. We had an extraordinary number of parents passing away, for instance. There were I think two heart attacks and two suicides, one drowning, and four killed together in a car accident. One stroke. And we had the usual heavy mortality rate among the grandparents, or maybe it was heavier this year, it seemed so. And finally the tragedy.

The tragedy occurred when Matthew Wein and Tony Mavrogordo were playing over where they're excavating for the new federal office building. There were all these big wooden beams stacked, you know, at the edge of the excavation. There's a court case coming out of that, the parents are claiming that the beams were poorly stacked. I don't know what's true and what's not. It's been a strange year.

I forgot to mention Billy Brandt's father, who was knifed fatally when he grappled with a masked intruder in his home.

One day, we had a discussion in class. They asked me, where did they go? The trees, the salamander, the tropical fish, Edgar, the poppas and mommas, Matthew and Tony, where did they go? And I said, I don't know, I don't know. And they said, who knows? and I said, nobody knows. And they said, is death that which gives meaning to life? And I said, no, life is that which gives meaning to life. Then they said, but isn't death, considered as a fundamental datum, the means by which the taken-for-granted mundanity of the everyday may be transcended in the direction of—

I said, yes, maybe.

They said, we don't like it.

I said, that's sound.

They said, it's a bloody shame!

I said, it is.

They said, will you make love now with Helen (our teaching assistant) so that we can see how it is done? We know you like Helen.

I do like Helen but I said that I would not.

We've heard so much about it, they said, but we've never seen it.

I said I would be fired and that it was never, or almost never, done as a demonstration. Helen looked out of the window.

They said, please, please make love with Helen, we require an assertion of value, we are frightened.

I said that they shouldn't be frightened (although I am often frightened) and that there was value everywhere. Helen came and embraced me. I kissed her a few times on the brow. We held each other. The children were excited. Then there was a knock on the door, I opened the door, and the new gerbil walked in. The children cheered wildly.

LANA

HAYDEN CARRUTH

Last night I dropped in at the Con-
      cord. Out on Erie? You
know it, like all the other joints
      along the strip there, glu-

cose and styrofoam, but it's Greek,
      and they got baklava
that Lana likes—that's Lana Schom-
      bauer—so I'm there a

good many times already. God
      knows I've looked at that same
painting on the wall enough, in
      that shiny fake-gold frame,

only of course it's not a painting
      but one of those repro-
ductions they do now with the raised
      up surfaces, like so,

to make it look like brushstrokes. Made
      me think of '52
when the wife drug me all over
      half of Paris to scru-

tinize all those pictures. Should have
   done it years earlier
when we were young enough to learn
   something. Well, you don't per-

fect your sensibilities in
   law school, I can vouch for
that. Yuh, I'm a lawyer. Or I
   was. Got what they call tor-

pedoed. I was a bit too close
   to the politics of
the business. Busted and disbarred.
   Sure, it was undercov-

er, so to speak, but I had to
   take the fall. I didn't
deserve it, but who does?—and maybe it's not important—

I did my time down in Ossin-
   ing, and whatever you've
heard about life on the inside
   you can double it, move

it on up to the fifth power—
   in spades. So get through and
out, o.k.? I did it. Survived.
   I give myself a hand

for that, though it wasn't the worst.
   You know what it's like being disbarred? It's like they threw you
   out of everything, de-

clared you persona non grata
   in the whole world. I get
by, the boys take care of me, a
   clean check each week, it's bet-

ter than social security,
   and sure, they know I took
a bum rap, but that's not the
   only reason they look

out for me. They do it because
   they *like* me, they can talk
to me, and we're all scared together. So there I am gawk-

ing at this picture out at the
   Concord, and it's flashy,
cheap, I know enough to know that,
   too bright, colors like ne-

on signs. You know? You've seen the same
   in half the feeding joints
in America. It's a scene
   with a buck, fourteen points,

standing next to a frozen stream
   with snow everywhere, some
white birches, a mountain in the
   background, a platinum

sky with a trace of pink like a
   real winter sunset. Awful, nobody would hang it on
   their wall, even a law-

yer. But then all of a sudden
   I saw it for real, out
of its frame, just like I saw it
   once hunting, up about

five, six miles above Old Forge, beautiful, so beautiful
I couldn't move and the buck broke
   and jumped off, gone double-

time through the birches and first, puffs
   of snow drifting down, and
I didn't even mind, I just
   looked and kept looking, stand-

ing until it was near dark and
   my feet near frozen. But
if that was beautiful, how come
   the picture is so ut-

terly ugly? They're the same, I
   tell you. Well, the picture
lacks something, don't ask me what. Then
   Lana. I looked at her

gray hair and wrinkled face, and all
   of a sudden I saw
like an aura around her she
   was so beautiful, claw-

ing her napkin to wipe the honey off her mouth, she was
beautiful, she was—but I can't
   describe her now because

already I can't remember,
   like something I read long
ago when I was a kid, or
   maybe dreamed, or a song

I heard once. Who, Lana? No, not
   her, I don't have a wife
any more. She's a steno down
   at the courthouse. Her life—

well, it's not exactly great ei-
   ther. Schombauer, Lana.
We go Dutch. The movies, then the
   Concord for baklava.

THE LIFE AND DEATH KISSES

ALLEN GROSSMAN

ibant obscuri

The chroniclers ceased, they ceased . . . until I arose—
Out of the infinite unborn, one of the born who lived,
And out of the number of all who have lived and died,
One of those yet alive,
And among all who are yet alive, one of us not in the greatest
Pain, not demented, not buried and awaiting rescue without hope
Under a cruel weight, and not mourning inconsolable losses
Night after night, or enraged by the treachery of women,
Or subjected (not for *this moment,* thank God!) by the evil
Power of J—

Arose, in truth, because it was time, punctually,
At three in the afternoon, from where I was sitting without
Thought on an obdurate bright bench of varnished rattan
In the last car of a train—leaning and slowing as on a curve—
Beside a honey-blond woman of indeterminate age whose
Eyes were strange—
Amidst the blandness of air and the thin light of destination.
It was in the middle-western state of X—Land of Lakes—,
Somewhere on the western, unbuilt limb of the central city
Where lordly factories, and highways, and nursing homes were
Transparent with hesitation between then and now in sunlight
Whiter than it should be

Because the foul windows of the old train were crowded with
Papery faces—like bleached leaves fallen to the bottom of
An empty pool, one upon the other; or like ocean waves blown down
White by the silent hurricane, waves breaking out of sight of land,
Unsurvivable by ships—
Human beings with the faces of leaves or fallen water:
Near at hand the faces that *can* appear, and behind them also
The ones that *cannot* appear, in their multitudes, white faces
Receding into the whiteness of the light and the flat landscape
Of the Great Plains of the dream.

I rose to get down, for the train had stopped and it was
Leaning in the light. And I looked on my right hand to the woman
Who sat beside me—the stout, blond woman with strange eyes—,
Thinking, "She will know the way. This is her country."
But I saw she was blind.
She was blind. I knew by the hesitation of her body as she
Lifted it like something very large with separate intentions
In another world. She took hold of me and we entered the dark end
Of the car, and then she kissed me with life and death kisses
Amid a great rush of air mingled with odors of metal,
And the slamming of doors. And out of her mouth a stone passed
Into my open mouth.

"This is the stone of witness," she said, "that stops every heart."
Thereafter, I turned to the left hand and went down. In the sunlight
A Spring snow was rising and falling on the plain, and the rails
Where the train had been
Were brimming with silver. I would have lingered in the light
For the interest of the empty scene, but I was wearied out
By the silence of life and death, and the kisses of the Fate.
And I lay down among the leaves like a young soul bewildered,
Beneath a sun that was as a stare of the finest eye. And then,
The life stopped in me, and the witness-stone divided my throat.

THE SURGEON

From the novel *Island People*

COLEMAN DOWELL

He had thought, right up until the end, that he was going to be allowed life.

That last evening he listened to his wife and thought about Moselle. His mind branched into twigs and buds and leaves, though a striving for singleness of idea and intent had pierced him with continual pain for a long time.

Once he had thought it the essence of the miraculous the way a mind could keep separate and distinct so many pieces of itself, those twigs and leaves and branches, no two alike; the likeness of a man to a tree was his clearest article of faith. He practiced it when he was tending wounds, lopping branches, painting, cementing, caulking winter's ravages and the galls of time.

A MAN IS LIKE A TREE could have been the wording on his shingle, if he had had a shingle. Now, even as sap was swelling fibers, nourishing new growth, so did his own sap still mindlessly push up and out when he thought of Moselle.

For the first time in two years his wife was giving him a signal, one long sought, even prayed for, and to fight the sudden terror of the signal, he thought about Moselle.

He thought about Moselle and listened to his wife, and then it was as though he were listening to Moselle (with his sap, his blood) and thinking of his wife, as she had been: never a nag, over a respectable span of years; never one to administer advertent hurts, for even after the trouble she pained him through inadvertence, sometimes ignorance, a forgivable failing. He had thought she had tried her damndest to be a mother and a lover, and yet he had tried time and again to leave her, first mentally, in sporadic dry runs, and then spiritually and bodily. He began to see, as she spoke and signaled, that she would have to leave him first, she, and the kids.

The signal was outwardly simple, inwardly cancerous: she was willing. Behind the signal and the meaning he saw the reason for all the unwilling lives around him, that puzzled and finally broke him: lives begun from such willingness rendered by time devoid of meaning. Such offspring would be, were, true inadvertencies, without roots.

His thoughts focused, gathered like moss on a tree around the central idea: she would have to leave him first, she, and the kids.

"She, and the kids" had always been divided by a septum. Leaving his wife was one thing, renouncing his kids meant another, a denial of the fruit of his manhood, a reversal, a renunciation of his great natural function, his dehiscence. A man in middle age, setting out to produce a second family from the womb of a young wife— as part of an enforced new order, that was all right. But for a man voluntarily to do it . . . and arriving at that point he always would force himself to see that what he mainly felt for Moselle was a kind of unconquerable lust, needles in the hide, fire in the bowels, a seizure like epilepsy. What he felt for his children was a thing too big to be tagged, a something as horizonless as night.

He saw the world: an immense hollow globe, reverberating with the roar of winds and restless directionless energies. And then he saw his children as tiny as seeds set down smack in the middle of the hollow ball, which he recognized as a fancy figure for his mind, and those tiny objects calmed the acoustical anarchy, softened and deadened the huge sounds so that a whisper could be heard—"Pa"— and he was at peace. Over the tumult of Moselle he would think to himself about his children: *They are the furniture of my mind.*

Self Argument:
A man can live without furniture. The further into the Eastern hemisphere you go the sparser the furnishings of a man's house,

and black tribes get along with a pot in one corner to cook their messes in. Furniture is a part of acquisitiveness, stand-in for desire too abstract to be formulated, maybe a shadow of a shadow of lust for the souls of one's fellows. A house is a copy of a brain, divided into chambers. The living room is the conscious mind and from there one moves downward: the lethal bathroom with shelves of death and tools of murder and suicide is probably the subconscious, and the bedrooms have equivalences peculiar to the occupants. The kitchen will mean one thing here, another in that household: Julia Child's kitchen and the Borgias' being example enough. Such as reading rooms, pantries, storage areas, music places, stand for various protuberances and depressions of the brain, individual to each man. At times in a man's house one can feel, on the threshold of a room, what that room means to the host, and it is usually a piece of furniture gone graphic as country speech that gives the meaning away.

Thus, without furniture—is this a syllogism?—a man would be safe from detection.

A Trial Predicament:

Caught and tried. He saw the courtroom, his judge-wife, the jury of three, two towheads and one as swart as Heathcliff: he'd be the troublemaker. First son: try those words on the tip of your mind, leaving the heart, that satchel of confusions, out of it, and if you are straightforward the words are like salt on meat, drawing juices to the surface, heightening discernment. Divorce emotion, pack it off without alimony, leave Pride penniless, give Traditional Expectations five minutes to get out of town, then feed to the computer-cold mind the equation FIRST SON. Whirr whirr as each bin is dipped into, each band pillaged, every bank robbed of infinite associations. FIRST alone is an agitator of large dimensions; SON alone rouses the sleeping rabble of atavism; FIRST SON is a major revolutionary figure with an aura of Christ and death. And of eternal life.

To be tried by your own children, to be granted or denied freedom by them, unbiased weighers of evidence; if this were standard procedure, would a man so freely seek release? To be tried by a jury of his peers . . . but how difficult to imagine yourself the equal of your children when you are attempting desertion, how the scale tips, then! No, not difficult; impossible. And so a trial becomes unthinkable because undemocratic and thus its own anti-matter.

What you are really dodging is evidence—having to present it or witnessing its presentation to your first-born: that the corespondent, Moselle, is closer to his age than yours; a high-school sophomore who waves to you, as you greedily wait each day at noon, surreptitiously flapping her hand behind her back at the cafeteria window, the cafeteria of the same building that holds his eighth-grade agonies, his gallant losing bouts with parsing and Pythagoras.

"*Moselle?*" You hear his incredulous voice that shards like a brittle urn which held his childhood. Moselle, who shared his classrooms and study halls in the small Island school, who marched with him in the band. His comic's voice that betrays his pains as nothing but jokes, that soars and plummets and plops with the hollow smack of a bladder, saying, trying out the words of imaginary introduction with Moselle as their object: "This is my *mother?*"

History:

Moselle was seventeen that January when the words of a song he liked, about needing more than wanting, and wanting for all time, became reality.

She had been his lover for a year. They celebrated her birthday with love in a field, a night when the populous sky was like a city. His shadow across her was mystical to his eyes, the shadow of a century raping an infant year, the abstraction of an eclipse, the sere breath of low-ebb January.

That night he operated less from lust than at any time with her. His new tender, terrible awareness of *who* she was to him made her seem fragile, recalled to him her two-year absence from school with the weight and aftermath of a curious fever upon her, her emergence as pale as the wine of her name, but as mysteriously matured, so plainly so that a fellow worker, watching her pass, said to him, "How'd you like to try that vintage?"

He saw that day that she was not beautiful, not voluptuous, but what he saw was a knowledge to match his own, that only the knowing can detect in others: of the relationship between death and life-as-sexual; the cavern between death and sanity. And he saw her desire to contain and be contained by the knowledge. She was not flirtatious when he stepped forth, formally, and they spoke for a while. She was direct in speech and her gaze was like a Fourth of July sparkler on his spine, for it seemed to tell him of her need. Not for some man; for him.

In a fantasy which may have had to do with middle age, dangerous in a man, it was said, he had watched her watching for his truck from the store porch, the tall girl two years behind in her classes, conscious of being with younger people. Their first alliance, they discovered, had been formed thus, with eyes that pretended to others not to see, and through a fantasy that each imagined was his or hers alone. But one day, as she walked home from school and he down-shifted to stop and offer her a lift, her back told him that she knew who he was, and that she was ready for him.

She told him in her pale voice how she had come to know the sound of his passing as she lay bald and listless before the fever had gone, and how she imagined that the fever had only moved down her body and settled where it remained, for him, because when it seemed to go and she overheard that she was to live, she had been thinking of him and not of dying, and the new fire of life was in her sex because of him; and she came to believe that thinking about him, and wanting him, had saved her from death. She told him this when they were one body and her breath and words were as hot as desert air on his face. The skin of his face had seemed to tauten with her whispers; all of his body had tightened and hardened until his bones were all he was aware of. It was as though her words had stripped him down to his essential self like a tree in winter. There was nothing superfluous, he was all bone and need to survive, and survival meant that she should flesh him out like leaves and cover his bones.

The first and consequent times with her, he had worn her thin pliant body like a foliage whose heat he had not imagined.

He had been an early lover, had never been celibate even as a pubertal boy. From early boyhood, which he placed sexually-retrospectively at about nine years, a spoken word or a written one, a glance between people, a thought, all were flint to his tinder. But the heat of Moselle's responses and the actual heat of her inner body exceeded his most hopeless imaginings. Thin, white, blue-veined, fragile; and an equator in her loins and upon her tongue.

When he had finished his first labors with her, she had collected moisture from him and with her fingers had rubbed it on her lips, and with no restorative pause he had plunged again.

Enclosed with her in the safety of their passion like a high impenetrable wall beyond the reach of laws, he told Moselle that in another time she would have been called lewd and lascivious and condemned to burn for a fraction of what she said and did with him. She was solemn at his jest, engrossed, he somehow knew, in plans to further prove him right.

One of her solemn pleasures was in his mystification: he had taken her as a virgin with ample proof of virginity, not only blood but a hymen as thick as a monastery wall, and her scream, turning inward, became part of the deep implosion that seared and claimed him. But eventually she told him that she had never touched herself, except with her mind; with him in her mind. Yet, with him in her mind, through the long illness and the liberating delirium, feeling her hair grow and the paling of the shell-like marks on her face, her sole moments of rationality brought about by the penetrating sound of his truck, there was nothing she had not done, and in doing, perfected.

His sensuous life had been copious as to partners, but circumspect, limited by the willingness of others, which had proved limitation enough. Therefore in a way he and Moselle came together as equals, truly experienced only in their imaginations. He, preoccupied with nature, had thought it a vain dream to find another person so free that deep roots were necessary to keep that person from diving headlong into heaven. He felt his own roots, deep and dark as such essentials. Moselle, floating in the delirium, growing filaments of hair, obsessed him.

The Surgeon Attempts a Philosophy:

The natural, or pagan, impulse, then, was toward a rivening ecstasy with heaven its goal, or perhaps, the ecstasy itself was the heaven, and the essential order was in the fostering and placement of roots. He could envisage a world new in creation where trees floated in the still-heavy air, their fibrils silklike, and as he gazed, these thickened and grew and touched earth, drawing the trees downward and placing them firmly. It was God's plan, that taste of freedom before order, and it was out of such a memory that the dream of airy heaven was formed. Counter to it was the underlying order, a conspiracy between God and the human race.

It was in the subsurface that enduring relationships took place, down where the roots met, and increasingly in his life he had come to suspect that others lacked such fundamentals, and until Moselle he had groped for that chthonic mystical touching with growing bewilderment. It was as though others sought to be blown away by the first storm to bid for them.

He said that it was wars that did it, so many wars in his lifetime, dispersing people over the face of the earth with their roots left behind in other countries, other times. He did not mean family, for frequently they migrated en masse, nor did he mean race, for the same conditions applied. What he meant was that mental tag in Latin or Greek that told you what you were.

A tree spore carried to a distant place by the wind took hold and produced itself a network of stability, but people no longer seemed to do the same. They appeared, in fact, to long for any chance to dissassociate themselves from their pasts and from each other. As he observed them, on television and in newspapers and in person on the Island as summer brought them in hordes, they invented chances and reasons. It invaded their educations, this need to live on air, their books were composed of it, and their sentiments and clichés, songs and slogans.

The massier the movement, the less connection there seemed to be just under the surface between its proponents. No unity prevailed, and at last, whatever the cause, there were factions broken off from factions without a fiber to show where the splintering had occurred, proof to him of the lack of connection to begin with.

But Moselle and he were Philemon and Baucis, and in the darkness of the earth they touched, and when he thought that way, his children—their need for him and his need for them—became finally the airiest spirits of an upper region, in no way bound or binding, and they and he were free of each other, and there was only himself and Moselle.

Trained to detect unsoundness, he found the sophistry, and despaired. He saw his despair as the denial of God, as essential disbelief in maintained order. Caution wthout purpose became pointless.

Moselle and the tree surgeon were discovered one warm May night, entwined beside the fresh-water pond, by a mob of her contemporaries. There were giggles and some vituperation and a hail of small stones from the boys. One stone each marked the man and the girl, he on his face, she on her breast. As a townsman remarked, after the courtroom exposure of Moselle's breast, "It's a good thing it wasn't the other way around. Who'd have wanted to see *his* tit in court."

The Surgeon Sums Up:
Love is condemned. It has been taken from us and condemned publicly. It was immoral, amoral, criminal, punishable. It was a third creature on trial, it was love that received the sentence. He and Moselle were only its parents, perpetrators, owners or trainers of the beast gone wild, rampaging, trampling civilization.

A high part of the trial, to which he had been brought by Moselle's parents, was when the tree surgeon spoke haltingly, seeming to address his words to his first-born, about roots, one of which he said was love between man and a fellow creature. A voice called out: "It's your root that got you in this mess," and court had to be dismissed for the day.

The sentence was commuted, as sentences frequently are in small islanded communities, out of consideration of the scarcity of good men to do the necessary work. But the man and the girl were marked, butts of jokes and crude epithets, and the girl, pregnant, was given in marriage to an off-Islander and moved away.

The man Moselle married was no bad bargain, a little older than her lover, the owner of good property and a sound house, and he had little or no lust in him. As he told her father, what he mainly wanted was a good housekeeper and an heir, and in Moselle, miraculously, he had found both. He was secure enough in his relationship with church and community not to care about gossip, and he promised Moselle's mother that he would keep his wife busy enough, once the baby came, not to have time to think about her past, and her good example, in church and out, would influence others to reform.

The tree surgeon saw the death of her youth as his own murderous act.

He moved his family out of the house that had witnessed his birth and his father's birth, and his wife's bewilderment that was a kind of birth, too, for she had emerged from the trial and the revelations a bent and bitter tuber, forced to the surface by elements and deformed by prolonged exposure. The familiar rooms held darkness for her. He would find her standing by a window, and seeing or hearing him in the room she would begin to speak in a low voice, recalling how she had stood thus waiting for him past midnight, past many midnights: the night in May when he and Moselle were discovered; the January night when he said his truck had broken down on the Shore Road; the night was in the house with them. In the familiar house the sun no longer stood above the horizon of its windows. Within it was always mörketiden, which, as her forebears knew, infected the brain.

When, in need or dreaming, he turned her to him, she cried out in her sleep. She could not be penetrated. Lying in the darkness, talking softly, she would recall for him how she had labored at his body's need, forcing pliancy when each bone ached after the long day's work. She told him how after the wedding night she had suffered the prospect of a life spent in that particular service. As she razed the structure of their mutual illusions, the darkness seeped deeper into him like a blight. At last, afraid the house would not withstand the inner pressures, he sold the old place and moved his family into the manor house of a sea captain turned farmer, dead a hundred years.

The house was nearly two hundred years old, but in elegant repair, thanks to the money of the last occupant—owner, still—a known queer. The house stood on a traveled road, and its tall windows sucked in the first and the last sun of the day. The surgeon had barbered its old trees, saved its new mimosas wind-riven at the crotch in their third year, broken and bent and arched into an allée the toxic spiney limbs of its great walls of osage orange, which the man told him was called bodark in the South, a corruption of bois d'arche. The owner had called the finished walkway, bricked and bordered beneath the arches with sun-shy mountain flowers, his Via della Spina. As the tree surgeon worked about the place, the owner and his birthmarked lover walked hidden within the vaulted greenery, shirtless. Once, as though teaching a baby to venture further into the world, the man had drawn his lover into the sunlight, and the tree surgeon had seen the curious formation on the lover's back: the map of an unfamiliar world that could still stir the memory.

He came to love the house, and when the owner had gone, refusing, by staying on an extra winter, the scandal the Islanders tried to force upon him, the tree surgeon continued to minister to the gardens and orchard, and after his own ordeal he saw the house as a refuge. He believed that no aura of perversity, or of the one-hundred-fifty-year-old murder whose stains were still in its attic, could so badly discolor its light and air as his own house was discolored by events of the past years. He could picture his wife in the sewing room, lit by the southern sun, and he thought he could hear her humming. He could see his children carefree in the orchard and himself pruning the espaliers, apt examples of deformity transformed into beauty.

Making the move, he concluded that he was joining the human race, for he was cutting off his own past to become a liver-on-air, to save his life and the lives of his family.

The Surgeon Concludes:

In so doing, an act of enormous unnaturalness for him, he lost his final connection with them. Only Moselle and he were still joined, the runners of their union having pushed beneath the waters of the separating Sound, and he saw that it was not so, not possible; that it was only his memory posing as the solution when it was the problem. It was Moselle he would find in the sewing room, pale full-bodied wine sparkling in the sunlight, a decanter he could never again touch. In the orchard it was Moselle and his child romping in silhouette, refracted in the blossoms, while his wife rocked by a window in a north room, guarding the possibilities of her womb until no guardian would be necessary.

Like a pointing finger, one fact was protrusive: in two years no Island child had been born. The only child formed of an Island union lay secure by Moselle's side in a house whose acres touched the edge of the sea.

No young of any age were enticed by the full moon to make love by the fresh-water pond, and he knew if they stumbled on love they would denounce it. In his brooding conclusions he saw that this was worse than loveless venery, fornication, all the excesses of old destroyed cities.

In solitude, the Islanders spent their evenings in front of individual television sets (the only rooted things left, their cables an intricate tracery under the soil), took their solitary meals there, living with Lucy, an old ghost no longer comprehensible to them. As he prowled around their houses, watching them through windows indifferently uncurtained—who had anything to conceal?—no laughter at the clown, except the laughter on the soundtrack, was heard. Lucy's predicaments, innocent and predictable, were founded on man's delight at his saving vulnerability. The tree surgeon's neighbors were invulnerable on their islands, invulnerable to gunshots and screams, moans and confessions and pleas for mercy. He watched them stolidly eating off trays, expressionless, lone but unlonely, and saw in windowpane and mirror the reflected violence from the T.V. screens, sometimes in color, mostly in the pale gray of nothing, of fog, limbo, and his ashen deductions.

And yet some old rationality persisted in him and made him suspect his conclusions, which seemed, after two years of nocturnal research, too final. As a man of the earth, he did not, had not believed in finality. Checking on himself, he climbed ladders, broke into outhouses, rowed out to boats promisingly bobbing in the harbor. A flashlight became an extension of his hand. He was already a criminal; nothing was beneath him.

That night, two years after Moselle had gone, when their child would be a year and five months old, that May night of anniversary lit by a full moon, the tree surgeon, pointedly rejecting his wife's signal, gone old and weak as a radio wave from another solar system, sent his family to bed and took his shotgun, his pick-up truck, and a small arsenal. One by one, slowly and with grace of motion and intent, for it was an offering, he killed everyone on the Island, five hundred and seventy-two people. He was a perfect shot, taking his roebuck, his ringnecked pheasant, his mallard in season with one clean shot, but he had never before taken so large a bag, and when he was finished his shoulder was torn and bleeding freely.

Before he killed his own family and himself (it was then past dawn, the horizon that pearly hue of a great dangling raceme of honey locust) he treated his barked shoulder with tenderness, and bound it. A momentary thought of precedence occurred: who first? but it was only an echo of order across the chasm of chaos.

Before he shot them, he grouped his family together so that in case he was wrong and there were still roots, they might intermingle long after flesh and the last signs of their blood had vanished.

The promise of the warm barrel in his own mouth was as sweet to him as the memory of Moselle's nipple.

FIVE POEMS

ROBERT CREELEY

FORTY

The forthright, good-natured faith
of man hung on crane up

forty stories with roof scaffolding
burning below him forty feet,

good warm face, black hair,
confidence. He said, when

the firemen appeared, he said
I'm glad to see you,

glad not to be there alone.
How old? Thirty, thirty-five?

He has friends to believe in,
those who love him.

ROOM

Quick stutters of incidental
passage going back

and forth, quick
breaks of pattern, slices

of the meat, two
rotten tomatoes, an incidental

snowstorm, death, a girl
that looks like you later

than these leaves of
grass, trees, birds, under

water, empty passage-
way, and no way back.

HOTEL

It isn't in the world of
fragile relationships

or memories, nothing
you could have brought with you.

It's snowing in Toronto.
It's four-thirty, a winter evening,

and the tv looks like a faded
hailstorm. The people

you know are down the hall,
maybe, but you're tired,

you're alone, and that's happy.
Give up and lie down.

ECHO

Back in time
for supper
when the lights

"ICH BIN . . ."

Ich Bin
2 Öl-tank

yellow squat
by railroad

shed train's
zapped past

round peculiar
empty small

town's ownership
fields' flat

production towered
by obsolescent hill-

side memory echoing
old wornout castle.

THREE POEMS

CID CORMAN

1

Myself: pocked pimpled
skin—doubling chin—
mouth straight and thin—eyes

knit by wrinkle—
forehead almost all
gone to skull. But

in the glass the child
awakens to
his absence. Not what

anyone pre-
dicted—merely what
everyone knows.

2

The difficult thing
is to say nothing
and mean it—or more
give it no meaning.

3

It isn't for want
of something to say—
something to tell you—

something you should know—
but to detain you—
keep you from going—

feeling myself here
as long as *you* are—
as long as you *are*.

COMRADES

FREDERICK BUSCH

We began to feel better after we had wrecked the cobalt-blue pitcher on our hardwood kitchen floor and like bad children bent on not being caught, our mouths open with fatigue, we had kneeled together to pick up shards. That night, we drank coffee together, grinding dark beans and pouring heavy cream into a small brown pottery jug. We sat in our denims while birch burned in the air-tight stove. We agreed that what surprised us most was our feeling of ease. To be sure, her knee was black and blue, my forearm was yellow with bruising; there would be scabs above my ear and on her bicep. But, drinking coffee and talking sensibly, we agreed that we hated the pitcher from Mexico, given us by friends in Green-wich Village long ago. We also agreed that such a symbol of marriage, and that's what it clearly had become, would need to be broken, now that we had so violently concurred—and here we gave a sort of corporate laugh—that we ought to be divorced.

In the week afterward, we spoke briskly and were kind. We felt compact and healthy, and we didn't weep upon each other, or at each other, or in places where one was overheard. We called each other *Love* a lot, as in "Pasta with bacon and pinto beans for dinner, Love."

I worked for a mildly leftwing journal of politics and the arts, and Berry often called me *Comrade*. I once had detested hearing her say it, although I'd understood the tensions it derived from—for when we were to be married, her most intimate confession to her parents, and my most threatening trait, was that I was a registered Liberal. *Comrade,* in the second week after our agreement to divorce, replaced *Love.* Each time we said it, we smiled.

After twelve days, we had planned everything but the details of our journey from Wilton, Connecticut, to Athens, Ohio, where our daughter was a college freshman. We agreed that we should not summon her home. We agreed that we should travel to her together. We agreed that we should stay with her a while and then drive her back with us to Wilton if she wished us to. And then with no verbal agreement, but with a sudden strong sense of necessity, we postponed the trip. For it became very clear that Berry had to see her mother first.

That was where we went on the second weekend after our glad decision to divorce. We had grown more fatigued by the Thursday of that week, and Berry had called me *Comrade* less and *Love* not at all. I told her, over coffee before the Saturday drive from Wilton to Montpelier, Vermont, that I was worried about us.

"You're worried about yourself, Bob," she said. She was in a russet corduroy suit and loafers with little heels, and she looked like someone a man should be happy to know.

"No, Ber," I said. "I'm serious."

"Don't you think I am? You're afraid of what my mother will be like. You're afraid of what we'll tell her about us and what she might say."

"Ber, your mother isn't going to care. She isn't going to know."

"My mother isn't the issue, Bob."

"There is no issue. Did you notice I was wearing corduroy also?"

I was in my brown wide-wale sports coat and khakis, good Saturday clothes for anyplace, and surely for a nursing home in Montpelier. She shook her head. She pulled at the square bottom of my brown knit tie. I made my teeth show, as if the tie were connected to a switch that she had tugged. Berry laughed. She had forgotten, I'd have sworn, everything, for just the duration of that knot-tightening. So I said, "Comrade: it was you."

"What?"

"Really. That I was worried about."

"All right," she said.

I said, "You sometimes don't look happy anymore. I mean, as happy as you did last week. All things being equal."

Berry said, "Elegance is not my strongest suit. Neither is fakery. Neither is pretense. You put them all together, you get what we got last week. All things being equal. You get folie à deux."

I said, "No, not yet. We'll order later."

"What?"

"It was a very bad joke. It was a menu joke. A waiter joke. It wasn't a joke. Never mind."

Berry nodded. The lines remained at the bridge of her nose and at either corner of her mouth. She smiled the smile I had just finished smiling in response to a tug on my brown knit tie. She shrugged, still smiling. I, smiling back, shrugged too.

And as I started the car, I wondered how we could have endured the last two weeks, and how our daughter would endure the other weeks, and why we were bent on driving together toward what was just more separateness. I drove us that way nevertheless.

Everybody's parent's old-age home is probably pretty much the same, I thought, when we arrived. I wondered if that meant that everybody's parent is pretty much the same. Or, I wondered, does it mean that oldness is the same for everyone. And, therefore, I thought, youth can't be so awfully individual either. I actually grew afraid as we walked up the steps. For there had to be *something* different, at some time or other. Most specifically, there had to be a happy divorce. So why not ours? I heard the answer, and in Berry's voice, inside my thoughts: Because we all are the same, Comrade. I thought of Barbara, our daughter, in her freshman dorm. I thought of the new side porch in Wilton, and of two storm windows I'd ordered.

It was early afternoon. The temperature in the home was comfortable, though slightly warm for me. Everybody's parent's old-age home is kept at approximately the same temperature. Berry walked a few steps ahead of me. I used to love her long stride. I should say that I still do. A stride is easy to love. She was ahead of me, and then she was bending above her mother. Everybody's bending above an aged parent is the same, no doubt, and we are all comrades in the having to bend, and in the boredom we share at having to hear about each other's bending. Berry bent, and so, at last, did I.

Berry knew what to say. Her mother was bulky under her pink quilted housecoat. Her face shone with medicines and cleanliness and seventy-six years come to something of a halt. Her brown eyes matched Berry's suit, I noticed. I reminded myself not to say that. She hated my noticing smallnesses when faced with large events. Their eyes were precisely the same color, and they matched Berry's suit. Berry said, "Hello. My name is Berry. I've come to visit you."

I said, "Hello. My name is Bob. I've come to visit you too."

The sweet smile shone, as it always did at such moments. I thought of a tug on my tie and my face's lighting up. Berry's mother said, "Hello. You've come to see me? Isn't that nice?"

"And we've brought you some gifts," Berry said.

I started to raise a box for her to see—it contained a pair of fleece-lined slippers, and it was prettily wrapped—when Berry's mother said, looking at her wrist on which there was no watch, "Oh, dear." She said it urgently. "Oh, dear," she said again. "You know, I have *got* to get back to work. I really must run. You're going to *have* to excuse me."

Berry said, "Mommy."

Her mother looked up quizzically. Perhaps the quizzical looking-up of one's faraway mother is also like the looking-up of everyone else's. But she did look up. Her face was sweet, her expression charming. She seemed prepared to be enlightened, and then to get away toward work.

All Berry said was, "But Mommy."

"Hello," her mother said. "I have to get back."

A nurse, I realized, had been standing behind us all that time. Her gray-gold hair was up in a knot and her hands were folded before her as grade-school teachers, when I was a child, used to fold their hands. She smiled, she shrugged just a little, and then she nodded when I pointed down the corridor into which Berry's mother had slowly walked, looking at her wrist as if a watch were strapped around it. Berry followed her mother and I followed Berry. We walked past a number of other people's parents, and we found Berry's mother in the solarium, where she sat in a very large red-leather and chromium chair, her back erect, as she had taught Berry always to sit, and her face as vacant of expression as Berry's now was filled. The tall windows behind Berry's mother were smudgeless, and their perfect cleanliness suggested that the windows had never been used. I wondered who ever looked in, from the outside of nursing home windows. Real sun came through them, but on the tan linoleum floor and the red chairs and the people who sat as if they were too small for them, the light looked artificial, and the solarium seemed an antique picture postcard, tinted into life.

"Love," I said to Berry. She looked up. She was furious with something. I realized that it might be me. I said, "Comrade. She's gone again. She doesn't remember. She can't. She isn't doing it on purpose. She would love you if she knew. She would love you if she could."

Berry, bent above her mother, as everyone else at some time must be bent, continued to look up. It must have hurt her back to crouch that way. She said, "Spare me, Comrade, the running commentary. Would you?" As if someone had pulled on a brown knit necktie, she smiled.

Berry looked down. I walked to them and bent down too. I said, "Hello. I'm Bob. I've come to visit you."

Berry said, "Hello. I'm Berry. I've come to visit you too."

I said, "We brought some gifts for you. Look."

Berry's mother, looking up and smiling, like everyone's mother who looks up to smile, said, "Oh. You've come to see me? Isn't that nice?"

"And we've brought you some gifts," I said, like all of their sons-in-law or all of their sons.

She lay her hand on the gay wrapping paper. The knuckles were swollen, and two of the clean white fingers with their frayed tips were permanently bent. Sometimes she made you forget that her body was also, in several ways, afflicted. Sometimes you thought only about her mind, and how far inside it she was hidden. She said, "Oh, dear."

Berry, in a lower voice than I'd heard that afternoon, though in a voice I had heard a great deal before our happy agreement to divorce, said, "You have to go back to work."

Her mother looked at the wrist that bore no watch. "I have to get back to work," her mother said.

Berry said, "Me too."

The nurse with gray-gold hair was with us. She took the gifts for Berry's mother and told us that the doctor would see us. He did. We asked the questions and he answered them. I suppose everyone asks questions like those. Everyone probably hears those answers. And everyone, then, goes down the corridor and through the lobby and into, in our case, a bright autumn afternoon in Vermont.

In the car, Berry said, "So there she is again."

"She's just the way we expected her to be."

"Really?"

"Well—you know."

"No," Berry said. "What if I expected her to say, *Hi, kid! What's cookin'?* That's what she used to say to me. I'd come home or I'd call her up, and she'd say, *Hi, kid! What's cookin'?*"

"I know. But she can't, Berry. It's natural to be angry at somebody you love who really gets sick. Especially a parent. But she really can't."

"Thanks, Comrade Doktor. But what if she won't? You know? What if she *won't?*"

"You aren't serious."

"No? What if she *will* not? What if she *wants* to hide away? And forget about us all. What about *that?*"

"And forget about *you* is what you mean, Ber."

"Yes," she said. "Forget about me."

You wouldn't have known, if you had been watching us, that soon we would drive to Ohio and tell our daughter about our divorce. Everyone driving a car very fast on a highway in fast-moving traffic looks like everyone else. I turned to Berry to say so. She looked like her mother. I turned back to look at the road. I drove and I drove and I drove until the sirens behind me, then the lights in the mirror, told me it was time to pause a while and look like other fugitives, slumped and pale, gripping the motionless wheel at the side of the road.

NIGHT SONG OF THE
LOS ANGELES BASIN

GARY SNYDER

    Owl
     calls
     pollen dust blows
  swirl of light strokes writhing
  knot-tying light paths
  calligraphy of cars

Los Angeles basin and hill slopes
checkered with streetways. Floral loops
of the freeway express and exchange.

    dragons of light in the dark
    sweeps going both ways
    in the night city belly
    the passage of light end to end
        and rebound,
    ride drivers all heading somewhere
    etch in their traces to night's eye-mind

    calligraphy of cars.

Vole paths. Mouse trails worn in
on meadow grass;

winding pocket-gopher tunnels,
marmot lookout rocks.
Houses with green watered gardens
slip under the ghost of the dry chaparral—

                    Ghost
                    shrine to the L.A. River.
                    The jinja that never was there
                    is there where the river debouches,
                    mouths out, the point of the moment
                    of trembling and gathering & giving
                    so lizards clap hands there,
                    only lizards come pray, saying
                    "please give us health and long life."

                         a hawk,
                         a mouse,

Slash of calligraphy of freeways of cars.
                    Into the pools of the channelized river
                    the Goddess in tall rain dress
                    tosses a handful of meal.

                    gold bellies roil
                    mouth-bubbles, frenzy of feeding
                    the common ones, bright-colored rare ones
                    show up, they tangle and tumble,
                    godlings ride by in Rolls Royce
                    wide-eyed in brokers' halls
                    lifted in hotels
                    being presented to, platters
                    of tidbit and wine,
                    snatch of fame,

                         churn and roil,

                    meal gone the water subsides.

a mouse,
hawk,

The calligraphy of lights on the night
freeways of Los Angeles

will long be remembered.

Owl
calls;
late-rising moon.

WAS PAPA HAYDN BORN APRIL 1ST?

GREGORY CORSO

If I, like Mozart
were instead Humphrey Bogart
seated at the clavier
with an unmendable hole
            in my silken pants
I'd glance at the Eumenides
            in adagio
smiling my cigarette smile at them
plonk-plunking like Sam'd play
ever ready to pull out my roscoe
and dust them away

RAPTURE

JAMES PURDY

"I wouldn't have known you!" Mrs. Muir spoke to her brother. "You've grown so tall, and you're so deeply tanned. Oh, Kent, it's really you then?"

Kent put down his two valises, and kissed her dryly on the cheek.

"You haven't changed much, though, Gladys. The same sweet smile, and sky-blue eyes." He hugged her ever so gently then.

Kent was Gladys Muir's half-brother. He had an extended furlough from the army, where he was stationed in West Germany. Before his assignment there he had been in the Middle East, and before that somewhere in the Pacific. But now, though still a young man, he was a few years over thirty, he was free from his military service at least for a while.

He had been given so long a furlough in order to see Mrs. Muir because the doctor had told him she was not expected to live for more than a few months at the most. Kent, as he studied his sister's face, was not certain if she knew how serious her illness was, and how brief a time yet remained to her.

"Here is Brice," Mrs. Muir said softly as her only son entered the front room of their Florida bungalow. "You've not seen him, Kent, since he was ten or eleven years old, have you?"

Kent stepped back a few inches when he set eyes on his nephew, and his right hand moved slightly upwards as it did when he saluted an enlisted man.

"This is your Uncle Kent," Mrs. Muir spoke to Brice as if her brother would not hear her prompting her son. Brice blushed a deep brick red, and looked away.

"Brice has so often spoken of you," Mrs. Muir went on. "He has kept all of the snapshots of you and he keeps them over his dresser. Especially the photo of you coming out from swimming in the ocean somewhere. That seems to be his favorite of you."

Brice looked away, and colored even more violently. He was then just sixteen and was shy for his age.

"If Uncle Kent will excuse me, Mother, I have to practice my cornet," Brice apologized. He almost bowed to his uncle as he left the room.

Mrs. Muir and her brother laughed in agreeable nervousness as the boy left them.

"Brice wears his hair quite long, doesn't he?" Kent said as they sat down, and began sipping some fresh lemonade.

They could hear the cornet now coming from the garage where Brice practiced.

"Say, he plays like a real professional."

"He does play with a very fine group of musicians," Mrs. Muir smiled. "But since he left school early, he has been working in a restaurant, you see. He gets up every morning before five o'clock."

Her brother clicked his tongue.

Mrs. Muir observed then how very short Kent's own hair was, though he wore rather long and well-defined sideburns which set off his deep-set green eyes.

"He does so much want to be a musician, Kent," Mrs. Muir spoke as if giving away a secret.

"How much have you told Brice about everything, Gladys," Kent wondered, wiping his mouth from the tart drink.

"Oh, nothing at all. He thinks I am just not feeling up to par."

"I understand," her brother said, looking at one of his finger nails, which was blackened owing to his having caught it in his car door that day.

"Let me show you to your room, Kent." Mrs. Muir led him up the stairs. "You'll share the same bathroom, if you don't mind," she explained. "The bathroom which should be yours has been out of order for a few days. So you'll share with Brice, if that's agreeable."

When Brice came home from work in the restaurant in the late afternoon the next day, Kent was outside up on a ladder cleaning out the eaves of the roof. Owing to the sudden spell of hot weather, his uncle had taken off his shirt. He had worked so hard, repairing some of the broken parts of the eaves, and also fastening down some loose tiles on the roof, that rivulets of sweat poured down his chest to his bronzed thick arms.

"Need any help, Uncle Kent?" Brice called up to him, smiling broadly.

In answer, coming down from the ladder, Kent ruffled up the boy's thick mop of hair, and grinned.

"All fixed now, Brice, so the water won't run out the wrong way."

Brice avoided his uncle's glance, but smiled continually.

Mrs. Muir, observing the two men from inside where she sat on a new davenport (she had purchased it expressly so that Brice would not suspect she was ill), smiled.

"Brice will be in good hands," Mrs. Muir spoke softly to herself. "Certainly strong ones."

Gladys Muir still did most of the housework, though the doctor had advised her against doing so. She always cleaned the bathroom immaculately, for she knew Brice liked it sparkling clean. On the shelf above the wash basin, Mrs. Muir always took down Brice's comb, in which every day four or five strands of his gold hair were left behind. She would remove the hair, and place it in a small box in her own bedroom.

But after Kent arrived, as she would go in to clean their common bathroom, she observed that there were no hairs now in the comb. The first time she noticed this, she stood for a long time staring at the comb. She lifted it up and looked under it. She felt, then, strangely unaccountably as if a load had been lifted from her heart.

She found herself from then on waiting, one might say, for the ceremony of the cleaning of the bathroom and the looking at the comb. But with each passing day, each time she picked up the comb it was clean, without one hair remaining.

There was a small aperture leading from the bathroom to a small closet down the hall, a kind of register which conveyed hot air from the furnace in winter. The next day when she heard Kent go into the bathroom she opened the air register. She was trembling so badly she was afraid he would hear her.

But Kent was completely occupied, she saw, in polishing his boots until they shone like a looking glass. But then straightening up, she saw him gaze at Brice's comb. He took hold of it with extreme care. He was completely absorbed in looking at the comb which she could see still held a few of Brice's hairs in its teeth.

Kent held the comb for a while close to his mouth, then lowering it, almost languidly, he removed the strands of hair and placed them in his khaki shirt pocket.

Mrs. Muir stole away into her own bedroom, and sat down heavily. She could hear her brother in his own bedroom, moving about. He remained there for only a short time, then he went downstairs, got into his rented car, and drove away.

When she felt her strength return, Mrs. Muir went into Kent's bedroom. She made his bed, and did some dusting and sweeping. Then very slowly she advanced to the dresser and opened each drawer deliberately one after the other. She left the top drawer for last, as if she must prepare herself for what she would find in it. There was a small mother-of-pearl box there. She opened it. At first she saw only the reproduction on its underlid of a painting of John the Baptist as a youth. But in the box itself, arranged in pink tissue paper, she spied a gathering of the gold hair of Brice Muir. She closed the box. There was a kind of strange smile playing over all her features at that moment.

Mrs. Muir felt, she did not know why, the same way she had when her father, the day of her wedding, had held her arm and they had walked down the aisle of the church together, and her father had then presented her to her bridegroom. She had felt at the moment a kind of bliss. She now felt she could give up her son to someone who would cherish him as her bridegroom had cherished her.

But when Gladys Muir began to talk with Kent about her "going," her brother became taciturn and embarrassed, and the serious commitment she wished from him was not made.

The days passed, and Mrs. Muir realized that very little time remained. She knew positively that she had now only days, perhaps only hours. The doctor had told her her passing would be so easy she would scarcely be aware of it, such was the nature of her malady.

As she felt then that the time for parting was imminent, she took Brice's comb in her handkerchief so that it could not be seen and joined Kent where he sat playing solitaire in the front room.

He stopped playing immediately she had come in, and stood up in a kind of military fashion. Brice was outside practicing his cornet in the garage, so of course he could not overhear what she might say, or what her brother might answer.

When Kent had put away his cards and was sitting on the new davenport facing her, Gladys Muir without warning brought out Brice's comb.

She saw the look of consternation on her brother's face.

"I want to tell you, Kent, how great a happiness I feel that you are close to my boy. The effort of speaking is very hard for me, as I believe I told you. So I have brought this to speak for me."

A deep silence prevailed.

"Take it, Kent, for I have an identical comb upstairs in my room." Kent took the comb. His eyes filled with tears.

"You will keep him with you, Kent?" Gladys managed to say.

She was pleased, grateful to see how strong her brother's emotion was.

"I don't ever want to leave him," her brother got out. "But do you think he will want to be with me equally?"

"I know he will, Kent. He has a kind of worship of you, and always has. So you will have one another . . . But what neither of you can know is the great burden that is being lifted from my heart knowing you will be close to one another."

"I will make him my life if he will let me," the uncle spoke in a kind of incoherent manner.

Mrs. Muir was sad she had forced it all upon him in so short a space, but then she saw that no other course would have been possible.

Kent was so blinded by his tears, tears really of joy, he later was to realize, and also tears of so many strange and powerful feelings that it took him some time to look over at his sister and then to realize she had gone.

At the very moment of his realization he heard the cornet playing cease. He went to the door as Brice was going through it. As if the boy read the meaning in his uncle's face, he put down his cornet, and threw himself into the older man's arms.

There was almost no one at the funeral. There was the minister, and a woman who played the organ and who sang one song in a faded alto voice, and then of course the gravediggers and the sexton.

Brice had put on his best Sunday suit, a little too small for him, and a brand-new tie which his mother had purchased for him only last week. Uncle Kent wore his captain's uniform with several bright colored citations across the jacket.

Kent noticed that Brice did not shed any tears at the service, and he looked very pale. His lips moved from time to time as if he were playing his cornet. They went to a very expensive restaurant later, but neither of them was able to eat very much. Neither Kent nor Brice drank at all, so there was nothing somehow to give them any kind of solace.

"I am going to take care of everything, Brice," Kent told him just before starting the motor of his car. "I don't want you to have to worry about a thing now."

It was only eight o'clock in the evening, but Brice said he must go to bed soon as he was due at the restaurant the next morning no later than five-thirty.

"You don't need to work there anymore, Brice," Kent said thickly as he was seated at the new davenport. "Unless you want to, of course," he amended his statement when he saw a look of uneasiness on the face of his nephew. "I have enough, you see, for both of us."

"I think, Uncle Kent, it might get my mind off of everything if I did go to work just as usual."

"All right, Brice. But remember, you don't have to. As I said, there's enough for both of us."

Kent stood up then, and made a motion to take Brice in his arms, but something in the way the young man looked at him caused him merely to shake hands with him and give him a husky goodnight.

It began to rain outside, and presently there was a distant peal of thunder, and flashes of silver and sometimes yellow lightning. Kent closed the door leading to the patio. He took out a pack of worn cards, and began his game of solitaire.

All at once it seemed to him he could hear his sister's voice as she showed him the comb with the gold strands of hair.

"She knew everything and was glad," Kent said aloud. "But then, after all, I am his uncle, and too old for him."

The rain had wet the top blanket on his bed, so Kent threw this off. He had his small transistor radio, and he decided he would just lie in bed and listen to some music.

The rain whipped against the roof and the windows. Kent felt very restless and edgy. His sister's sudden death did not seem real, and he kept seeing her showing him the comb. He could not believe Gladys had meant what she had said, but then what else could she have meant?

He had dozed off when a noise wakened him. It was, he soon realized, Brice taking a shower, and the sound of the water in the shower mingled with the sound of the steady downpour, outside, of the rain. He dozed off again, and then he thought he heard someone call. Rising up in bed, he saw that Brice had entered his room. He had no clothes on. At first the thought crossed the uncle's mind that he was walking in his sleep, but then he saw this was not true.

"Can I come in, Uncle Kent?" Brice's voice reached him as if it came from a far distance, and sounded like a small child's in the dark.

"Please, Brice."

"You don't drink or smoke, do you, Uncle Kent?"

He nodded. They both listened to the radio which was playing a waltz.

"May I sit on the edge of your bed," Brice inquired.

"You're crying," Kent said throatily. "And you're still wet from your shower."

"No, it's from the rain. I stepped out on the porch for a while. I felt so good with the rain coming down on me . . . But I shouldn't get your bed wet."

"The rain got my top blanket wet also before I turned in," Kent explained.

He suddenly took Brice's outstretched hand in his.

"It's all right to cry in my presence," Kent said, but he had hardly got the words out before Brice threw himself into his uncle's arms. He began weeping very convulsively, almost violently.

Kent held him to his chest tightly.

"You're shivering, Brice. Get under the covers for a while at least."

The boy obeyed, and Kent found himself holding him very tightly under the blanket as the boy sobbed on.

Kent all at once kissed the boy on his cheek, and as he kissed him some of the tears came into his mouth.

The sobs began to subside.

"I feel very close to you, Uncle Kent," Brice said. "Do you to me?"

"I do," Kent heard his own voice coming, it seemed, from beneath the floor boards, and unrecognizable as his own.

"I told my mother how I cared for you," Brice said, after a considerable effort, and as he said this he kissed his uncle on the mouth and then let his lips rest there. "She told me to stay with you if you would want me to. She said you loved me."

"If I would want you to." Kent spoke almost in high anguish, deliriously.

"Yes, she thought you might."

"Oh, Brice," the uncle stammered, and he kept his mouth against the boy's. "If you care for me," Kent went on, "it will be beyond my wildest dream."

"Why is that, Uncle Kent?"

They kept their lips close together.

"*Why is that?*" the uncle repeated. He kissed him over the face now.

"You are drying up all my tears," Brice told him.

Then:

"I loved you when I first saw you, Uncle Kent," Brice whispered.

The uncle shook his head, but held the boy very close to him. He felt he was dreaming all this. No one had ever loved him before, neither women nor men. He had given up any hope of love. Then he had found his sister's boy's comb full of golden hair, and now he held this boy to his breast. It could not be true. He must be asleep, fast aslumber, or he was still across the ocean and his sister and her son whom he had so seldom seen were far away from him, unknown persons against time and distance.

Then he felt the boy's burning kisses on his body.

They grasped one another then with frantic passion, like men lost at sea who hold to one another before the final breaker will pass over them.

"Is this true, Brice," Kent said after a while in the midst of such unparalleled joy, "are you sure you want to be with me?"

Brice held his uncle in his desperate embrace, and kissed him almost brutally on the mouth.

"I said you had dried all my tears," Brice told him. He kissed his uncle again and again, and his hand pressed against the older man's thigh.

"I hope in the morning I will find you against my heart and it will not be just a thing I felt in slumber," Kent said.

He sensed his nephew's hot breath and wet kisses against his chest, and he plunged his thick stubby hard fingers through the mass of gold hair.

Outside the lightning had turned to a peculiar pink, and the peals of thunder came then more threatening and if possible louder, and the rain fell in great white sheets against the house and the spattered windows.

THE SIGNATURE OF ALL THINGS

KENNETH REXROTH

1

My head and shoulders, and my book
In the cool shade, and my body
Stretched bathing in the sun, I lie
Reading beside the waterfall—
Boehme's "Signature of All Things."
Through the deep July day the leaves
Of the laurel, all the colors
Of gold, spin down through the moving
Deep laurel shade all day. They float
On the mirrored sky and forest
For a while, and then, still slowly
Spinning, sink through the crystal deep
Of the pool to its leaf gold floor.
The saint saw the world as streaming
In the electrolysis of love.
I put him by and gaze through shade
Folded into shade of slender
Laurel trunks and leaves filled with sun.
The wren broods in her moss domed nest.
A newt struggles with a white moth
Drowning in the pool. The hawks scream,
Playing together on the ceiling
Of heaven. The long hours go by.
I think of those who have loved me,

Of all the mountains I have climbed,
Of all the seas I have swum in.
The evil of the world sinks.
My own sin and trouble fall away
Like Christian's bundle, and I watch
My forty summers fall like falling
Leaves and falling water held
Eternally in summer air.

2

Deer are stamping in the glades,
Under the full July moon.
There is a smell of dry grass
In the air, and more faintly,
The scent of a far off skunk.
As I stand at the wood's edge,
Watching the darkness, listening
To the stillness, a small owl
Comes to the branch above me,
On wings more still than my breath.
When I turn my light on him,
His eyes glow like drops of iron,
And he perks his head at me,
Like a curious kitten.
The meadow is bright as snow.
My dog prowls the grass, a dark
Blur in the blur of brightness,
I walk to the oak grove where
The Indian village was once.
There, in blotched and cobwebbed light
And dark, dim in the blue haze,
Are twenty Holstein heifers,
Black and white, all lying down,
Quietly together, under
The huge trees rooted in the graves.

3

When I dragged the rotten log
From the bottom of the pool,

It seemed heavy as stone.
I let it lie in the sun
For a month; and then chopped it
Into sections, and split them
For kindling, and spread them out
To dry some more. Late that night;
After reading for hours,
While moths rattled at the lamp,
The saints and the philosophers
On the destiny of man;
I went out on my cabin porch,
And looked up through the black forest
At the swaying islands of stars.
Suddenly I saw at my feet,
Spread on the floor of night, ingots
Of quivering phosphorescence,
And all about were scattered chips
Of pale cold light that was alive.

VISIONS OF JESUS

JEROME ROTHENBERG

Let's say it was Jesus. Who is Jesus? Why should Jesus be the name
now celebrated, entering the poem?
Or let's say it wasn't. That I have the key to make it open
like a sound. Each sound's a rage.
Each page a turning over. I am writing this
the way a preacher speaks the word out on a prairie.
Visions of Jesus everywhere.
Sweet Jesus, says the song, to which the mind says
archly, darkly "sour Jesus,"
& the poem begins with that.
Pink Jesus. Tiny Jesuses
on every bush, the world of sagebrush now a world of tiny Jesuses.
Soft Jesus maybe. (Is there a sexual aspersion in it
or only another way of saying "tender Jesus"?)
Jesus in Oklahoma
with his beard cut off. A weepy girl
named Jesus. She opens up her breast,
the moon pops out. O menses, colored glass
& papers, birds with messages
of love, tra la, on metal wings. His other name
is Rollo, Baby Winchester
or Baby Love. Jesus with a cow's head
on his shoulders, candles reaching from
his fingertips. Jesus in his one-eyed ford.

Squawk squawk, the preacher cries.
Eyes of the congregation turning white. The pinwheel
shooting sparks against his lap.
Jesus in furs. Jesus in Oklahoma,
growing old.
Hot & glowing Jesus. Jesus on the ace of hearts.
Alfalfa Jesus.
I am writing this the way a gambler cuts his name
into the table. Jesus in formica.
Drinking in the morning, playing coon-can
with his brother James.
Other names of Jesus.
Jesus H. Jones or Jesus in the woodpile.
Tomtom Jesus.
Jesus who aims a bullet down his mouth.
His children hang his body from a cross.
Three Jesuses in Ypsilanti.
Three in Tishomingo.
Jesus buried in Fort Sill.
His suffering has left their bodies
empty. In the night sky past El Reno
Jesus becomes his pain & flies,
aiming to leave his eyes for others.
Mother Jesus.
Her children have forsaken her.
She learns to cry & plays
nightly at mah jong, dropping her tiles
into the bottomless lake.
The man who chews his wrists down to the bone
is also Jesus. Jesus
in a feathered skull cap. Tacking stars
onto his vest, o cockeyed Jesus,
wanderer from Minsk,
he squawks the language of the little merchants,
squatting at their campfire he stirs
their coffee with *his* tool. How like his grandfather
he has become. Coyote Jesus.
Farting in the sweat lodge, tight
against his buttons

in the bride's room. Ponca City
Jesus. Pawnee Jesus.
He is staring at the eyes of Jesus
staring into his.
Their eyeballs spin around
like planets.
Visions of Jesus everywhere.
Gambler Jesus.
Banker Jesus.
Flatfoot Jesus with a floy floy.
Jesus shuffling.
The soldiers guard his silent fan,
tacked up, beside his rattle.
Jesus on the pavement. Jesus
shot for love, the powwow over,
naked, crawling toward you,
vomit on his beard. His father's milk
is dribbling—plin plin—in the cup
called Jesus. Ghosts
unhook the breast plate, draw
two streams of milk out,
mix them, opening
the mother's womb. No midwife
comes to her, she gives birth
like a man, & holds him
in a dream. Old song
erupting in the gourd dance,
in the storefront church
at night, among the hapless
armies. Two plus two is
Jesus. Five is Jesus.
Jesus in Okarchie,
driving. Jesus in his one-eyed ford,
arriving for the dance in Barefoot.
Visions of Jesus everywhere.
Jesus wrapped up in a woman's shawl.
Jesus in a corner,
stroking his tight body.
Masturbating Jesus.

Jesus sucking on a ball of fat.
There is no language left for him to speak,
only the humming in his chest,
a rush of syllables
like honey. Pouring
from every orifice, the voice
of renegades & preachers
without words.
Pink Jesuses in Oklahoma,
emerging with the spring.
Catfish Jesuses.
A beetle with the face of Jesus
scribbled on its back, squashed flat
against the dance floor.
Jesus squawking with the voice of angels.
I am writing this the way a man speaks without words.
Wordless in the light he pulls
out of his mouth. In the holes he hides in.
Wordless in praises. Wordless in peyote.
Wordless in hellos & hallelujahs.
The freaky Jew slips in beside
his bride, asleep forever, counts up bears
& cadillacs
under a leaky sky.

WILD CLOVER

GUY DAVENPORT

BLUE THISTLE

Here, said Gerrit, making an *iks* with the toe of his hiking boot where the meadow thinned out into the alluvial gravel of the shingle spit, *jo?* We'll be across the wind, with the *landtong* and inlet to see from the front of the tent, meadow and wood from the back. What quiet! was Petra's observation. She saw beebalm, and the grandmother of all thistles. Nello, easing his shoulders from under the straps of his tall pack, sighed, sagged, rolled his arms, and stomped.

LA GARIBALDIENNE

Brainy steelrim specs, Garibaldi cap, Padvinster shirt with patches for woodcraft, swimming, hiking, botany, sewing, geography. Blue seven in a yellow oval on her shirt pocket. In boy's white short pants, big shoes and thick socks, Petra was straight up and down boy except for the flossy snick along the keel and sliding look she gives you when she doesn't believe a word you're saying. Raised on Kropotkin and Montessori, she was great buddies with her folks, anarchists of some kidney. Quiet, said her brother Nello, hundreds of cubic meters of solid silence. Spiffing, our blue tent, nickelbright frame and yellow rigging. You can, Petra said, hear mevrouw and mijnheer Vole messing about, it's that quiet. Smell the meadow: clover, mint, grass, river.

3

Beyond the spinney there, back of the rocks, was where we camped,
Gerrit pointed. Promised myself, I did, that if I came again I'd
camp on this spit, with the meadow. Erasmus, said Petra, is nice
but spooky. That jiggle in his turned-in eye, the flop of hair all
over his forehead, shapely meat all over, but he's strange. Because,
Nello asked, he lives with Strodekker, Nils, and Tobias? Of course
not, Petra said, with one of her looks. I mean the way he talks
brainy and then runs out of something to say, fighting sleep. He
blushes pretty. Nobody should be that good-looking. He's OK,
Gerrit said, when you get to know him. Hans had told me that,
and it's hard to fool Hans. It was his idea to winkle Erasmus loose
from his tribe, his buddy Jan off to Italy, talk about a funny family. It was Rasmus's scheme that we not wash. Strodekker holds
to a germ-free nursery, peroxiding the depths of ears, crusading
against dirt under fingernails and crud between toes. The whole
house floats with shampoo bubbles and is loud with the gushing
water of showers. Also, he'd had it with sex, said he was being
kissed to death. Tell all, Petra said, but later. Rocks in a ring for
the fire, the spit, pots and pans.

4

Everything's off somewhere else, Petra said, giving her hair a toss.
We're here. The meadow's here, the river, the woods over there.
Gerrit's wrinkling his nubble nose. Cornelius has the tent as ship-
shape and trim as a bandbox. Whistling *The Red Flag Shall Over-
come*, she studied the page of the *Boy Scout Handbook* that shows
how to lay out a campfire. Dinky aluminum pots, she muttered,
nests of cups. Water from the spring in the spinney. A sprig of
clover in her teeth, eyes calmly honest, Petra edged her panties
down. Pink butt, Cornelius said, soon to be tawny goldeny bronze.
Gerrit, swallowing hard, politely stared. Prude, Petra said. Let's
see what the river's like. And Gerrit in the fetching altogether. The
river shines this time of afternoon.

GOLDBUTTONS

Petra drawing plants in her sketchbook, saying the names of parts
to herself, bract, umbel, petiole, said to Gerrit who came to watch,
they're alive. They're out here on their own, as independent as
Frisians. They were here before we were, I mean before people

were, at all, them and the insects, so it's their world we're visiting, intruding on. Time is so grandly slow. No, said Gerrit, it's just that there's so much of it. What I like, Petra said, is a thing minding its own business, like this little goldbutton here. Greeny white roots, a hard stalk, its flowers eight to the line here at the bottom, five on the next level up, three, two, one. It's just tall enough to live in with the grass and still eat lots of light, and get enough water through its toes. Axial, but not strictly: you can't lay a ruler along any of its lines. The orangey yellow of the flower matches the dandelion green of its leaves: they go together.

6

Mitochondria, Petra said, cytoblasts. Everything may be a symbiosis of the two. Every once in a while, Cornelius said, my weewee goes weightless, floating. Because we're britchesless, I suppose. The earth, Petra said, was deep in bacteria once upon a time, making the oxygen for our atmosphere. Erasmus last summer, Gerrit said, called Hans an elemental sprite, or djinn, a hybrid of whacky Toby and serious Nils. The weeds out here, Petra said, are not weeds. This is their place, their meadow. Erasmus said his predicament was that his hormones turned on early, with the help of a camp counselor, a buttermilk-fed weightlifter who believed in flying saucers and extrasensory perception, and told his charges that it was good for their souls to whack off until their brains were sodden. Showed them how, and lectured on the hygiene of it all. Some people, Cornelius said, have all the luck. Nello, Petra said, wants you to believe that we're afflicted with stuffy parents when we're not. Why then, Nello said, am I so shy? Look, Petra said, how plants make colonies, like islands, and don't mix in with each other.

7

Happy dimples and merry eyes, Nello said, is what Gerrit has all over his face, and Petra can't kiss for laughing. Don't niggle, Petra said, we're doing our best. Straight face, puckered lips. Close your eyes, Nello said. I'm pretty certain you're supposed to close your eyes. A squint will do, like that. Side by side, prone, Gerrit's feet riding up and down in a swinging kick, Petra's toes dug into clover, they kissed again, rocking their lips, Nello counting to sixty, one and abra, two cadabra. Nello hummed. Sixty abracadabra. A whole minute. Peppermint, Petra said, rolling onto her back and stretching. Gerrit walked his elbows closer, grazed Petra's lips with his, and mashed into another kiss. Both heels rose. He ventured a hand over a breast. Nello kicked into a headstand and watched upside down. If you like it, you like it. If you don't, what are you doing it for? Sixty and five, sixty and six. Two minutes and one, two minutes and two. Blood's rushing to my head and I'm going to croak in a fit. Three minutes. Gerrit lifted, but Petra pulled his head back, and kept her hand in his hair.

LANDTONG

The feldspar and quartz pebbles derive from Precambrian gneisses or granites and the small fragments of tourmaline and garnets from crystalline schists. The general inference, therefore, from the pebbles is that the beds in which they occur were unconformably related to certain Precambrian gneisses and certain slates, limestones, and quartzites of Cambrian or Lower Silurian age.

SYCAMORE

The *Jules Verne* stood tethered in the spinney beyond the meadow, its yellow drag tied to a boulder, valves leaking steam. Its girdling panels of zodiac, polychrome asterisks, and Laplander embroidery were as benign an intrusion among the trees of the grove as a circus wagon on the street of a Baltic town, a flourish of band music into the domestic sounds of a village. Quark in a Danish student cap, American jeans, Lord Byron shirt with ample sleeves, was picking blueberries in a school of butterflies. Tumble and Buckeye had climbed into a sycamore, walking its limbs as easily as cats. Tumble sat, hooked his knees on a horizontal branch, and hung upside down. Well, he said, there's the begetted eightness of unique nuclearity. Sure, said Tumble, noneness or nineness, or there's no dance to the frequency of the wave. Quark, overhearing in the blueberries, shouted that numbers are numbers. Zero one way, zero the other, scattering butterflies by drawing a goose egg in the air. The zero in ten is a nine pretending it's under one to be beside it and generate a progression of nine again. Tumble, parking his Norwegian forager's cap over a spray of sycamore leaves, said two four six, three six nine is what you get in a multiplication by threes along the one to niner line, but by four gives four eight three seven two six one five nine before you get to four again. He pried off his sneakers, tied the laces together, and hung them from a stout twig. Into each sneaker he stuffed a sock, white, striped blue and red at the top. By five, said Buckeye, gets you five one six two seven three eight four nine, which leaves a space between numbers for landing in when you leapfrog back from four to one. Quark, down among the blueberries, had sailed his cap to the boulder with nonchalant accuracy, and pulled off his shirt, which he made into a ball, tossing it over his head to land behind him in a patch of goldenrod and rabbit tobacco. By six, he shouted, six three nine, six three nine, over and over, out to infinity. Tumble, upside down, squirmed out of his sweater, like a bat peeling itself, as Buckeye remarked, and let it drop far below. Bet you can't shuck your jeans, Quark dared him, while hanging upside down by your knees. Bet I can, said Tumble, watch. Unbuckling and zipping down, he sang, or zipping up, considering, I lift my left leg off the limb, so. And slide my left leg out, ha. And latch on again, squeezing good, with left knee while easing right leg out, and what was the bet, Quark old boy? He did it! Buckeye said. But your face is red as a tomato. Feel lightheaded, too, Tumble said, lifting his arms to the limb and scrambling onto it, astride. Woof! By seven, he said, seven five three one eight six four two nine. You lose two every step except from one to eight and two to nine, where you add seven. That's the best yet, Buckeye said, and with a bet won to boot. Think of something good and nasty. By eight, Quark said, eight seven six. Changing the subject! said Tumble. As for the bet, I was thinking. Eight seven six, Quark shouted him down, five four three. I was thinking that. Two! One! Nine! That, said Buckeye, has its tail in its mouth. The eight's on one end, the nine on the other, and the in between's reversed. I was thinking, Tumble dogged on, that as long as my jeans are fifteen feet down, where, as soon as they're off, my underpants will follow, there, have followed, *whee!* right on top. By nine, Quark sang, nine nine nine nine nine nine nine nine nine.

LEAVES

Wild tansy, Petra said, Roman wormwood. *Ambrosia artemisiae-folia.* Not, I think, Theophrastos' *apsinthion*, which is *Artemisia*, genus and species swapping places as in a dance. This is a new

world weed with pinnatifid leaves, very Greek, very acanthus. The
flowers go on and on up the stem, shishkabob of yellow ruffles,
tight little green balls when they begin. She leaned over the wild
tansy, spraddle-legged, hands on knees, Gerrit's long-billed red cap
on the back of her head. Carrotweed, said Gerrit, finding it in the
book. Stammerwort tasselweed ragweed tall ambrosia. Ambrosia is
what the Greek gods ate, and at our house it's orange slices bananas grapes pineapple and coconut wish I had some now. Nectar's
what they drank and now bees drink it. I like being naked, I think.
Artemisleaf, said Petra. Of course. Because it has a leaf like Artemisia, toothy lobes in a nineteenth-century neoclassical spray. You
look good naked, long brown legs and big square toes. Botanists
are nice people, gentle, with queer names. Sereno Watson. Blue-
eyed grass, said Cornelius. Artemis was the Greek goddess of hunting and women and young animals. Women when they're young
animals, said Petra.

DOUBLE FLOWER OF BRISTOW, OR NONESUCH

This glorious flower being as rare as it is beautiful, is for roots
being stringy, for leaves and stalks being hairy and high, and for
the flowers growing in tufts, altogether like the single nonesuch:
but that this bears a larger umbel of flowers at the stalk's top, every
flower having three or four rows of petals, of a deeper orange,
adding more grace, but blossoms without making seed, like other
double flowers, but overcomes this defect by propagating from the
root.

SNUG

What I like, Petra said in the sleeping bag, is a dark sleety winter
afternoon when I can go from school clothes to flannel pyjamas and
wool dressing gown and get snug in the big chair with a blanket
and something good to read, and can see outside. You've got so
many worlds at once: memory both recent and far, the house with
supper coming along and talk and Papa coming in, and your book.
You know where you are. A cat's view of life, Cornelius said.
Thanks, said Petra. Where we are here, Gerrit said, is the backside
of nowhere, under all the stars, at the edge of a meadow, near a
river, all three in two sleeping bags zipped into one, Petra in the

middle. Straight down is New Zealand. Did you see the mouse on a stem of broomsedge, holding on with four fists? Petra did, but Nello missed him.

A STRING OF SPANISH ONIONS

Candlelight in our tent, and every sound an event to itself, spoon's clink on a cup, and our voices. Hansje was happiest that we weren't going to wash, and kept saying we'd stink. Erasmus was cool about it. Take off socks, briefs, a shirt, he said, and into the laundry basket it goes. It's good to wear dust and mud, pollen and leaf-trash. Hansje pointed out that we didn't know what dirty was. And, besides, naked and dirty was different from wearing dirty clothes. Places, Erasmus said. The meadow can't be dirty. I said that it could. Dump city trash on it, atomic waste, industrial crud. Understod, Erasmus said. But we, sweaty and dusty and with oniony armpits, are clean in the same way the meadow is clean. We're natural. What if we hadn't brought toilet paper? Well, Erasmus said, we have a river, and even dust. We could powder. like birds. Every culture has its own sense of clean and dirty. Every part of a city. Every family. But the day your socks are yours, comfortable and friendly, is the day parents snatch them away from you. Then Erasmus made a speech on dirt: which he said was anything out of place, like seasand in the carpet, dust on shelves, egg on a necktie. But it was Erasmus who rolled in dust when he was sweaty. Petra didn't need to say a word. Her eyes said it all.

RISE AND SET, AUTUMNAL STARS

So, Petra said, Hiroshige. What's happening at a place. A tree, and it's there through the seasons. It has its life, from seedling to ax or lightning bolt. But it's there. And then, all of a minute, when Hiroshige chooses to have us look, a peasant carrying two bundles of firewood on a yoke across his shoulders passes the tree. At the same moment, a monk, a lady on a horse, they are also passing. Our meadow here was under snow last winter, and hares made tracks across it, and the mice burrowed deeper and all the grass and flowers were dead. And now we're here with our blue tent and each other. And last summer, Gerrit said, Erasmus doing a hundred push-ups at a time, counting in Latin, betting Hansje he couldn't do a hundred and five. And unmentionable things, Petra said. No, said Gerrit, that was part of the game. Pure thoughts all the way, like us.

15

The sleeping bags zipped together, as with Hans, Erasmus, and Gerrit before, Gerrit's plan, one less sleeping bag to tote, and, as Petra explained to her folks back in Amsterdam, proof of their freedom. Me in the middle, Petra said. Liberal parents are the stuffiest. If ours were a Calvinist enclave where sex is never mentioned except to deny its existence, not an eyebrow would raise at three innocent teenagers camping in a meadow, two of them brother and sister, the other a friend from the playpen forward. Liberals are the new Calvinists. Those Danes, Nello said, in Jugoslavia. I'm still trying to figure out what they were doing. Four girls and one boy in the one tent back of the textileless beach. Squealed all night, that lot.

PARNASSIA PALUSTRIS LINNAEUS

Flowers, fragrant as honey, are interesting in that five of the original stamens transform into staminodes split into narrow gland-tipped segments, which attract insects. The five fertile stamens alternate with the petals and mature before the stigmas, but in a remarkable way. The anthers face outwards and ripen in succession, each in turn lying on top of the ovary with the pollen side facing upwards. After several days, when the anthers are all empty of pollen, the apical stigmas become receptive and occupy the former position of the anthers. Knuth's *Handbook of Flower Pollination* says that the stalked glands of the staminodes attract insects by their glistening color, as if they had abundant nectar. Intelligent insects are not deceived, but flies and beetles are, and effect cross-pollination. Many smaller flies are also attracted. They lick the nectar but are ineffective in transferring pollen.

CAMPFIRE

Minimal possessions, Gerrit said, maximum order. Last summer, Petra said, we had maximum possessions at camp, carloads of stuff, and most likely minimal order, no matter how loud the games mistresses shouted at us, as muddled as we were. One reason, among others, when Gerrit went off here with Hansje Keirinckx and Erasmus Strodekker, I saw that camping could be something quite different from a giggle of girls talking boys, television, clothes, and homework. So here we are. Nello will live down going camping with his sister. Never, said Cornelius. A knowing smile will serve, Petra said, if not an invitation to mind one's business. Well, Gerrit said, we're different. We have hygiene, sort of. It was Hansje's bright idea that we go native and swear off soap and water, as a corollary to Erasmus giving up sex. He said one morning that waking up out here's fun because the mind's an idiot and thinks it's where it usually is when you wake, when it, by happy surprise, isn't. He stole that from Proust, Petra said. There's a famous passage about finding yourself again when you wake in a strange room. It couldn't be in Proust, Gerrit said, when Erasmus would look out all four sides of the tent and say he's seeing a rabbit, a whirl of gnats, a brace of meadowlarks landing and taking off, up down. I slept in the middle, like Petra now, being the neutral element, though Erasmus would reach across and knit fingers with Hansje, and shove and push, by way of some kind of understanding they have. Erasmus was rollicking in our outing because he wasn't, as he said, being hugged and kissed to death. No Toby and Nils rooting and pranking in the bed of a morning. No fights. Just the freedom of the out of doors, and friends who were just friends.

IMPATIENS BIFLORA

The pod has evanescent partitions, with anatropous seeds along a thick axis. Five valves, elastically coiled, spring open when dry, shooting out the seeds.

19

Well, Petra said, there was this poster in a shop across from the Centre Pompidou in Paris. A man it showed, with a great body, about twenty, in the buff, holding a baby out in his arms, looking wise and happy, as if it approved of his daddy having an extensive babymaker hanging out and down over tight fat balls, for all the world to see. But behind these fetching two, crossways the poster, were two boys, also britchesless, lying in a hug. Ha, said Gerrit. Anything printed on the poster? Nello asked. No words, Petra said, just the photo.

20

Hair muddled, eyelids thick with sleep, Gerrit raised himself on
his elbows in the sleeping bag, and said, There's a mist off the
river. Whoopee, said Nello, eyes still closed. Petra lay batting her
eyes and smiling. Hello, said Gerrit. Don't look, he said, after leaning to give her a kiss, I've got to nip out to pee, and have sprung
one. Let's see, said Petra, reaching. No, said Gerrit, blockading
with knees. Close your eyes. Petra closed her eyes, looking as soon
as Gerrit was out. Wow, she said, straight out and up, and with its
hood back. It does that, Nello said, as you know good and well,
when the bladder's about to pop. Learn something every day,
Petra said, lifting the tent flap and looking out. Gerrit's peeing up.
A silver arc, pretty in the mist. Me too, said Nello, scrambling
out. Hey, Petra, Nello hollered, it won't go down. Breakfast, said
Petra. A fire, water, mush, raisins. I'm impressed. Gerrit, half embarrassed and half pleased with himself, scrounged around in his
napsack until he found briefs, which prodded out in front when he
put them on. Bashful, said Petra. Water jug, coffee packets, and
come here. I liked kissing all day yesterday. Poor Nello's left out.
Don't anybody kiss me, Nello said. As they stood kissing, Petra
pushed down Gerrit's briefs, and, squatting, took them off, batting
Gerrit's hands away from trying to pull them up again. No clothes
we agreed, she said. I'm mortified, said Gerrit.

LUPINUS CALCARATUS

Erect, high, silky pubescent throughout, leafy. Leaflets 7 to 10,
linear lanceolate, acute, mucronate: stipules ovate, acuminate, per-
sistent: flowers in rather close and short raceme, bracts subulate,
deciduous, calyx deeply spurred at base, minutely bracteolate, the
upper lip short, double toothed, white, the lower larger, entire,
acute: banner and wings somewhat pubescent externally, the keel
ciliate: pods hairy, with four seeds. Flowers white, the spur ex-
ceeding the pedicels.

22

House wren of the Grenadines, said Tumble, mockingbird banana-
quit Carib grackle. Buccament, said Quark, Sion Hill Cumberland
Questelles Layou New Ground Mesopotamia Troumaca. Angelfish,

said Buckeye, spotfin butterfly. Finite but unbounded, O over under by and through!

23

Fainthearted, no, said Petra, but do be fair. Kissing's fun. I'm not looking, Nello said. I'm just here, browning my butt and listening to the meadow, the buzz of it. So what are you doing? Fondling, said Gerrit. Feeling better all the time, said Petra. Everything, anyway, has become unreal. Time has stopped. I think the meadow and river have drifted away from where it was when we came. It's us, Nello said, who are different, and getting differenter all the time. How different will we get? Running around bareassed is not all that peculiar, and that's not what's doing something to us. We've only each other to say things to: that's a big difference. Last summer Erasmus said all manner of things I'm certain he would never have said back home. We think differently, Petra said, breathing deep after a long kiss. Snuggling on the sunroom couch or at Betje's when she has the house all to herself is always a dare when hands stray to critical places, like now. I'm not looking, Nello said. Why not? Gerrit said. Unfair, Petra said, is unfair, sitting up and monkeying over to Nello, pressing a kiss on the back of his neck. Tickles, he said, after a suspicious silence. But feels good. Does it now! Petra said, neither tease nor mischief in her voice. Gerrit's next. Gerrit's next what? asked Gerrit. Kiss Nello, Petra said. Why ever not?

SURVEYOR

Gerrit, in his scout shirt because of the morning chill, with Corbusier Homme Modulor shoulderpatch, said once they were off the bus at Knollendorp, honest Hans asked Rasmus every tactless question that sprang easily to his liberal mind. In less than ten meters of hiking to the sandspit, he pried into Rasmus's standing as Strodekker's newly adopted son, happy older brother to Nils and Tobias, their involvement with the Vrijheid cadres, why he wanted to get away from them for a few days to change the pH factors of his soul, length of his weewee, who his real parents were, if he did it with girls too, how much he got for an allowance, what they did in Denmark and the Federal Republic, why one of his eyes was off center and jiggled, the length of Strodekker's weewee, and on and on, until Rasmus was shaken inside out but not in the least pissed off. He's as honest as a dog. This is his shirt, from the wild scout troop Strodekker runs. It was when Hansje asked Rasmus if he didn't think that Strodekker's just a mite gaga that I changed the conversation and got a shoulder squeeze of gratitude. What I did was ask Hansje the same questions about his buddy Jan, who was with his folks, and heard more about him than I really needed to know. So, Petra said, why do you have Erasmus's shirt? He gave it to me, Gerrit said.

TREES

Four trees upon a solitary acre
Without design
Or order, or apparent action,
Maintain.

The sun upon a morning meets them,
The wind.
No nearer neighbor have they
But God.

The acre gives them place,
They him attention of passer-by,
Of shadow, or of squirrel, haply,
Or boy.

What deed is theirs unto the general nature,
What plan
They severally retard or further,
Unknown.

THREE PERSIMMONS IN A BLUE DISH

Klee Noordzee coast, the sandspit, a Boudin with Cornelius on it, sea blow cocking his hair into a crest of light. Early Mondriaan pine forest with blue shadows, the wood at the top of the meadow. Courbet, the spring. What's more, Gerrit said, is our telescoping aluminum flagpole here on the main brace, flying the Danish flag. For the bunnies, Petra said. They were wondering where we're from. Now they can say, Ah! Lutherans! Dutch flag tomorrow,

Gerrit said. Then Swedish, followed by the Norwegian. Today we're Danes.

27

The spinney explored, the meadow traversed twice, the sandspit inspected, the rivermouth waded in, they came back to the tent. Bread, cheese, and hot soup, said Petra. We're getting to be the color of gingerbread. And Gerrit's spirited virile member sticks straight out, sort of, rather than toward heaven. Does it feel good? A grin and a blush together are wildly becoming. Cakes and apples, sang Nello, in all the chapels, fine balonies and rich mellow pears. Last summer, Gerrit said, and I'd have been a zoological exhibit, with commentary by Hansje and Rasmus.

PATROL

Quark on reconnoiter in the wood met Wolf, her gazing eye silver and soot, silent of paw as she strode. Sabina! Quark said in the old Latin, mama of Quirinus, chaster than Vesta, cunninger than Minarva. *Hrff!* said Sabina, *et lactentes ficos et gutulliocae.* Carissa! said Quark. I saw you playing with the frogs and crickets, pretending to dance and pounce, laughing all the while. *Archeotera,* said Sabina, *unde haec sunt omnia nata.* But, said Quark, these are good people, over yonder by the water, the three cubs in a cloth house. They live in a town of canals and lightning run through threads, where they learn, not much, but something, numbers and tongues mainly. I've smelt them, Sabina said, two toms and a bitch, potash and olive, sheep and cottonweed. Metal. Not to do you a mischief, Quark said. The metal is the frame of their house, cups, buckles and such. It is never prudent to be seen, O Consiliarius. The faith has been gone so long.

LA CHENILLE ET LA MOUCHE

From the *Jules Verne,* a hot-air balloon hanging unanchored six meters above the meadow, defying both gravity and its own radiant levity, its declinator lever set on *orbit,* hung a rope ladder up which Buckeye, Tumble, and Quark swarmed with the progress of swimming arctic wolves, knees and elbows in the same vertical plane, all three in midshipman's uniforms of the French navy. The propeller turned its four wooden blades idly, like a windmill dreaming. Two brass cylinders leaked steam. The crystal-set telegraph key was chittering patrol signals, asking for reports. Buckeye, standing a bouquet of meadow flowers in the teapot, sat down to the key and sent: *Le travail mène à la richesse.* Ha! said Tumble, that will really interest the dispatcher. *Pauvres poètes, travaillons! Travaillons!* sang Quark. *La chenille en peinant sans cesse devient le riche papillon.* Tumble, out of his sailor suit and into plus fours, red flannel shirt, sweater, scarf, aviator cap, goggles, and gauntlets, gave four dials a reading, poking each with a businesslike fiinger. Ion stream, he said. Neutrinos under however many atmospheres you get from rho over time, divided by the azimuth in hypernewtons. Twenty-three point six eight niner, said Buckeye. Fourier waves in sync. Somebody, Quark said, has been pressing weeds in the log. Now, said Tumble, send them the Fly. Never mind that they're asking for coordinates. That's microswedenborgs point zero zero one by four zero on the nose. The Fly, said Buckeye. *Nos mouches savent des chansons que leur apprirent en Norvège.* Quark, naked between naval togs and flight overall, said of his penis that it was sunburned, along with his behind, and probably his toes and the back of his neck. *Les mouches ganiques qui sont les divinités de la neige.* That ought to hold them until we can achieve drift. We're starting to spin. Rain on white dew, Buckeye recited, all the leaves are yellow. Wait awhile for that, said Quark, and where's the beebalm and cucumber salve for my member and butt, both as red as cherry wine. Look at the late afternoon sun on the inlet down there, Buckeye said, wrinkled quicksilver specked with green and blue. Get those weeds out of the teapot. Let's see it with biscuits and cheese, apples and chocolate. The log, said Quark, who had wrapped himself in a blanket, uncorked the ink bottle, and dipped the quill. Berrying, he wrote. Bees, caterpillars, flies, sycamore polyhedra, three families of fieldmice, from whom that peculiar joke we still haven't figured out. Gerrit and Petra kissed fifty-four times, or once every ten minutes for nine hours, with Gerrit's piddler going sprack at every kiss.

QUINCE, AUTUMN RAIN, AND MEDLAR

The Summer Bon Chretien is somewhat a long pear, with a green and yellow russetish coat, and sometimes red sides: it is ripe at Michaelmas: some dry them as they do prunes, and keep them all the year after. The Summer Bergamot is an excellent well relished pear, flat and short, of a mean bigness, and of a dark yellowish green color on the outside. The Primating Pear is moist and early ripe. The Russet Catherine is a very good middle-sized pear.

AND O A GYPSY AIR

From a haversack slung on the taffrail of the nacelle Tumble took a horn, Buckeye a banjo, and Quark a Jew's harp. The balloon was over the spinney, gorgeous and strange. The key of G minor, Tumble said, his hair all whorls and spikes still, as they had an urge in the middle of breakfast (honey, wheatmeal biscuits, and reindeer milk) for music. Where the cacklers, Buckeye said, but no grunters, continuo from Haydn, the tune on the Jew's harp, and I sing. Naked but for a shirt, he attacked the run that began the air with a voice like rung glass and the sweetest of tenor bells. Where the cacklers, but no grunters shall be set loose for the hunters, those we still must keep alive. Tumble rocked his shoulders and kept time with his heels as he played the ground, handsomely paced, on the horn. Aye, and put them forth to thrive in the parks and in the chases, and the finer walléd places, like Saint Jameses, Greenwich, Tiballs, where the acorns, plump as chiballs, soon shall change both kind and name. Proclaim them then the Kingses game. Quark broke into a jig, ringing the Jew's harp, and lolling his eyes. So the act no harm may be unto their keeper Barnabee. It will do as good a service as did ever Gypsy Jarvis. All instruments down as they sang the last lines trio, in glorious harmony. Or our Captain Charles, the tall man, and a part to of our salmon! Golly diddle dingle gunst, said Tumble. Tom Tickler on the tabor, who could bring the girls. Oof. Quark leaned over the rail with the big brass telescope. They're all kissing, time about, he said, and they're having mush and raisins for breakfast.

BOSNIAN MEADOW MOUSE

They sat in the meadow. Nello said that it could be described botanically, geologically, ecologically, geographically, aesthetically, historically, poetically, but that none of these descriptions would include what they were doing.

SILENCE, WITH CRICKETS

A throbbing owl call in the night. Talk about spooky, said Nello. Like doves, Petra said, they can swivel their heads all the way around. The little Athenian owl was the *strix*, compact as a jug, mewed from olives, flew sideways, wings as blurred as a hummingbird's. Makes it the cozier, Gerrit said, snuggled here as warm as toast. Admit however, Petra said, that the ground is twice as hard as a floor, and has rocks in it. I'm hungry, Nello said. I'm happy, Gerrit said.

MASTER JOHN TRADESCANTE'S ORCHARD

The muscadine, some call the Queen Mother Plum, and some the Cherry Plum, is fair and red, of a reasonable bigness and ripe about Bartholmy Tide. The Flushing Bullace grows in a thick cluster like grapes. The Morocco Plum is black like a damson, well tasted, and somewhat dry in eating. The Green Peasecod Plum is long and pointed, and ripe in the beginning of September. The Amber Plum is round and as yellow as wax, coming clean from the stone like an apricock. The Red Mirobalane Plum grows to be a great tree quickly, spreading thick and far, like the Black Thorn or Sloe.

THE SCENERY IS ROMANTIC IF IT HAS STEPS

There's a gerbil in the telephone, Quark said, eating goober peas. Give it a thump, said Buckeye. Josephine Geronimo and Virgilia Tardy were present at the planting of poplars in the marshes. The toms are coming from the spring in the grove, carrying a bucket of water between them, free arms out for balance and leverage. The one with thick dark hair that makes jug handles over his ears still has a stiff jubilator. It flops and bounces as he walks. The other, with hair the color of ripe wheat, is singing *Der Vogelfänger bin ich ja.* The *virguncula* is outside the tent pouring heated water into tin cups already containing dehydrated essence of cow milk, van Houten's powdered cocoa, and refined Jamaican sugar. She presses her lips against the lips of each of the toms when they bring her the water. Meanwhile, the family of rabbits in the spinney is out in the sun, nibbling. Buckeye, having made some persnickety adjustments to the rigging, touched a drop of oil to the propeller shaft, and advanced the roller map a smitch, began a little quickstep dance, snapping his fingers, singing softly but briskly, as if under his breath, in Faeroese. Tumble, climbing aboard up the rope ladder, swung a jeaned leg over the taffrail, wrecked Quark's hair because he was on the telephone, and joined Buckeye's dance, nose

to nose, knee to knee. Say what? Quark shouted into the telephone.
I have maniacs on board, unbuttoning each other's clothes. Yes,
Buck and Tumble, to be sure. There's no other patrol in this sector
closer than a star circle, is there? Didn't think so. Ariel by Hizqiyya!
Over. Out.

36

Two kinds of ants, red and black. They probably have wars. And
some of the mice have little white pants and some are cinnamon
gray and make round nests on stalks. We'll never get all the bugs
identified. Gnats are the neutrinos of the place. Meadow birds and
river birds. Highland grass, lowland grass: it's the sandspit and
the river that accounts for that. Time to kiss. Yuck, said Nello, but
if that's the game. Long hug, long kiss, Petra said, two full minutes,
and see if Nello's wizzle bobs its head again, and after three but-
ting throbs stands bolt upright. Bobtail dominicker, Gerrit counted,
little poll ram. Three zoll, four zoll, zickerzoll bam! Poker up on
four. Don't open your eyes, Nello niddy, and you won't get the
giggles. And your blushes turn your tan purple. Nello likes being
kissed, likes kissing. You're over two minutes. Better make it last,
Cornelius Bezemsteel, as I'm next, and on the mouth this time.

THE CAT'S WIFE HAS WHISKERS TOO

Jam, said Tumble, strawberry jam. I think I got the clothes wrong,
though. Cassock, or smock, belted over linsey-woolsy trews, and
hook-and-eye boots, are not period, and the old woman who sold
me the jam was still looking at the money when I left. I think
Wardrobe and Props tease us. Jam on Ryvitas, however, is good
stuff, yuss? It will give us a bellyache if we eat the whole jar. Rabbit, Quark said, showed me some sweetgrass today, a nice fresh
taste with a tang of ginger in it. She said it was excellent as a di-
gestive.

L'ACOUSTIQUE PAYSAGISTE

What, Gerrit said, if you knew everything. All music, all painting,
all writing, had met everybody, and been everywhere. You'd be
crazy, Petra said, humming more of the First Brandenburg Con-
certo that Gerrit had been whistling to an imaginary viola. That's
not what knowing's about. Of course you have to know enough to

begin to discriminate, but from there on out it's pick and choose. Besides, everything's not for everybody. There's temperament, and talent, and disposition.

39

The life! Nello said, roughing it, camping in a meadow, going bare-bottomed, grub all flavored with ashes, crick in the neck and back from sleeping on the ground. Chocolate bars, though wrecked in transit, Petra said, are not flavored with wood ash. Clover, bees sorrel, knotgrass, ants, partridges (*juck* is what they say, said Gerrit, if we were to see one, never mind hearing one), owls (heard, but not yet seen), gnats. But, said Nello, I absoposifuckinglutetively will not kiss Gerrit. Why not? Petra asked. Yes, said Gerrit, why not?

ANTONIO GRAMSCI IN PRISON

Milky blue at the horizon, the sky prospered toward a rich and solid azure overhead. Gerrit, a bandana around his forehead, its knot ducktailed out from his nape, stood at attention, pectorals squeezed in tight and flat, butt hard, hands flat on thighs, shoulders squared, the tucked corners of his mouth wry, fighting off hilarity, toes wiggling, tongue in cheek, eyes merry. Nothing, Petra said, think of absolutely nothing. White mind. They'll pay me to tell this, Cornelius said. It's worth trying, Petra said, if you want it to go down. I feel like a sexpot with red pouting lips and a raccoon ring of mascara around my eyes, steamy at the crotch, rather than the stickstraight begoggled plain Socialist brainy wonder that I am. This is what happens when you're the only girl around. Hormones in well-behaved boys know I'm here, nip down to your gonads with chemical messages to trigger spermatogenesis, which has given you satyriasis. Feels good, said Gerrit. You don't think our kissing for days and days has had anything to do with it? Oh no, said Cornelius, nor the rest of it. Now I'm getting one again.

WITTGENSTEIN ON A CAISSON

Humming Beethoven. The sky rotten with a bilge drift of clouds like squid ink coiling in milk. Lice in the seams of tunic and trousers. A red fungus burning between his toes. Death is not an event in life.

42

Mullein must have room enough to spread its fine rosette of basal leaves, if it is to erect its Jacob's staff. It cannot be crowded even by grass. It is a biennial, and cannot establish itself in cultivated fields. It is found in meadows and pastures and along fences that are not too much overgrown.

MEADOW

Aujourd'hui comme aux temps de Pline et de Columelle la jacinthe se plaît dans les Gaules, la pervenche en Illyrie, la marguerite sur les ruines de Numance et pendant qu'autour d'elles les villes ont changé de maîtres et de noms, que plusiers sont entrées dans le néant, que les civilizations se sont choquées et brisées, leurs paisibles générations ont traversé les âges et sont arrivées jusqu'à nous, fraîches et riantes comme aux jours des batailles.

TWO ACORNS, ONE GINGKO LEAF

The great things, Gerrit said, hair windsprung and sunny, a rust of sunburn across his nose, are how to get rid of wars, bombs, bankers, prejudice, hunger, meanness, and who was Jesus. When you two are kissing, Cornelius said, at least Gerrit can't talk. He purrs, Petra said. Erasmus, Gerrit said, woke one morning with an erection hard as a broomstick, complete with balls scrunched up tight, like mine. Like ours, Cornelius said. Hansje was all for hankypanky, but Erasmus put a damper on that. Poor Hansje, Petra said. But I'm glad there's somebody who can say what he can't do. We climbed practically all the trees in the spinney, explored the other spit over the hill there, swam, and generally mucked about, seriously silly, with forays into all those brainy things Erasmus and Hansje can carry on for days, like making endless lists out of their heads, history and science and films, with Hansje sneaking in the odd naughty bit. So like late in the afternoon, Erasmus said that if he whacked off he'd keep from gunking up the sleeping bag that night, and started in, offhandedly dextrous, so to speak, except that he's a lefthander. Offhandedly, Petra said. While walking around and talking, gathering sticks for the fire. Hansje's eyes were a study. Big and round, as if he had more schemes than he could deal with, and needed to hit on the right one first crack out of the box. Erasmus can laugh with his eyes better than anybody, also read minds. So he started this long talk about sheepwalks and Roman roads, and every once in a while he'd close his eyes because his wizzle was feeling so good, and slow his stroke, and gasp. All this to hypnotize Hansje, who was being cool like crazy, fighting off paying the least attention, because that was the rules of the game. Explain it, Petra said, reaching over to give Gerrit's balls a squeeze. Watch it, he said. Why? said Petra. Rules of the game, said Gerrit. In your story or right now? Cornelius asked. Both, said Petra. I want to hear why. It just was, Gerrit said. We had agreed to prove that we're the masters of our bodies, and not them of us, I'm quoting Erasmus, who gets all this day in and day out from his composite family, which sometimes seems to be a Roman bathhouse in the last five minutes of the empire, and sometimes a Montessori Kindergarten devoted to ethics and hygiene. Suntans of ultimate golden brown, fresh air, exercise, fellowship, life tough and simple, radical sweet innocence: Erasmus kept saying all this, and Hansje and I ate it all in, so that when he himself said he was slaking animal lust that was a natural function of the organism, how could Hansje and I be transparent copycats? Golly, Petra said, the things I don't know about. Nello, are you understanding this? Sure, said Cornelius, every word. I can finish the story. Erasmus was being a devil lording it over two innocents, for the fun of watching them squirm. You think? Gerrit asked. He said that it was the longest he'd gone without coming in years, and that it was a big thing for him to be in the sleeping bag with us as friends only, and to be barebutt with us all day. Confusing, said Petra, but only a bit strange, you know? Do I? Gerrit asked. I mean, know? Sure, Petra said. So finish the story. Ha, said Gerrit. When Hansje was about to fizz over and invite us all to join him in an orgy, Erasmus quit, shrugged his shoulders, and said maybe he didn't need to, after all. He really is a devil, Petra said. How long did it take him to drive Hansje and you crazy?

45

Quark on the telephone in the nacelle of the balloon. Yuss, he said, I know, but I'm more interested in a nest of crystals we found back of the spring in the spinney. The series is in fifths of a rotation, optimal foci of tetrahedra on a very long axis. What? I'm putting Buckeye on the thread. Here he is. Ho! said Buckeye, it's lovely.

They're asleep now, in a heap, arms and legs every which way. I was too shy to look. Here's Tumble, whose imagination it all rather caught. Hello hello, said Tumble. Well, nothing that would get into a poem by Catullus, but then they weren't arctic hares up on their hind legs batting at each other, either. Actually they're not in a heap, as Buck said. They're up and have the lantern lit in the tent, and have broken out biscuits and made cocoa, and are laughing and kissing all around. Sabina the wolf is scandalized, and the owl in the sycamore has offered comments also. Band two alpha for that, Ariel by Hizqiyya. They're talking about hot chocolate in a café in Amsterdam on a cold day, with sleet, Edouard Manet, Bishop Desmond Tutu, Petra's mother's fanatic housekeeping, the legs of Joaquin Carvalho Cruz, the failure of Danes to understand any joke whatsoever, bicycles, Mondriaan's admiration of Mae West, Queen Wilhelmina's battiness, Daley Thompson, Wittgenstein's chocolate oatmeal, Erasmus Strodekker's off eye and membrum virile, Mary Lou Retton, the boulevards of Paris, gosling motilities among the precocious, Petra's breasts by lantern light, the best ways to ripen pears, Gerrit's foreskin, the coziness of the tent, friendship's liberation from reticence, owls, zebras, Mozart, the quiet of the meadow in the middle of the night, why it was nobody's business if Gerrit kissed Nello, or Nello Petra, tennis racquets, the clarity of the stars seen through the tent flaps, how wide awake they were, and eyes blue with fate.